The FRED Files

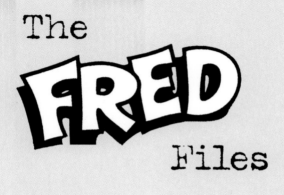

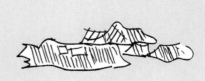

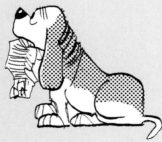

The FRED Files

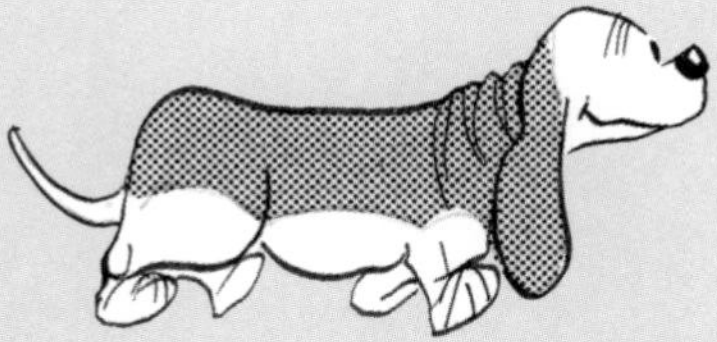

ORION

First published in Great Britain in 2005
by Orion Books Ltd
Orion House, 5 Upper St Martin's Lane,
London WC2H 9EA

10 9 8 7 6 5 4 3 2 1

A CIP catalogue record for this book is
available from the British Library.

ISBN 0 75285 976 5

Printed and bound in Great Britain by
Butler and Tanner Ltd, Frome and London

www.orionbooks.co.uk

The

FRED

Files

Foreword

by Mac

When as a struggling cartoonist many years ago I first met Alex Graham he told me about his working day. 'In the early evening,' he said, 'I jot down a few ideas. The next morning I draw them up and in the afternoon I play golf.' I was extremely impressed but, try as I might, somehow I could not emulate that enviable lifestyle. Instead I watched the hours of the mornings, the afternoons and the evenings disappear with perhaps only two finished cartoons to show for it and never even a glimpse of a golf course. He was the most prolific cartoonist, producing wonderfully funny gag cartoons for *Punch* and many other magazines. Then, forty-two years ago, he produced a cartoon strip which was to warm the hearts of dog lovers all over the world.

Fred Basset is the perfect dog. A thinker, a philosopher, and possessed with so many endearing qualities that it is no wonder he constantly wins the hearts of the judges at dog shows and carries away 'best in show' cups. This is quite an achievement, considering that, according to my calculations, he is now approximately 294 doggy years old.

Who wouldn't want to own a dog like Fred? As far as I can recollect, Fred, in all his forty-two years, has not been infested by fleas, has never regurgitated the contents of the compost heap on to the living room carpet two minutes before guests arrive, or tried to impregnate their legs. I can't recall his owner ever following him around on walks with a pooper-scooper and a plastic bag. Fred has always resisted sticking his nose into the crotch of the vicar, doesn't suffer from flatulence and amazingly, in all his long life, has not once cocked his leg. What a dog!

What Fred has done is to make me and millions of fans laugh each day as he battles with the Tucker twins, takes over the boss's armchair, steals food from the table and trails mud from the garden all over the newly-cleaned kitchen floor. He has been the leader of the pack, a television critic, the long-suffering audience to his master's piano playing ar rabbit chaser.

When Alex Graham sadly died some years ago, we thought that his doggy creation had gone with him. B heavens Alex, with his amazing output, had drawn months of strips in advance and whilst these were being a new artist was found. Working together with Alex's children, Neilson and then Arran, scrupulous attentior the original concept. It is nigh impossible to spot any differences.

Fred Basset is syndicated to newspapers all over the world. He is a film star who has appeared in several animated films, and throughout his long life has maintained his ability to make us laugh, to identify with his owners on the traumas and delights of having a pet in the house and, happily for a 294-year-old, he is still playful, affectionate and hasn't aged a bit. I suspect that somewhere in the attic of Fred's house there is a very dusty picture of an extremely wrinkled hound called Dorian Basset.

Introduction

by Arran Graham

The village of Ticehurst lies ten miles to the south-east of Tunbridge Wells. At its heart is a thirteenth-century church with a square tower. The bustling square has shops, two public houses, a garage and an ancient water pump under some trees. In 1963 our family home was on the edge of the village opposite the Ticehurst sign. It was a modern house that Dad had had built; most of the accommodation was on the ground floor but a steep staircase led up to the studio. It was from here in July of that year that Fred Basset sauntered into our lives.

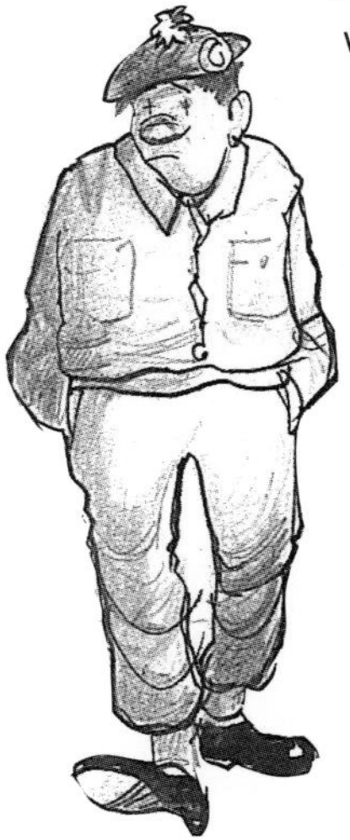

By 1963 Dad was already an established cartoonist. Born in Glasgow in 1917, he was brought up in a modest street in Dumfries only yards from the turnstiles of the Queen of the South football ground. Following a sound education at Dumfries Academy he entered the Glasgow School of Art, where he met my mother, Winnifred. It was from here – funds no doubt being short – that he began selling 'joke' cartoons (or 'singles') to various Scottish newspapers for ten shillings each. Following wartime service with the Argyll and Sutherland Highlanders, he created his first strip cartoon, Wee Hughie, in 1945. Such was the popularity of the character that the series was constantly recycled only coming to an end after his death. In the same year that Wee Hughie first appeared, my parents moved to London. It has always been a matter of family lore that Dad would walk Fleet Street during the day trying to sell his work, only to return in the evening to a one-bedroom attic flat in Ealing and a meal of bread and syrup. Once armed with

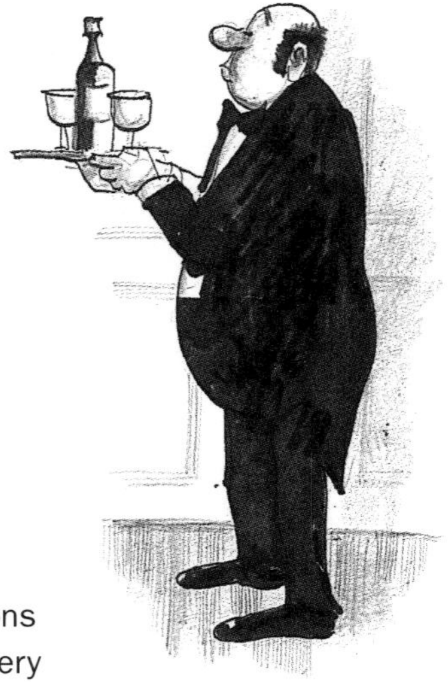

an agent, these early hardships did not last long as both *Punch* and *Tatler* magazines soon began to accept his work. Briggs the Butler in the *Tatler* was another early success and the strip ran for well over ten years. As work became increasingly regular with contributions to newspapers, magazines and books, the decision was made to move out of London and down to East Sussex.

A question frequently asked was: 'Where do all the ideas come from?' The answer was simple – from everything and everybody. With a keen, observant eye Dad could extract wry humour from everyday life. Sport, especially football and golf, provided a rich source of fun. Human foibles, often observed at parties and other social events, were another. Fellow cartoonist and *Punch* editor William Hewison once remarked that Dad had 'probably got more mileage out of the cocktail party than any other cartoonist'. Nothing escaped Dad's keen eye – not even my teenage years. Appearing first in *Punch*, a collection of cartoons was published under the title *Daughter in the House*. This book is very special to me, not least for its dedication, shown below.

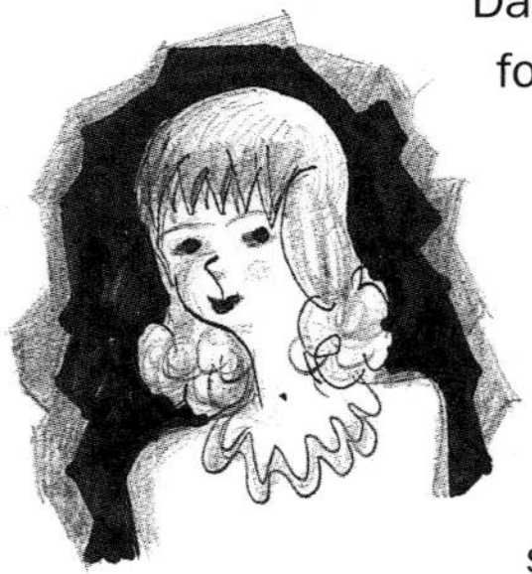

Although ideas came easily they still needed to be knocked into a shape that could be used to effect. This was a more difficult process and took place in the late afternoon, when, as children, my brother and I had to be as quiet as church mice. This was tricky during the school holidays but had its advantages in providing a regular framework for our homework during term time!

In early 1963 Dad was invited by the *Daily Mail* to create a strip cartoon with family appeal – a talking or thinking dog was suggested. Dogs had always been part of his life. Over the years he had owned a labrador, a collie, two poodles called Mac and Tosh and a

and apologies from

Daddy.

September 1969.

brace of boxers. Quite why he chose a basset, Fred only knows. What is equally astonishing was his inability to draw animals, let alone dogs! Examples of this can be found in *Punch* and in a series entitled 'Augustus and his Faithful Hound' which appeared in *Woman's Journal*. Lovable as these canine creations might be they certainly would not have cut the mustard at Crufts. So it was with Fred. It is well known that the *Daily Mail*, following a number of complaints from basset owners, bought him a basset called Freda so that he might draw from life. Freda was later joined by a Yorkshire terrier called Yorkie (well, I suppose he had to be!) and a little black poodle not unlike Fifi. Naturally, the dogs were important elements in the business, so our good friend and accountant, Simon Cryer, approached the Inland Revenue. He recalls that 'I had a lively conversation with them on Alex's behalf about the allowability of the upkeep of the dogs. We settled on a fifty per cent allowance for them'.

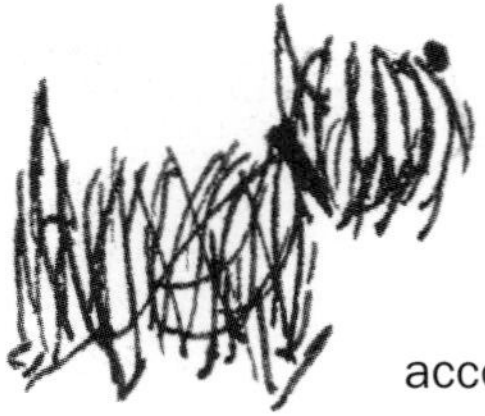

Fred very quickly settled into our household. My brother Neilson wrote a book called *Fred Basset and the Spaghetti*, illustrated by Dad, whilst my job was to apply shading to the strip, for which I received extra pocket money! Mum provided those most important of ingredients, support and encouragement. In later years she was often prompting Dad to put more background in the strip, as he was always keen to get out on to the golf course as soon as possible . . . Although not a member of the family, a warm thanks must go to Les Hulme, who lettered every strip for almost forty years.

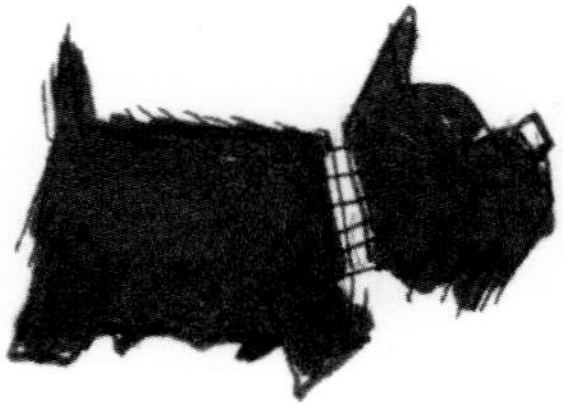

As the strip evolved, names for characters and locations had to be devised. There was little system to it. The names of family friends would often be jumbled up to fit a particular character. Tinkers Wood, a favourite location for the adventures of Fred and his two mates Jock and Yorkie, came from our first house, Tinkers Cottage. The Bull Inn was just across the lane from Tinkers Cottage and our final house, Huntleys, also gave its name to roads, avenues and closes. As for the rest, they came like the ideas – from anywhere and everywhere.

Fred Basset quickly established his popularity. Fans came from all walks of life and from all ages. Here is a typical letter from the countless received:

Syndication takes Fred all over the world – America, South Africa, India, Dubai, Australia and many European countries – although Fred doesn't always keep his name. He is Wurzel in Germany, Loreng in Norway and Pitko in Finland.

Since Dad's death on 3rd December 1991, Fred Basset has remained a Graham family affair. I work together with the talented artist, Michael Martin, who lives in France with his wife Debbie and children Sam and Mia. Fred's new adventures continue to appear every day and by becoming one of the longest running strip cartoons in the world, Fred Basset has firmly sat on the idea that you can't teach an old dog new tricks.

Well done Fred!

Arran

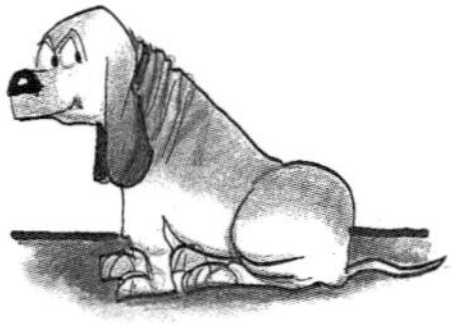

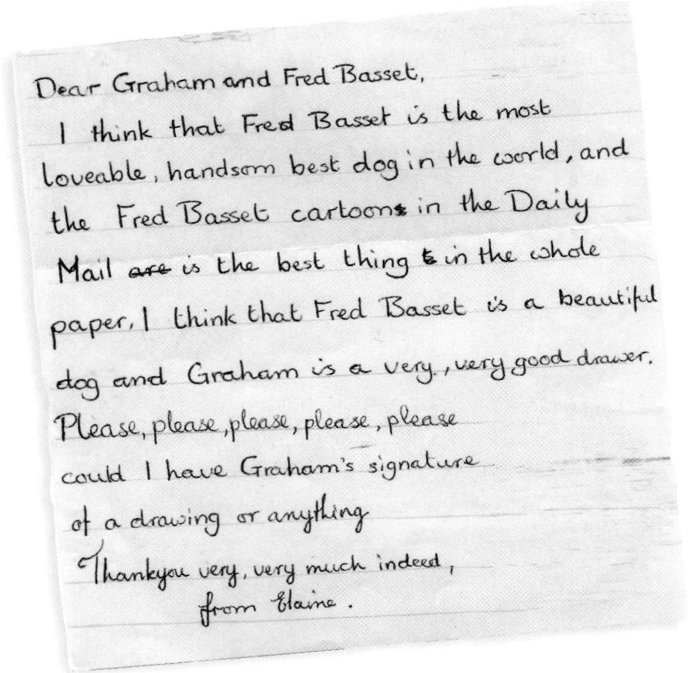

Dear Graham and Fred Basset,
I think that Fred Basset is the most loveable, handsom best dog in the world, and the Fred Basset cartoons in the Daily Mail ~~are~~ is the best thing ~~s~~ in the whole paper. I think that Fred Basset is a beautiful dog and Graham is a very, very good drawer.
Please, please, please, please, please could I have Graham's signature of a drawing or anything
Thankyou very, very much indeed,
from Elaine.

Alex Graham, with Freda, a gift from the *Daily Mail*.
Yorkie wasn't going to miss out on the photo call!

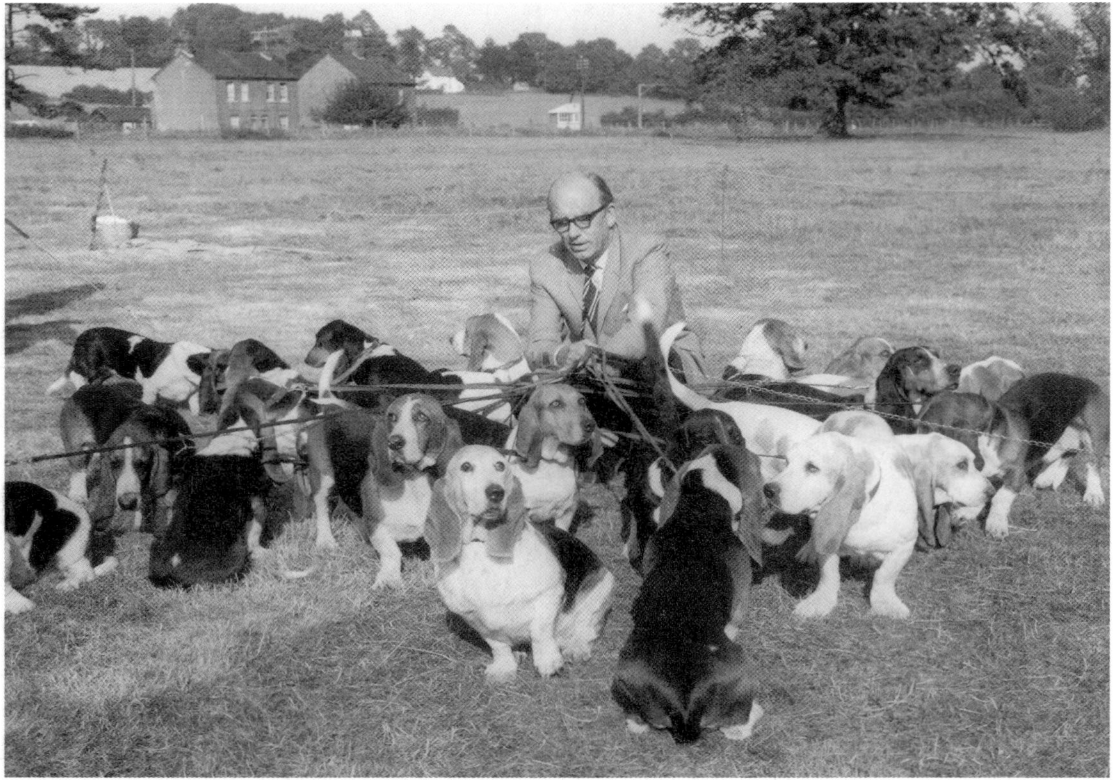

Alex Graham with a few of Fred's friends . . .

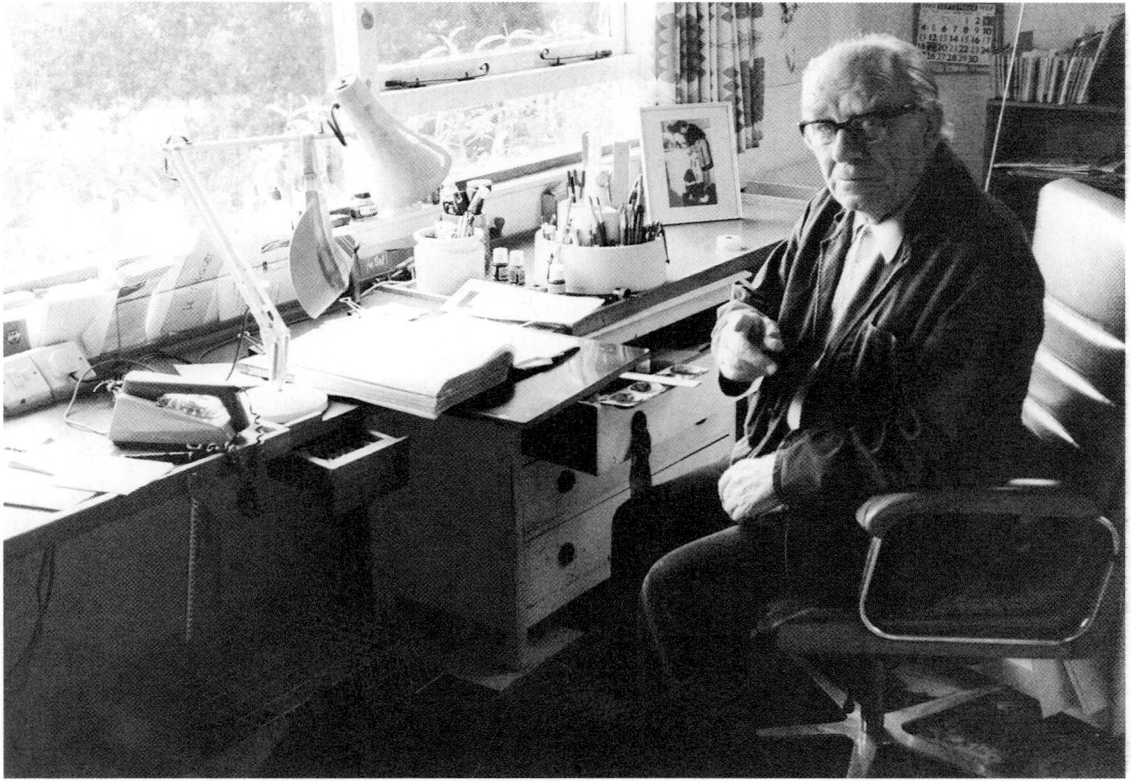

Alex Graham at work in his studio in the garden at Huntleys, Ticehurst.

How It All Began . . .

Interview with Alex Graham

The following is taken from an interview with Alex Graham, which originally appeared in Cartoonist Profiles in 1976. The first question asked how the Fred Basset cartoon strip came about.

It was going to be a family strip, first of all, and I produced some roughs on a six months contract, and he's been there ever since.

But it was you who decided to make it a Basset?

Yes, I suppose Bassets were possibly becoming popular then, and they've rather expressive faces – they didn't look like other dogs, they were a unique type of dog. There are lots of terriers but only one Basset type of dog.

How do you see the character of Fred? I mean, he's a little bit cowardly, a little bit cunning . . .

I think he's a little bit of everything. I mean, if you've got to carry on a daily strip year after year, he's got to be a bit of everything – sometimes he's cowardly, sometimes he's brave, sometimes he's slow and sometimes he's quick. I think that if you look through it over the years, he's everything.

But the basis of the humour is that he's a dog but he's behaving like a person?

The basis of the humour is that he's a dog who *thinks* like a person. I think the unusual thing is that he's the character in the strip who is commenting on the behaviour of the other characters in the strip.

The rest of the 'cast' came on slowly, Jock, Yorky . . .

Just happened – I mean there was no deliberate intention – they just came and then they became sort of built-in.

You hadn't drawn a lot of dogs before the strip began?

I had done a few dog drawings for *Punch* but I wasn't very good at drawing them.

But for the purpose of this strip, the Daily Mail bought you a Basset?

Yes – because in the first week or two, so many people said it didn't look like a Basset that they thought they'd better buy me a Basset!

Now just give us an outline of your working day – you have it structured so that you can work at certain times?

Oh, yes. I work in the mornings and the evenings purely. I don't work in the afternoons. In the mornings I do the actual physical thing of drawing – I mean, I could have the radio on if I wanted it. Then in the evenings for about an hour and a half, two hours, I do pretty intensive inventing. I would never think of trying to invent anything before 5.30 in the evening.

Now getting away from Fred for a moment, of course you were doing lots of work for many years before Fred came along and you still do lots of other things. The only regular one I can think of is 'Briggs the Butler' for Tatler. ***Any other regular ones?***

When I started with the *Daily Mail* I was doing three strips actually – one I started during the War in Scotland, one for *Titbits* and the weekly one for *Tatler*, but then I pared this down and now I only do one strip in fact. But the one I did in Scotland which started in 1945 still continues but I don't do it. In fact they bought the rights and repeated it – I did that for 25 years. I think it's probably the longest running strip in the country. It's called 'Wee Hughie'.

Do you ever have 'off days', when you can't produce a single idea, or very few?

Well, occasionally, but I generally know if it's an 'off day' and I wouldn't even start. It may well be that I'm tired. I may have been playing golf all day and it comes to half past five and I think – 'No, not tonight'. Then I have days when I have a great sort of rush.

And being a canny Scotsman you like to have a good many strips in hand?

Being a canny Scotsman, I'm a year ahead!

Your father was an engineer. Any other artists in the family?

None whatsoever.

And you decided to go to art school did you, after being at school?

I decided when I was about twelve to be a cartoonist in fact. Then I went to art school when I was seventeen – a very long time ago. I found that they didn't teach cartooning but rather posters and that sort of thing. I didn't like that so I switched to drawing and painting and did rather well.

I understand you did very well. In fact, you won prizes for the best oils, the best portraits and landscapes. Is there an advantage

for a cartoonist in having academic training?
I don't think there's any advantage. The only advantage in my academic training was the ability to draw quickly – and also I think it helps you to compose, to fill a frame properly, fill a picture properly.

Was there ever a conflict as to whether you'd be a painter and do cartoons in your spare time?
Oh yes. I started doing cartoons during the War, when I happened to be lucky enough to occasionally be in a place where I could. I sold my first drawing when I was at school, but having done fairly well as a painter I didn't know quite what I was going to do. Then I took the step and came to London. I wasn't very good at cartooning then. It just happened that there weren't very many about just immediately post-War.

You just sent cartoons to a paper?
I got an agent, actually, and he knew of so many little markets that I'd never heard of that he practically sold everything, bad as it was, that I produced. During the War I was in the Argylls [Argyll & Sutherland Highlanders] and immediately post-War I came to London just on spec. I was just newly married, we were expecting our son, and we shared a flat in London with a Scots girl at 12/6 a week.

So another good thing to come out of the Glasgow Academy of Art was your wife Winnifred!
Indeed, yes. We were students together.

She was also an extremely good artist and also taught didn't she for a time?
She taught after the War but she never touched a paintbrush after she left art school and she hasn't touched one since.

Jud Hurd was talking about some of his cartoon friends, who have methods of work consisting of discussing ideas with colleagues or friends – snowballing, or kicking ideas around. You've never really done that, have you?
Never done that at all – I don't even discuss it with my wife – in fact, if I finish work in the evening, I can't remember within ten minutes what I was working at last! I can't possibly discuss it with anybody if I've forgotten it already!

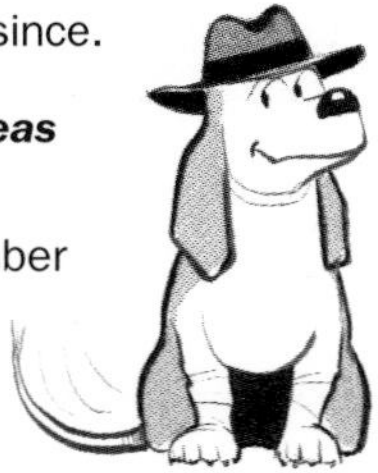

From Sketchbook To Artwork

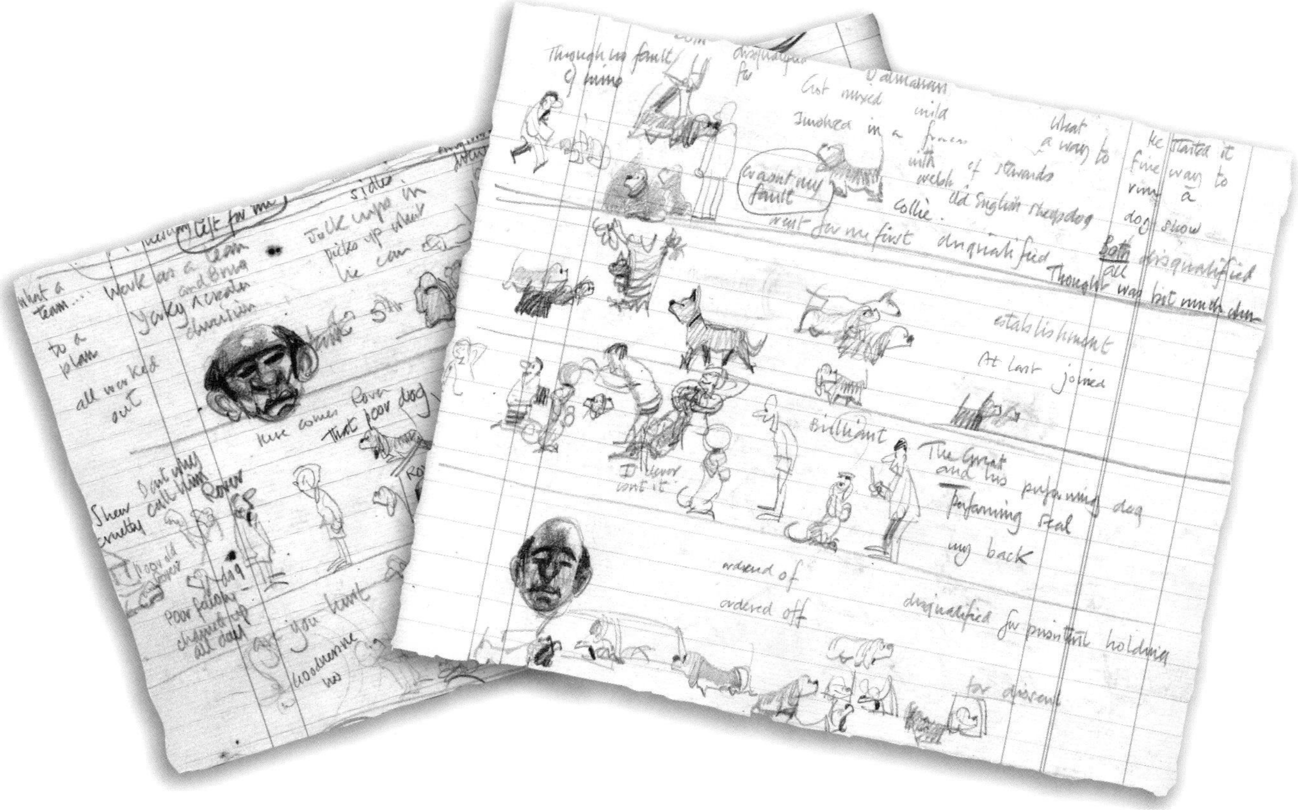
Wasn't my fault
Old English sheepdog
collie
establishment
At last joined
Brilliant
The Great and his performing dog
Performing seal
my back
ordered off
disqualified for positional holding

An excerpt from one of Alex Graham's ideas books. These incorporated storylines, doodles and the odd self-portrait!

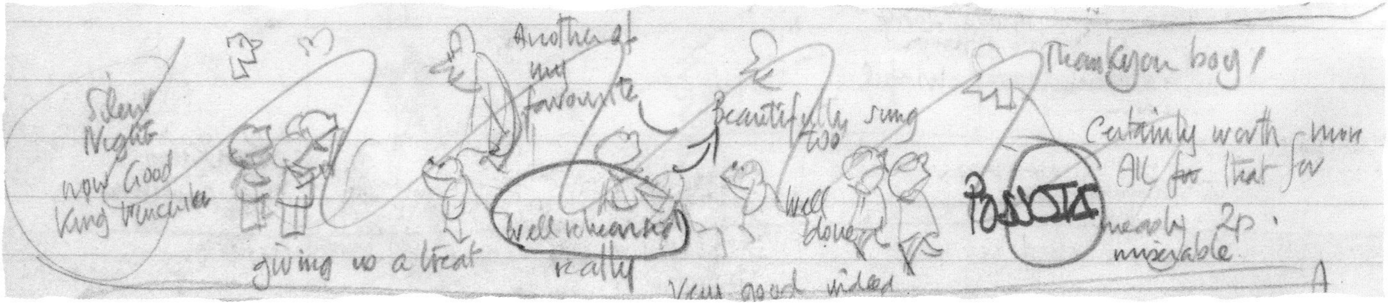

Silent Night
now Good King Wenceslas
giving us a treat
Another of my favourite
Well rehearsed
really
Beautifully sung too
Well done
Thank you boy!
Certainly worth more
All for that for
POSSOK
nearly 2p.
miserable

Carol Singers – the doodle. Note the circle on the right with the word POSSOK. This was short for Possibly OK.

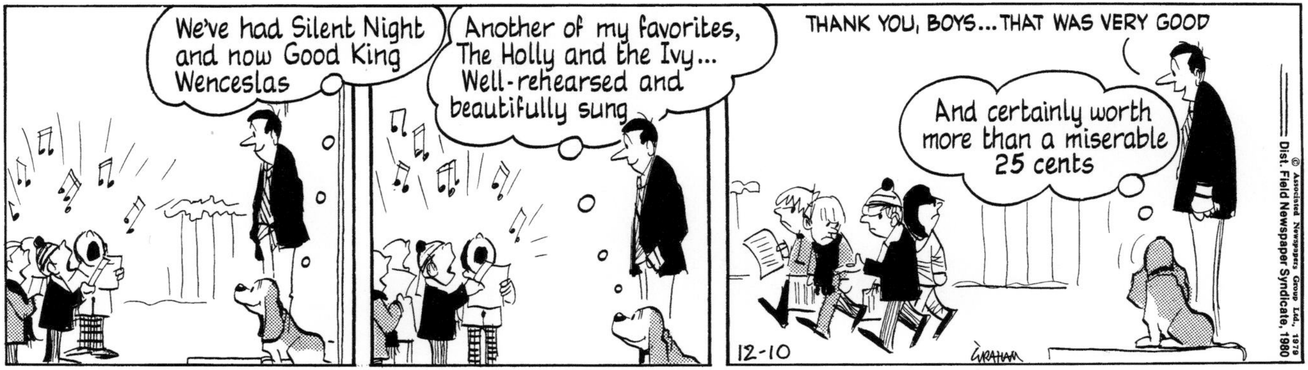
We've had Silent Night and now Good King Wenceslas
Another of my favorites, The Holly and the Ivy... Well-rehearsed and beautifully sung
THANK YOU, BOYS... THAT WAS VERY GOOD
And certainly worth more than a miserable 25 cents
12-10
GRAHAM
© Associated Newspapers Group Ltd., 1979
Dist. Field Newspaper Syndicate, 1980

Carol singers – the finished strip. Fred's international appeal is apparent, as the 2p has been altered to 25 cents, and American spelling used, for the American newspapers.

How Fred Has Changed . . .

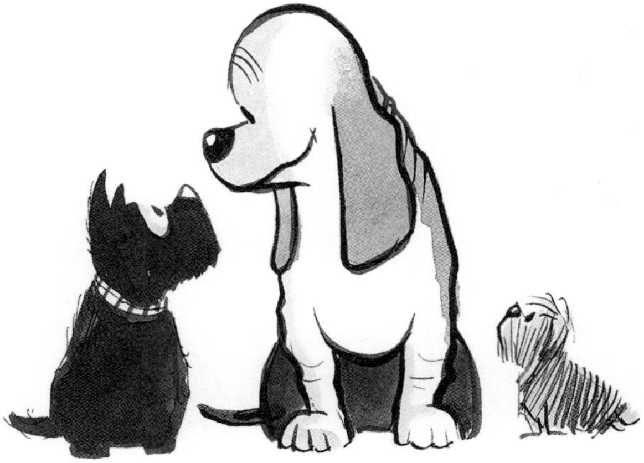

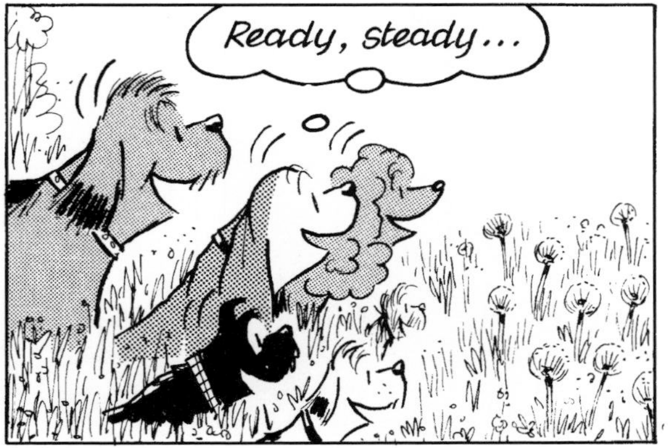

Ready, steady...

Fred Basset has evolved over the years, as can be seen from the contrasting styles of the 1970s' version on the left with the 2004 version.

FRED BASSET
by GRAHAM
THEY SAY THERE'S A WONDERFUL VIEW FROM THE TOP... SHALL WE HAVE A LOOK...?
Good idea
374
COME ON, FRED
Huh...?
Aren't we taking the car...?

Strip 374 was published in 1964. The overall style is very different . . .

HERE WE ARE
I wonder?
SUNNYSIDE GUEST HOUSE
We have!
A room with a view!

. . . to that of the present day.

Fred Branches Out . . .

Over the years, fifty-six Fred Basset books have been published and they still continue today. The early editions had distinctive yellow and black covers and have now become collector's items.

In addition to the books, Fred has inspired a variety of other spin-off items, including calendars and greetings cards. Just like the strip, some ideas work immediately, and need no attention before being drawn up as finished artwork, whilst, as can be seen overleaf, others need teasing out . . .

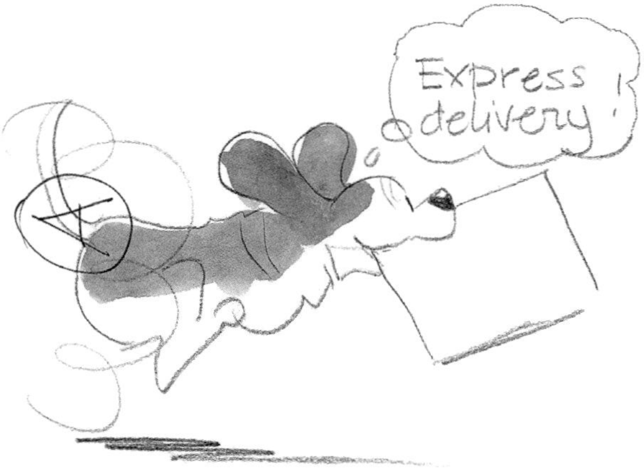
Express delivery!

[left] Rough sketch for the front of a birthday card.

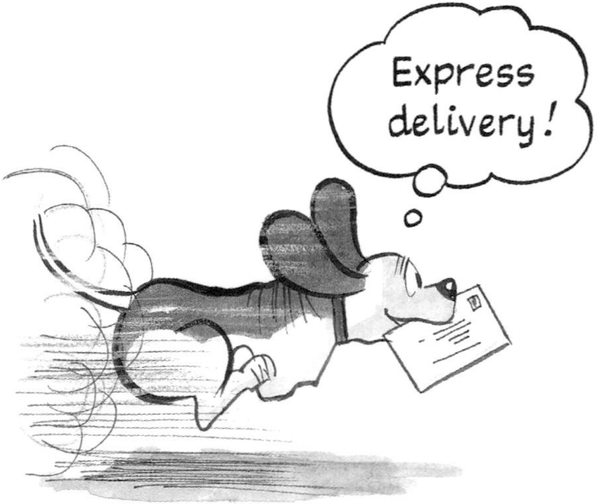
Express delivery!

[right] The finished artwork, which has scarcely changed at all.

Happy
Birthday

The rough sketch and finished artwork for inside the birthday card show a distinct change from concept to final design.

It's for you!
HAPPY BIRTHDAY

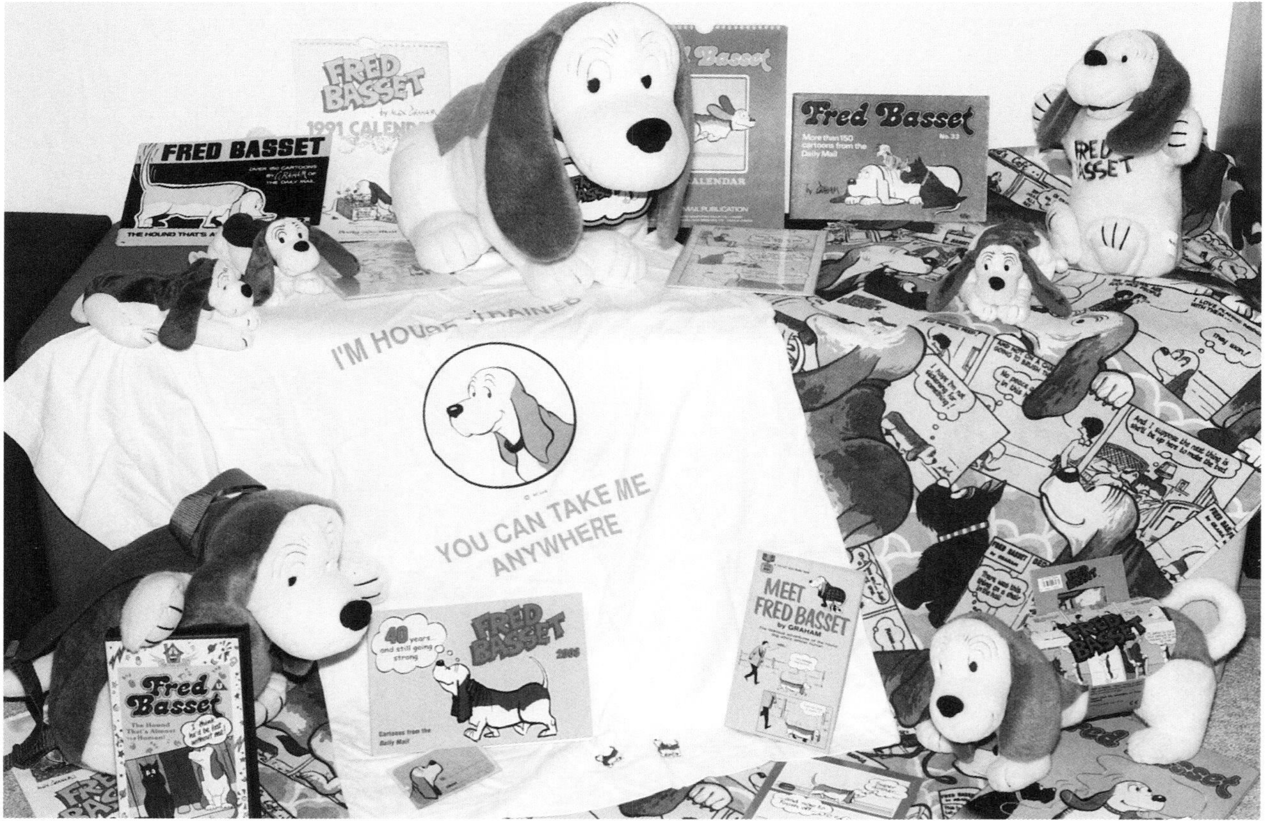
FRED BASSET
OVER 150 CARTOONS BY GRAHAM OF THE DAILY MAIL
FRED BASSET
Fred Basset
More than 150 cartoons from the Daily Mail
YOU CAN TAKE ME ANYWHERE
40 years... and still going strong
FRED BASSET
Cartoons from the Daily Mail
MEET FRED BASSET by GRAHAM
Fred Basset
The Hound That's Almost Human!

Photograph © Alan Ewers

Over forty-odd years there has been a variety of items available, including material for curtains, cushions and bed linen, toys, calendars, badges, pendants, a children's book and much, much more. Many of the items have been used for exhibitions, for example at an international exhibition of cartoons held in 2004 in St. Gaudens, south-west France.

In the mid-1970s, Fred Basset hit the small screen, when the BBC broadcast a series of five-minute films just before the six o'clock news. The voice of Fred was that of the actor Lionel Jeffries, and the series was later released on video. This isn't Fred's only brush with television: he once put in an appearance on the American quiz show *Jeopardy*. Asked to complete Fred's name, the poor contestant looked flummoxed, before inspiration struck, he answered correctly and received a substantial cash prize.

Fans Of Fred

In 1977 Alex Graham and Charles Schulz met in London. Here the two cartoonists are shown, together with their famous creations, Fred and Snoopy. Spare a thought for Fred as it is the only occasion that he has appeared in public without his characteristic shading! These two men retained their friendship through correspondence over a number of years.

Alex Graham considered P. G. Wodehouse his 'hero as humorist'. It gave him great pleasure to receive letters from his hero and to learn that P. G. Wodehouse followed Fred's escapades in his local Long Island newspaper. Indeed, in 1968, when the *Long Island Press* dropped the strip, they had to reinstate it after pressure from many of the residents, including Mr Wodehouse himself.

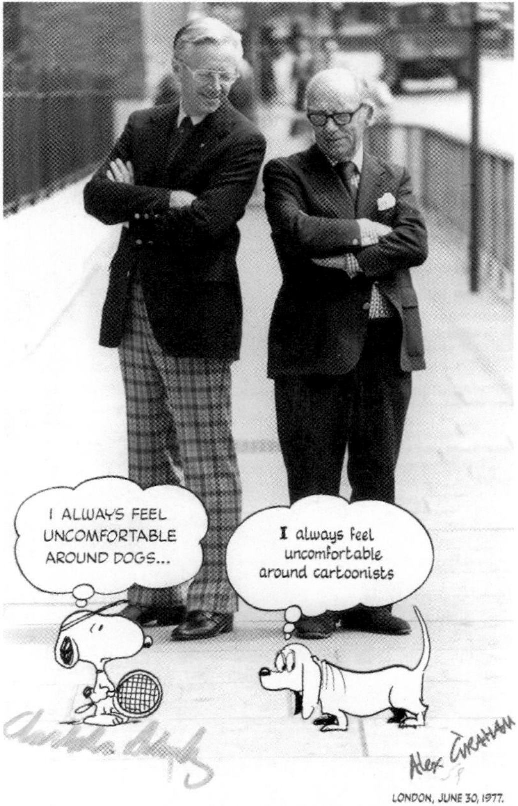
I ALWAYS FEEL UNCOMFORTABLE AROUND DOGS...
I always feel uncomfortable around cartoonists
Alex Graham
LONDON, JUNE 30, 1977.

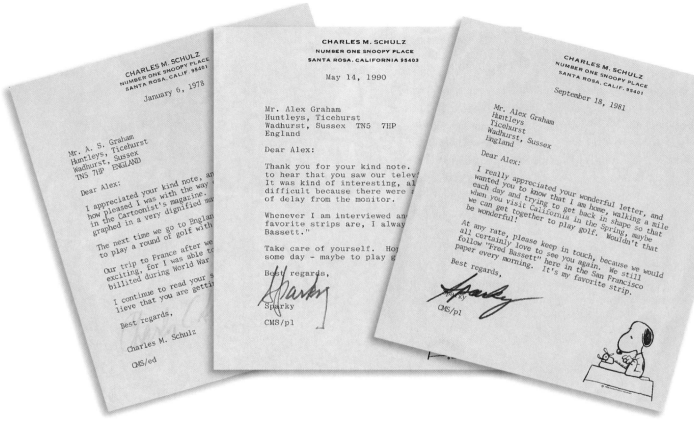

CHARLES M. SCHULZ
NUMBER ONE SNOOPY PLACE
SANTA ROSA, CALIF. 95401

January 6, 1978

Mr. A. S. Graham
Huntleys, Ticehurst
Wadhurst, Sussex
TN5 7HP ENGLAND

Dear Alex:

I appreciated your kind note, an
how pleased I was with the way
in the Cartoonist's magazine.
graphed in a very dignified ma

The next time we go to Englan
to play a round of golf with

Our trip to France after we
exciting, for I was able to
billited during World War

I continue to read your s
lieve that you are gettin

Best regards,

Charles M. Schulz

CMS/ed

CHARLES M. SCHULZ
NUMBER ONE SNOOPY PLACE
SANTA ROSA, CALIFORNIA 95403

May 14, 1990

Mr. Alex Graham
Huntleys, Ticehurst
Wadhurst, Sussex TN5 7HP
England

Dear Alex:

Thank you for your kind note.
to hear that you saw our telev
It was kind of interesting, al
difficult because there were a
of delay from the monitor.

Whenever I am interviewed an
favorite strips are, I alway
Bassett."

Take care of yourself. Ho
some day - maybe to play g

Best regards,

Sparky

CMS/pl

CHARLES M. SCHULZ
NUMBER ONE SNOOPY PLACE
SANTA ROSA, CALIF. 95401

September 18, 1981

Mr. Alex Graham
Huntleys
Ticehurst
Wadhurst, Sussex
England

Dear Alex:

I really appreciated your wonderful letter, and
wanted you to know that I am home, walking a mile
each day and trying to get back in shape so that
when you visit California in the Spring, maybe
we can get together to play golf. Wouldn't that
be wonderful!

At any rate, please keep in touch, because we would
all certainly love to see you again. We still
follow "Fred Bassett" here in the San Francisco
paper every morning. It's my favorite strip.

Best regards,

Sparky

CMS/pl

A few of the letters from Charles Schulz . . .

36

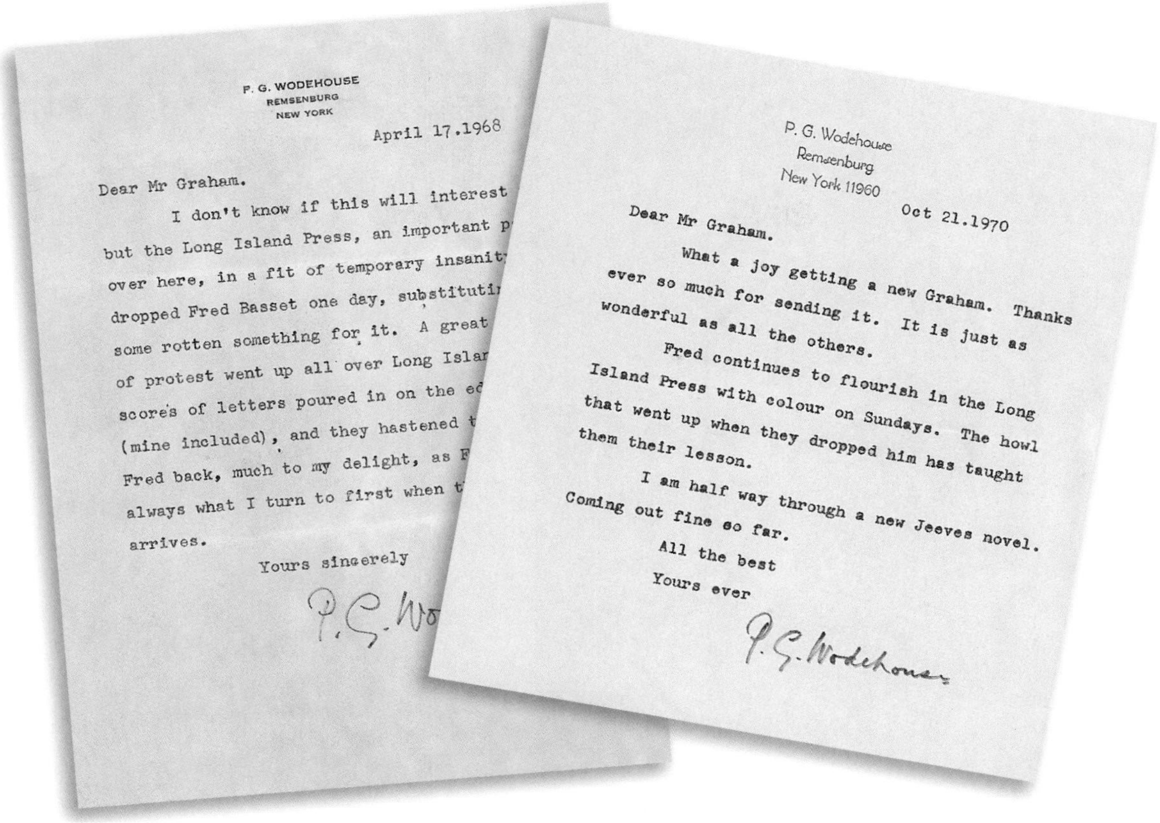

P. G. WODEHOUSE
REMSENBURG
NEW YORK

April 17.1968

Dear Mr Graham.

I don't know if this will interest
but the Long Island Press, an important p
over here, in a fit of temporary insanit
dropped Fred Basset one day, substitutin
some rotten something for it. A great
of protest went up all over Long Islan
scores of letters poured in on the ed
(mine included), and they hastened t
Fred back, much to my delight, as F
always what I turn to first when t
arrives.

Yours sincerely

P. G. Wo

P. G. Wodehouse
Remsenburg
New York 11960

Oct 21.1970

Dear Mr Graham.

What a joy getting a new Graham. Thanks ever so much for sending it. It is just as wonderful as all the others.

Fred continues to flourish in the Long Island Press with colour on Sundays. The howl that went up when they dropped him has taught them their lesson.

I am half way through a new Jeeves novel. Coming out fine so far.

All the best

Yours ever

P. G. Wodehouse

. . . and P. G. Wodehouse.

Fred Around The World . . .

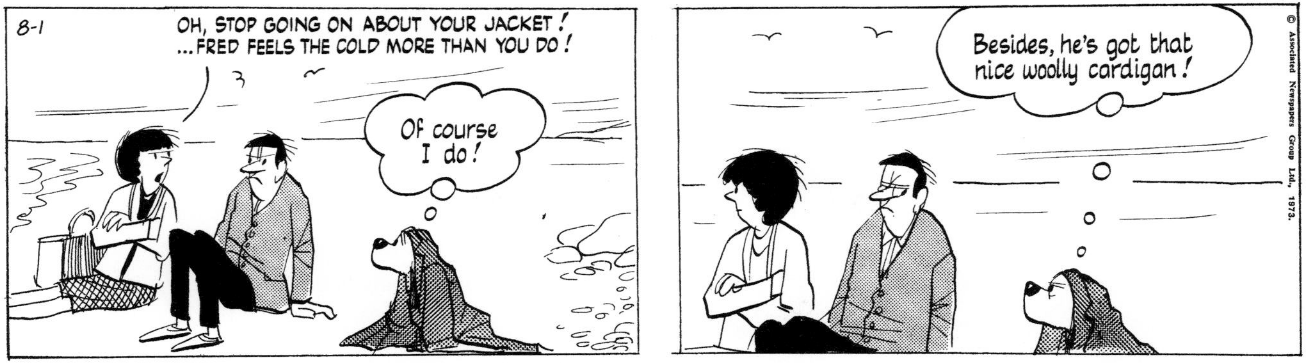

8-1
OH, STOP GOING ON ABOUT YOUR JACKET! ...FRED FEELS THE COLD MORE THAN YOU DO!
Of course I do!
Besides, he's got that nice woolly cardigan!
© Associated Newspapers Group Ltd., 1973.

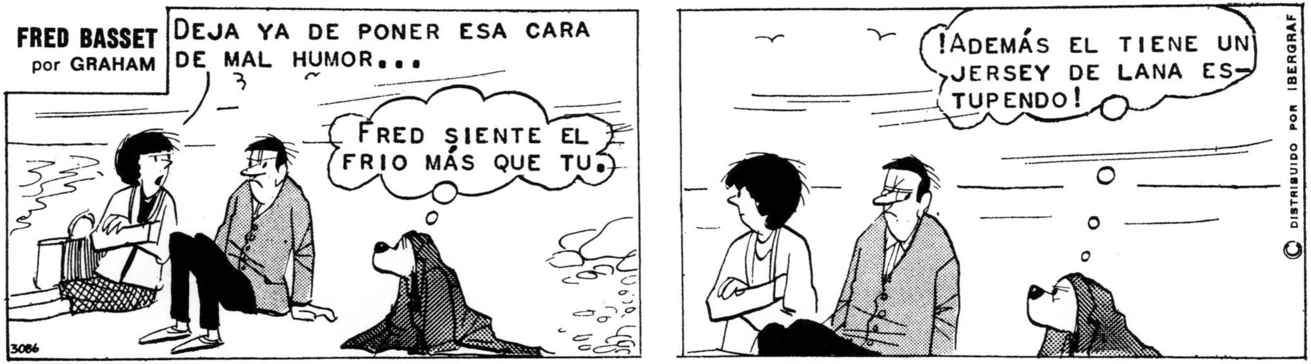

FRED BASSET por GRAHAM
DEJA YA DE PONER ESA CARA DE MAL HUMOR...
FRED SIENTE EL FRIO MÁS QUE TU.
¡ADEMÁS EL TIENE UN JERSEY DE LANA ESTUPENDO!
© DISTRIBUIDO POR IBERGRAF
3086

Syndication has taken Fred Basset to many parts of the world, including North and South America, Australia, South Africa, India, Malaysia, Bahrain, Saudi Arabia, Jamaica and many European countries. Here is a Spanish version, exchanging Camber Sands for the beaches of Benidorm!

Fred Basset was very popular in South Africa and for a time Alex Graham was honorary President of the South African Basset Hound Club. In February 1979 Alex, together with his wife Winnifred, was invited to visit South Africa.

On arrival at Johannesburg Airport he told an awaiting reporter that he was 'dog tired' by the flight, and yet forty-eight hours later he was in the hound ring as a judge. The winning basset received a tartan coat and an embroidered cushion and the proud owner was presented with fifty rand in cash and a year's supply of dog food!

Alex Graham and Fred in the *Cape Town Argus* during his South African trip.

The man behind lovable Fred

BET HE'S NOT LIVING ON BONES DOWN THERE!

FOR once Fred Basset takes a back seat to his creator Alex Graham. In Cape Town for a holiday of golf and visiting relations, Mr Graham had to leave his lovable hound behind. Fred, who in real life is actually Freda, makes a typically Basset comment on his owner's holiday habits. Fred(a) is sulking in kennels back home in England.

Fred Today . . .

Fred Basset continues in safe hands with Michael Martin's sympathetic artwork and Alex Graham's daughter providing that essential family flair. The two work closely together to create Fred's unique blend of observation and gentle good humour. The twenty-first century has brought new technology, changes to the English language and a more hectic and pressurised pace of life and Fred has never been slow in letting his audience know his own views on these developments. But there will always be the favourite pastimes of burying bones, chasing rabbits and taking a little time out to watch the world go by.

Ever since the first television series thirty-odd years ago, Fred Basset has thought of himself as a bit of a matinée idol and, with that little touch of vanity every star needs, he has even pointed out his best side when photographed by a speed camera! It is therefore with some pride that he can announce 'Fred Basset – the television show' is being developed by VGI Entertainment and will be coming soon.

All in all, not bad for a dog with short legs, long ears and a mind of his own . . .

The Very First Fred Basset Book 1963

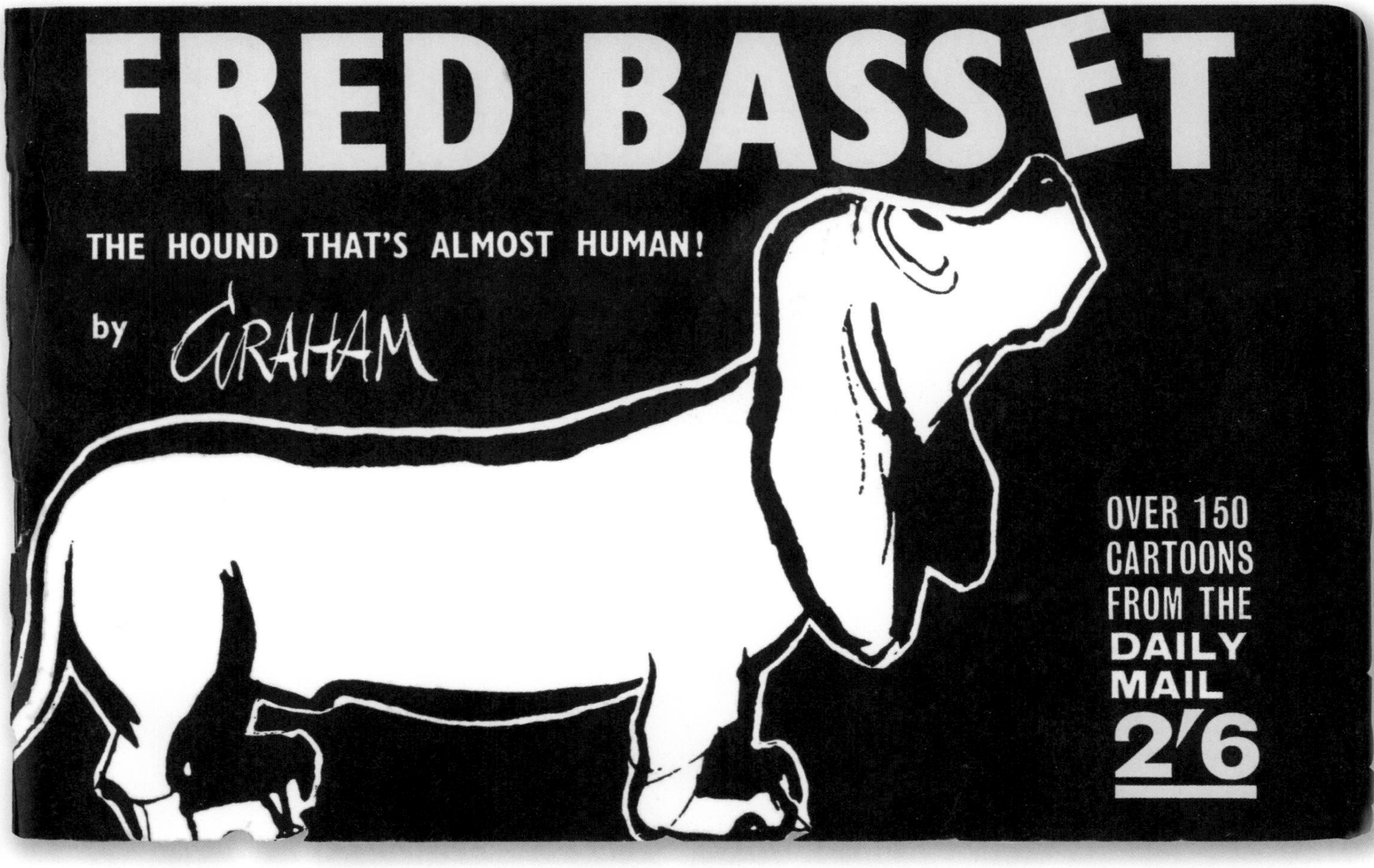
FRED BASSET
THE HOUND THAT'S ALMOST HUMAN!
by GRAHAM
OVER 150 CARTOONS FROM THE DAILY MAIL
2'6

FRED BASSET

Rarely has a new cartoon character seized the public funny bone with such swift and enduring effect as Fred Basset, the dog-shaped dog who thinks like a man.

Since he first appeared in the columns of the Daily Mail the inimitable Fred has been bringing a sharp eye and cynical tolerance to the human condition. By turns heroic, cowardly, gallant, rebellious, innocent and knowing, and a constant prey to insecurity, he mirrors so much of the infinite variety of human nature.

Here they are then, for new readers to enjoy and the connoisseurs to savour again at their leisure, the exploits of our best friend, the one and only Fred Basset. Enter Fred . . . thinking.

Published by ASSOCIATED NEWSPAPERS LTD. LONDON E.C.4. Printed by Cox and Wyman Ltd. London & Reading

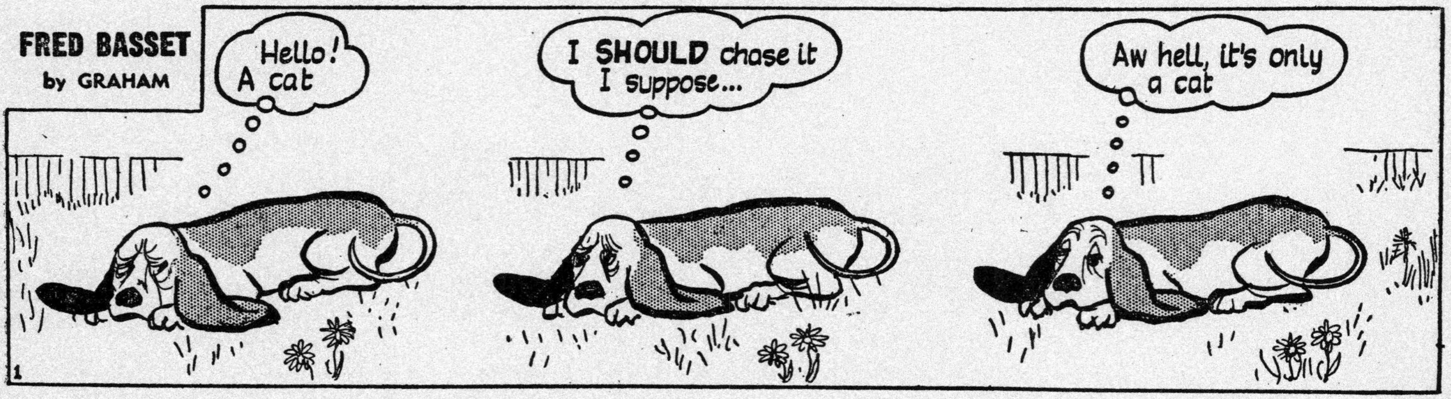
FRED BASSET
by GRAHAM
Hello! A cat
I SHOULD chase it I suppose...
Aw hell, it's only a cat
1

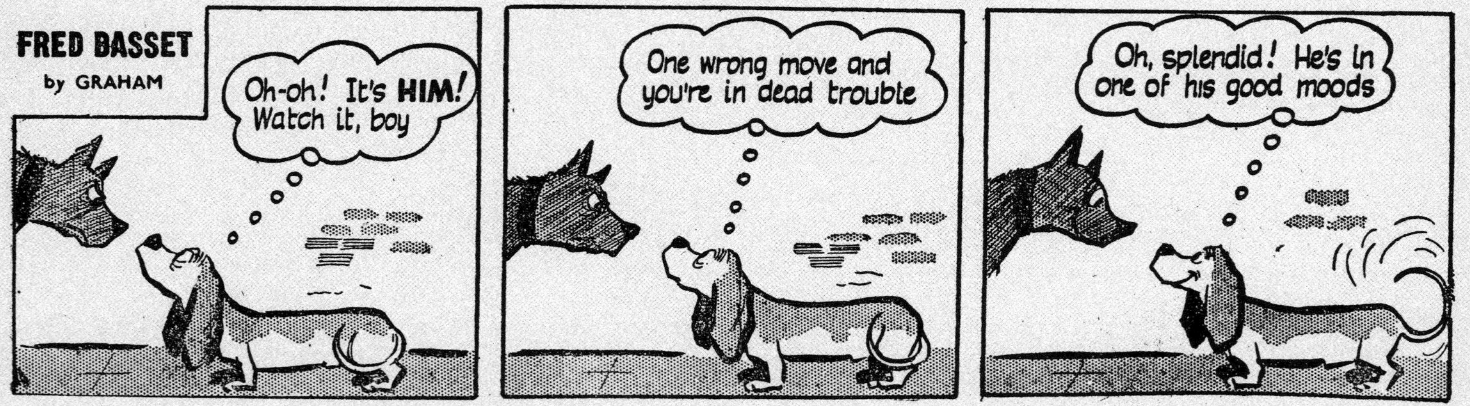
FRED BASSET
by GRAHAM
Oh-oh! It's HIM! Watch it, boy
One wrong move and you're in dead trouble
Oh, splendid! He's in one of his good moods

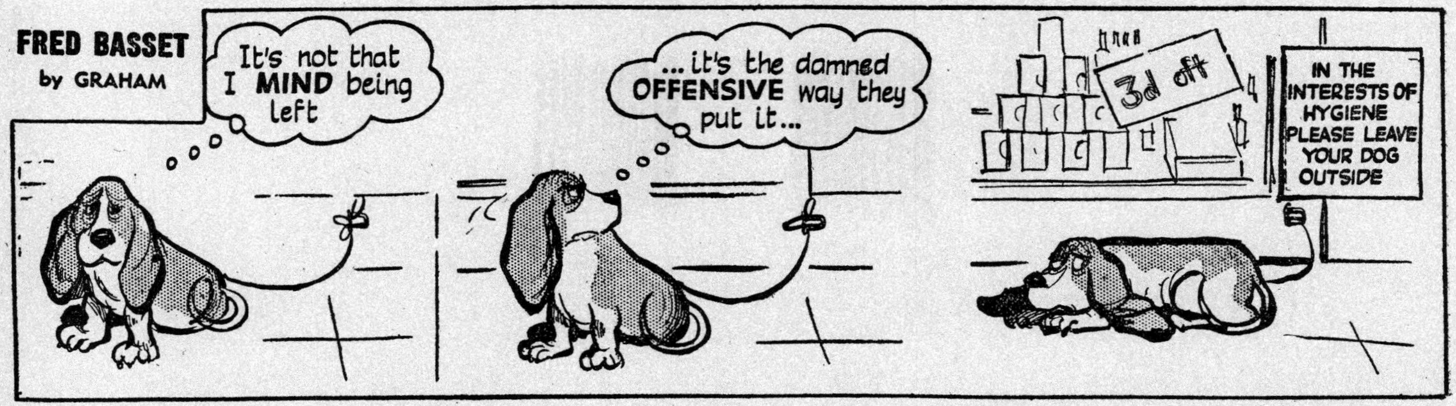
FRED BASSET
by GRAHAM
It's not that I MIND being left
... it's the damned OFFENSIVE way they put it...
3d off
IN THE INTERESTS OF HYGIENE PLEASE LEAVE YOUR DOG OUTSIDE

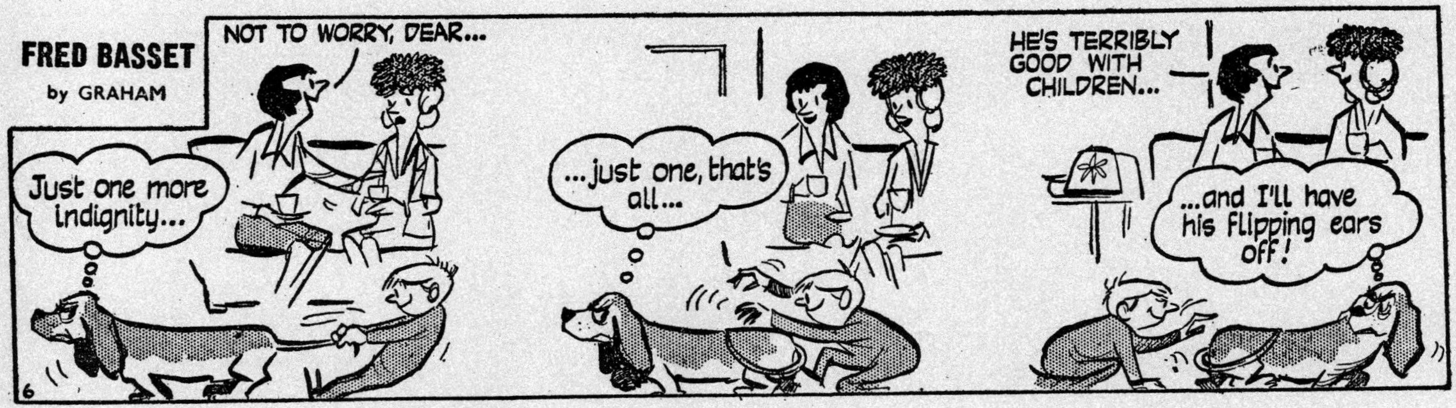
FRED BASSET
by GRAHAM
NOT TO WORRY, DEAR...
Just one more indignity...
...just one, that's all...
HE'S TERRIBLY GOOD WITH CHILDREN...
...and I'll have his flipping ears off!

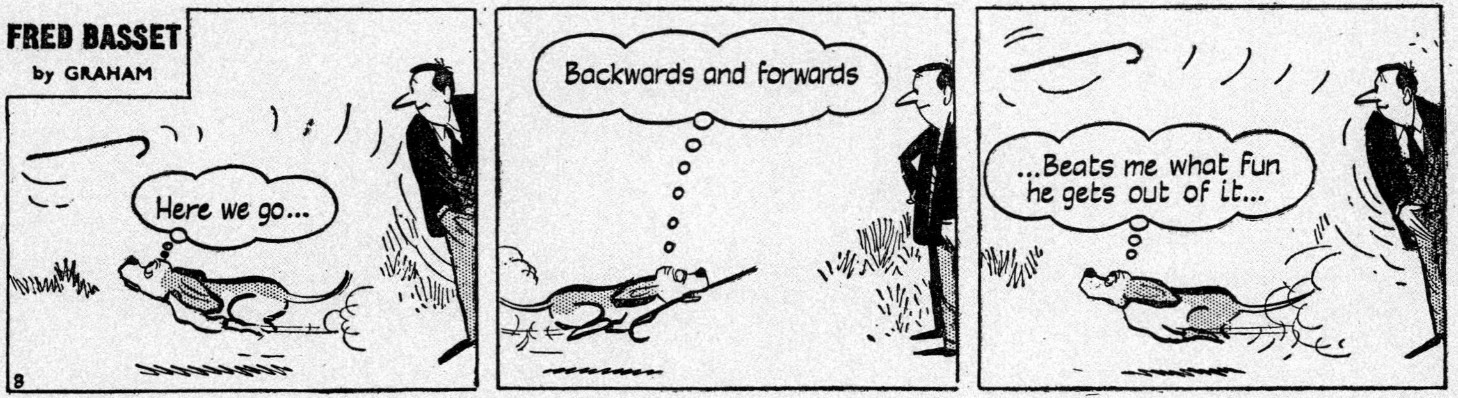
FRED BASSET
by GRAHAM
Here we go...
Backwards and forwards
...Beats me what fun he gets out of it...
8

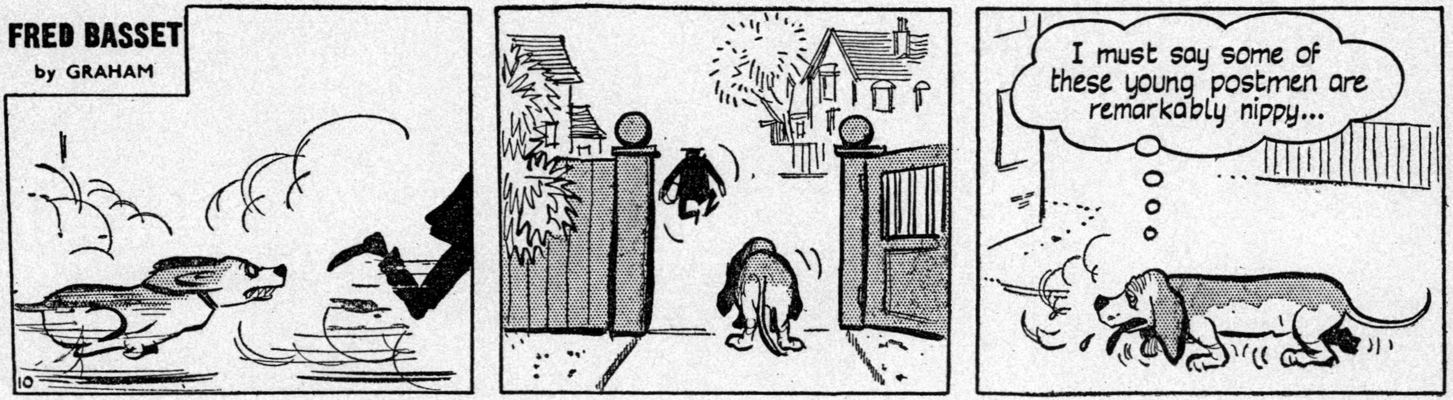
FRED BASSET
by GRAHAM
I must say some of these young postmen are remarkably nippy...
10

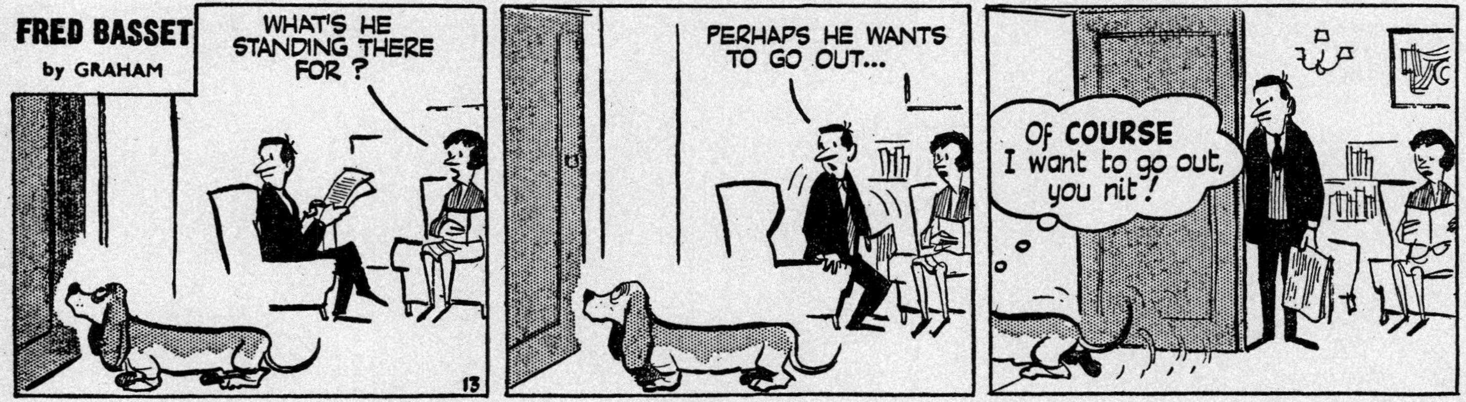
FRED BASSET
by GRAHAM
WHAT'S HE STANDING THERE FOR ?
13
PERHAPS HE WANTS TO GO OUT...
Of COURSE I want to go out, you nit !

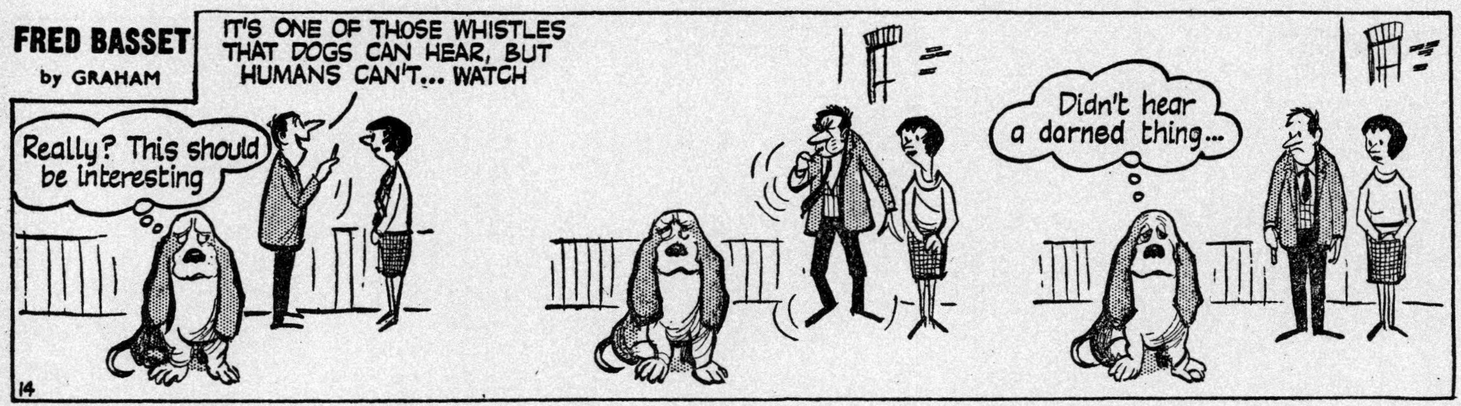
FRED BASSET
by GRAHAM
IT'S ONE OF THOSE WHISTLES THAT DOGS CAN HEAR, BUT HUMANS CAN'T... WATCH
Really? This should be interesting
14
Didn't hear a darned thing...

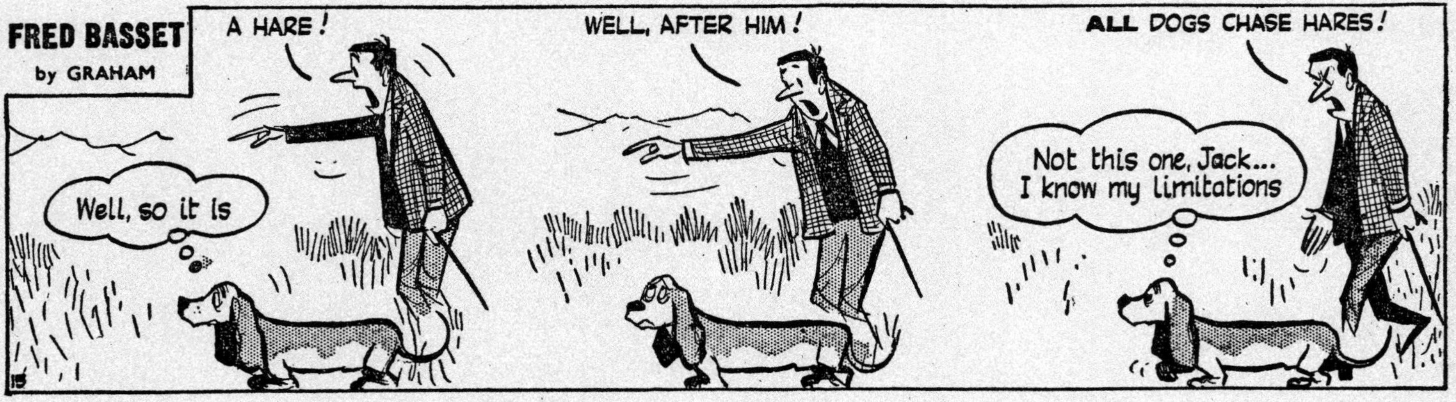
FRED BASSET
by GRAHAM
A HARE!
Well, so it is
WELL, AFTER HIM!
ALL DOGS CHASE HARES!
Not this one, Jack... I know my limitations
15

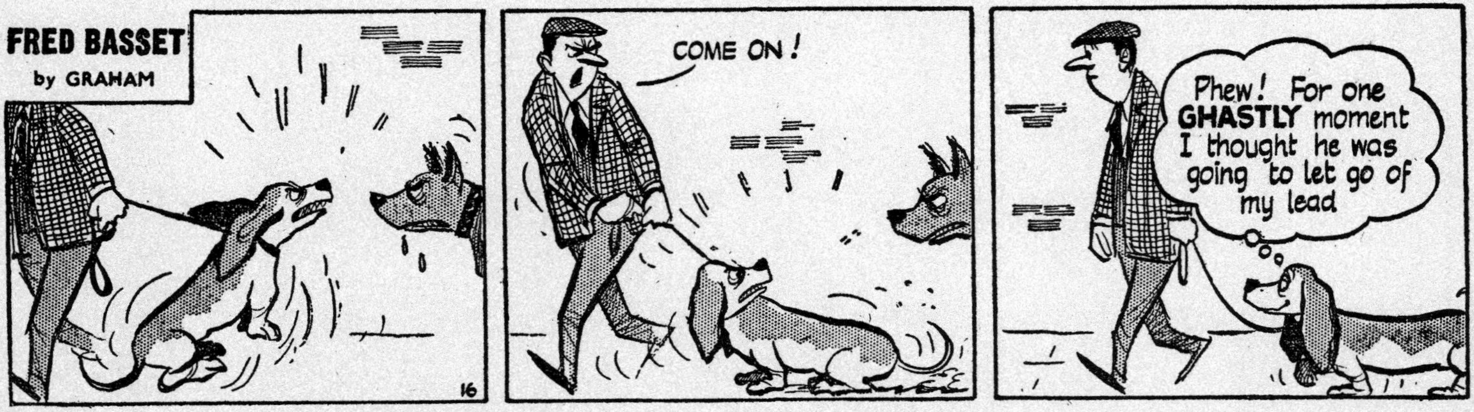
FRED BASSET
by GRAHAM
16
COME ON!
Phew! For one GHASTLY moment I thought he was going to let go of my lead

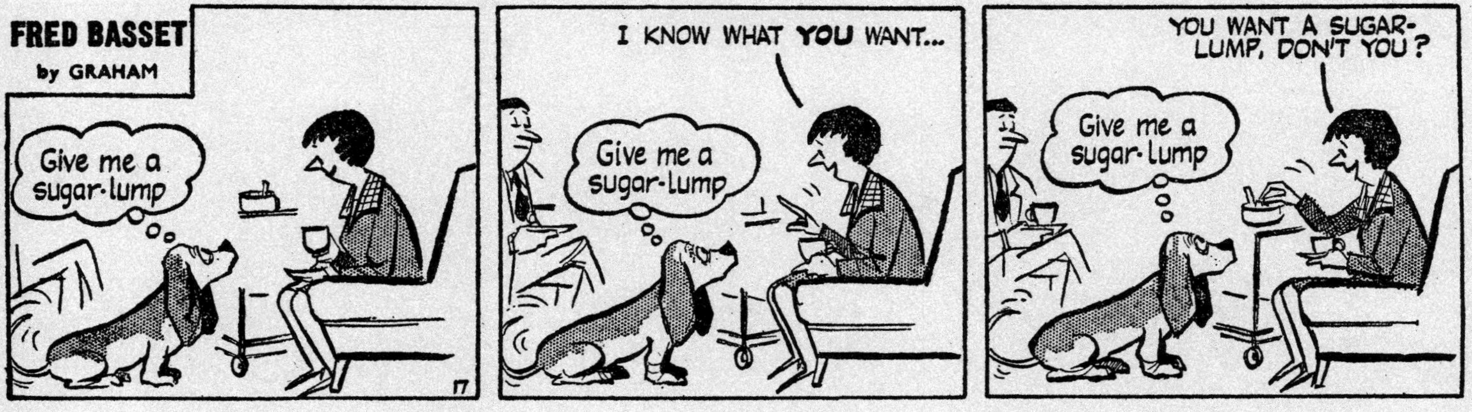
FRED BASSET
by GRAHAM
Give me a sugar-lump
I KNOW WHAT **YOU** WANT...
Give me a sugar-lump
YOU WANT A SUGAR-LUMP, DON'T YOU?
Give me a sugar-lump

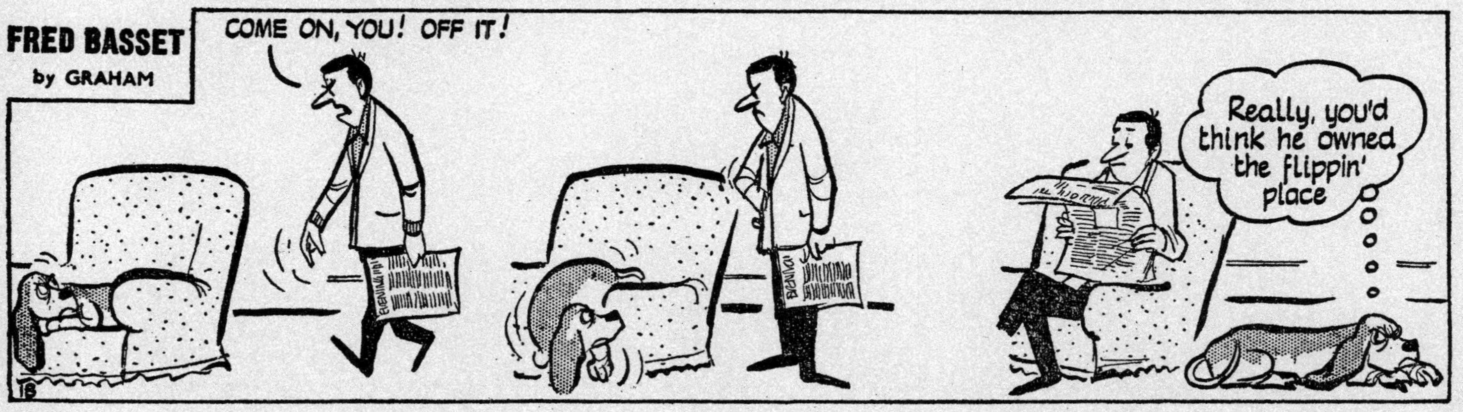
FRED BASSET
by GRAHAM
COME ON, YOU! OFF IT!
Really, you'd think he owned the flippin' place

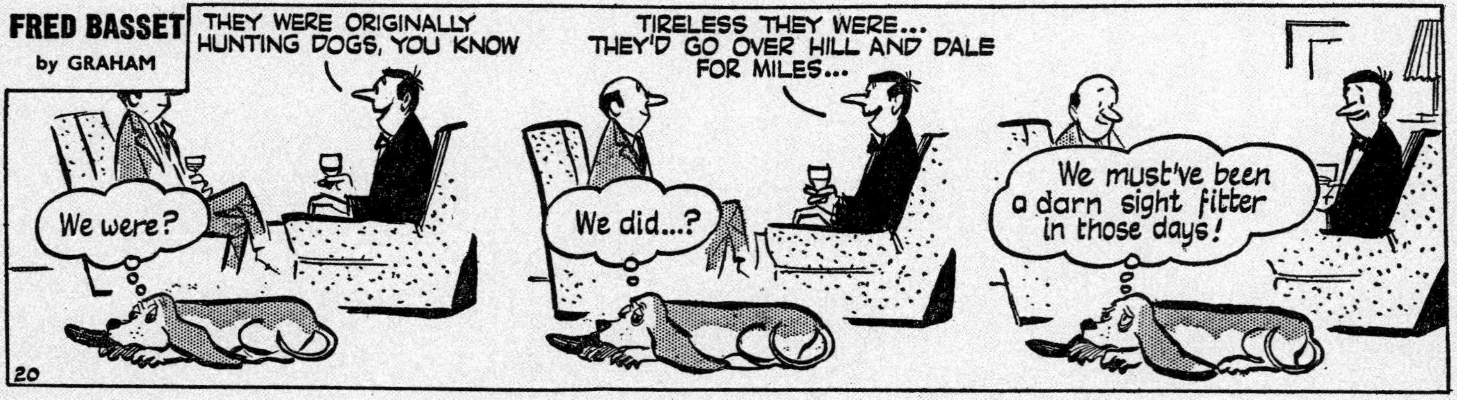
FRED BASSET
by GRAHAM
THEY WERE ORIGINALLY HUNTING DOGS, YOU KNOW
We were?
TIRELESS THEY WERE... THEY'D GO OVER HILL AND DALE FOR MILES...
We did...?
We must've been a darn sight fitter in those days!
20

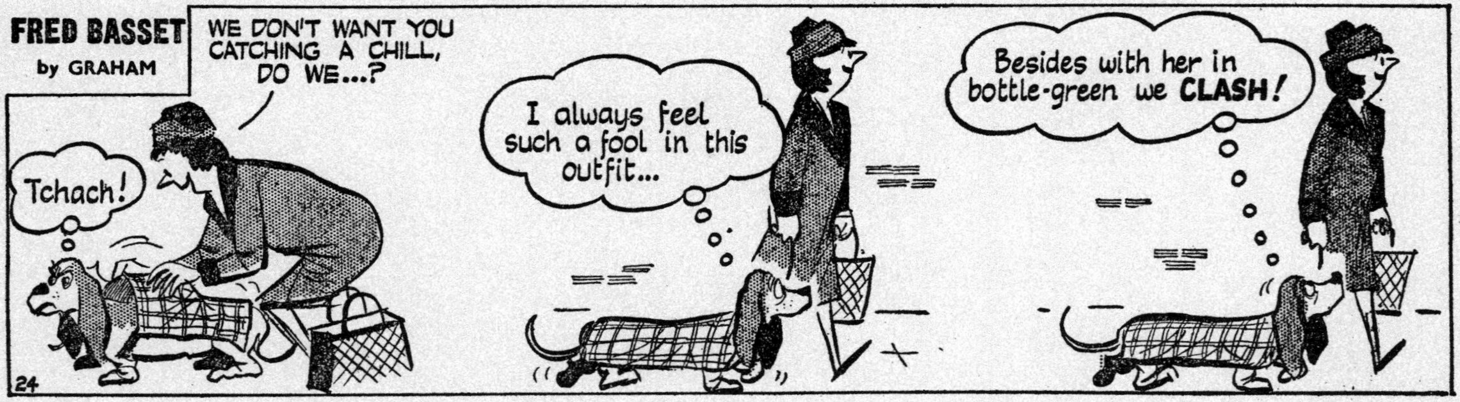
FRED BASSET
by GRAHAM
WE DON'T WANT YOU CATCHING A CHILL, DO WE...?
Tchach!
I always feel such a fool in this outfit...
Besides with her in bottle-green we **CLASH**!
24

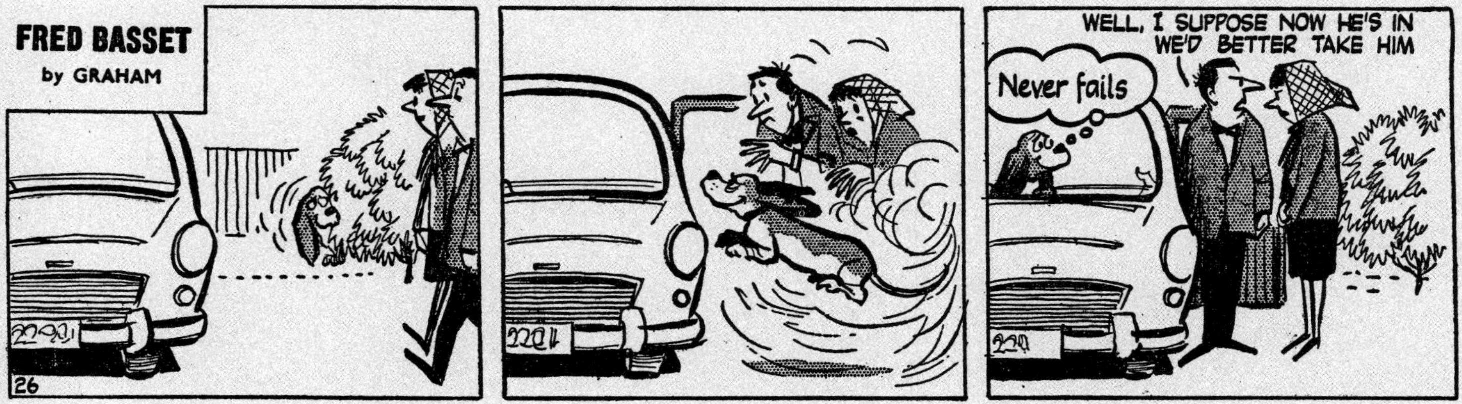
FRED BASSET
by GRAHAM
26
Never fails
WELL, I SUPPOSE NOW HE'S IN WE'D BETTER TAKE HIM

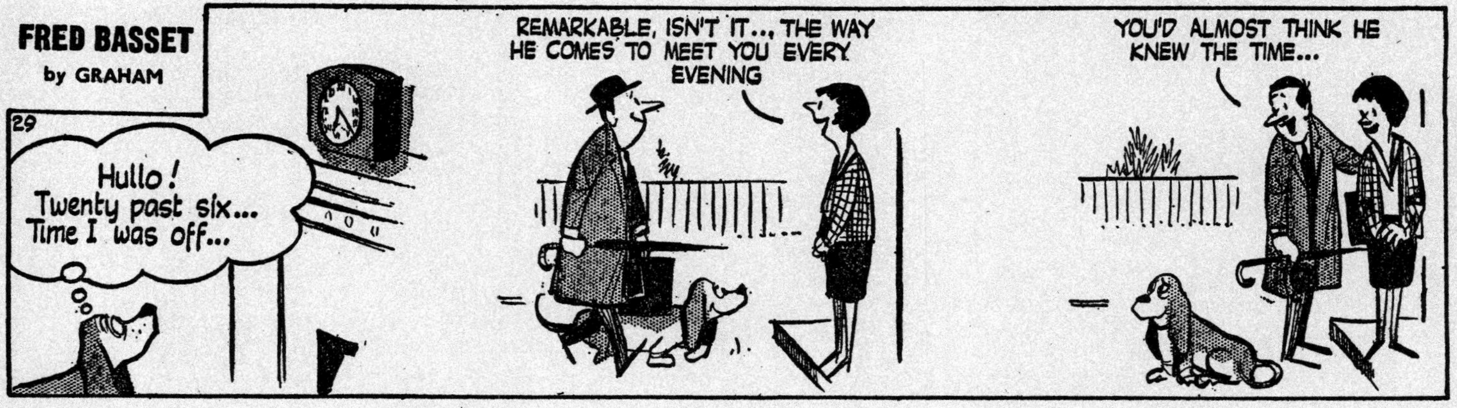
FRED BASSET
by GRAHAM
29
Hullo! Twenty past six... Time I was off...
REMARKABLE, ISN'T IT..., THE WAY HE COMES TO MEET YOU EVERY EVENING
YOU'D ALMOST THINK HE KNEW THE TIME...

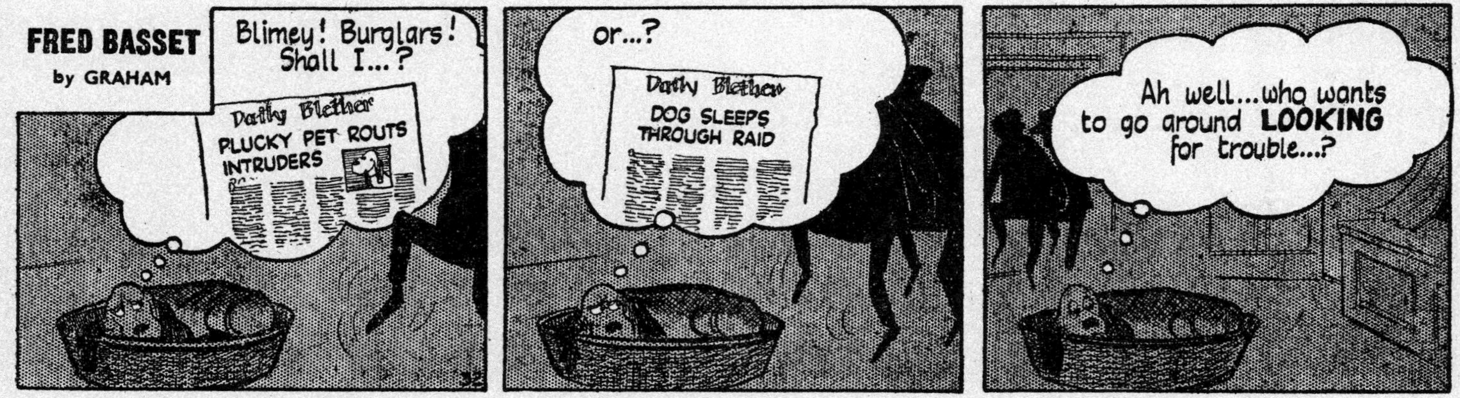

FRED BASSET
by GRAHAM
Blimey! Burglars! Shall I...?
Daily Blether
PLUCKY PET ROUTS INTRUDERS
or...?
Daily Blether
DOG SLEEPS THROUGH RAID
Ah well...who wants to go around LOOKING for trouble...?

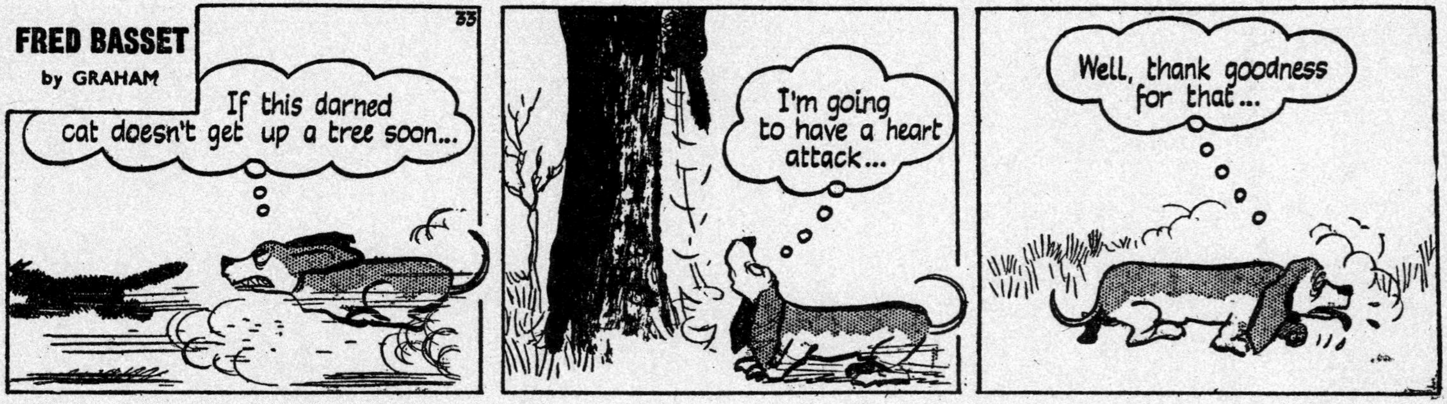

FRED BASSET
by GRAHAM
If this darned cat doesn't get up a tree soon...
I'm going to have a heart attack...
Well, thank goodness for that...

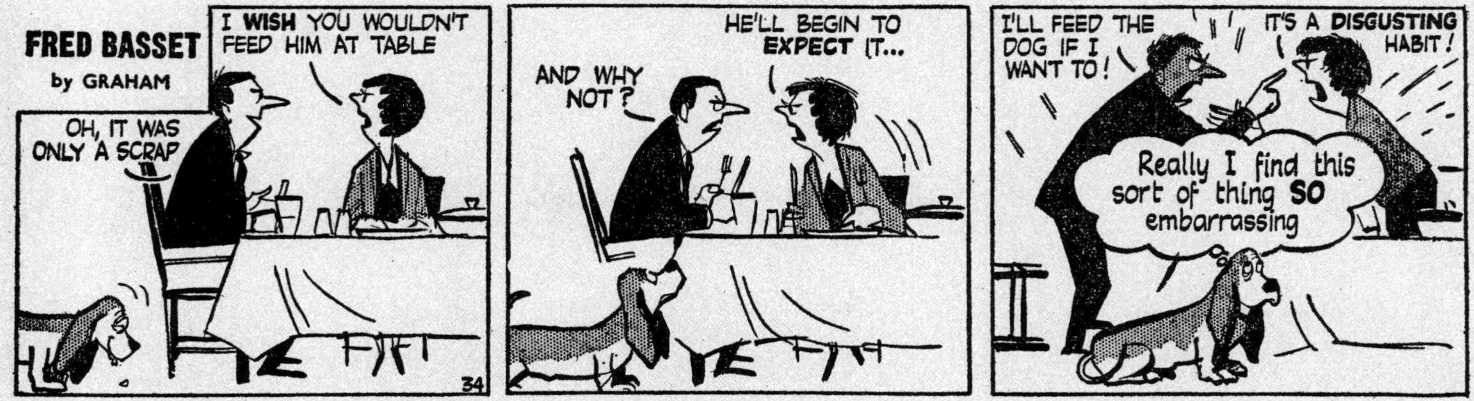
FRED BASSET
by GRAHAM
I WISH YOU WOULDN'T FEED HIM AT TABLE
OH, IT WAS ONLY A SCRAP
34
HE'LL BEGIN TO EXPECT IT...
AND WHY NOT?
I'LL FEED THE DOG IF I WANT TO!
IT'S A DISGUSTING HABIT!
Really I find this sort of thing SO embarrassing

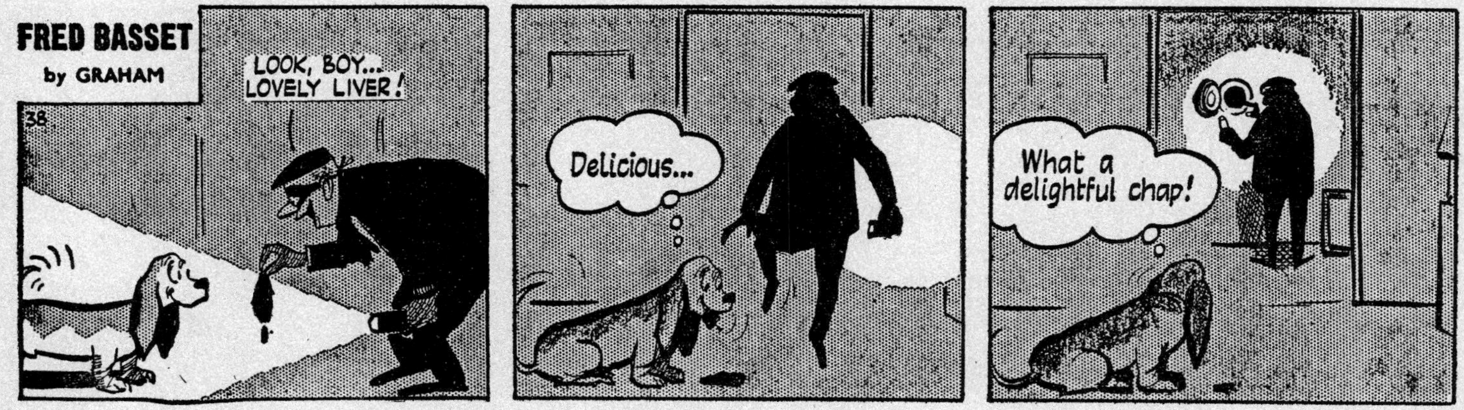
FRED BASSET
by GRAHAM
38
LOOK, BOY... LOVELY LIVER!
Delicious...
What a delightful chap!

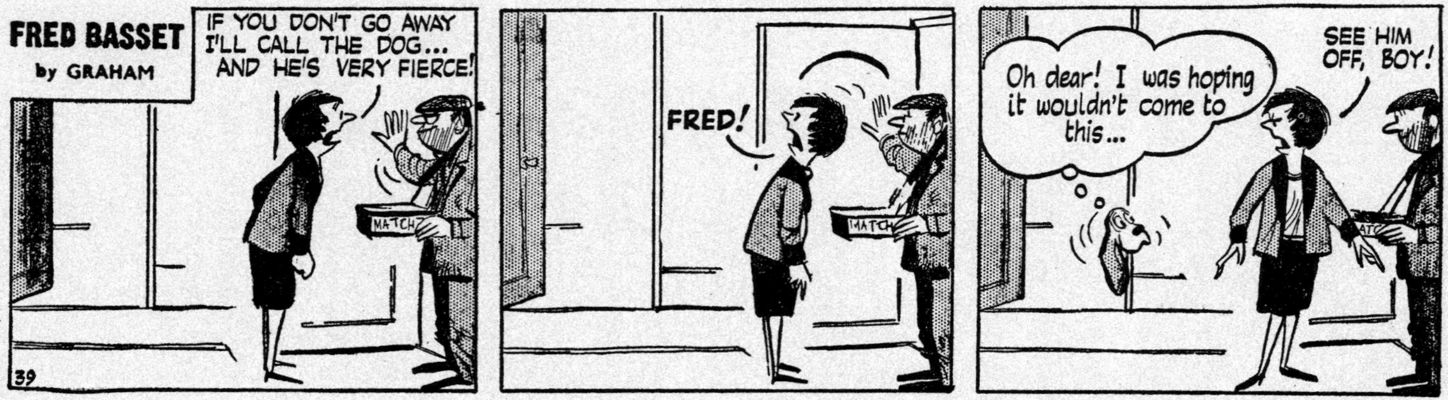
FRED BASSET
by GRAHAM
IF YOU DON'T GO AWAY I'LL CALL THE DOG... AND HE'S VERY FIERCE!
MATCH
39
FRED!
MATCH
Oh dear! I was hoping it wouldn't come to this...
SEE HIM OFF, BOY!

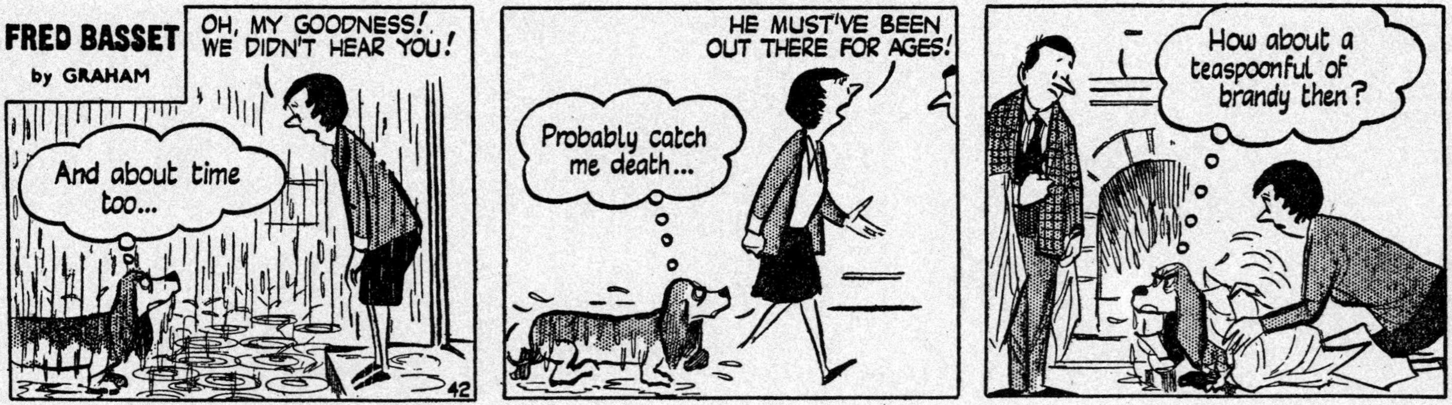
FRED BASSET
by GRAHAM
OH, MY GOODNESS! WE DIDN'T HEAR YOU!
And about time too...
42
HE MUST'VE BEEN OUT THERE FOR AGES!
Probably catch me death...
How about a teaspoonful of brandy then?

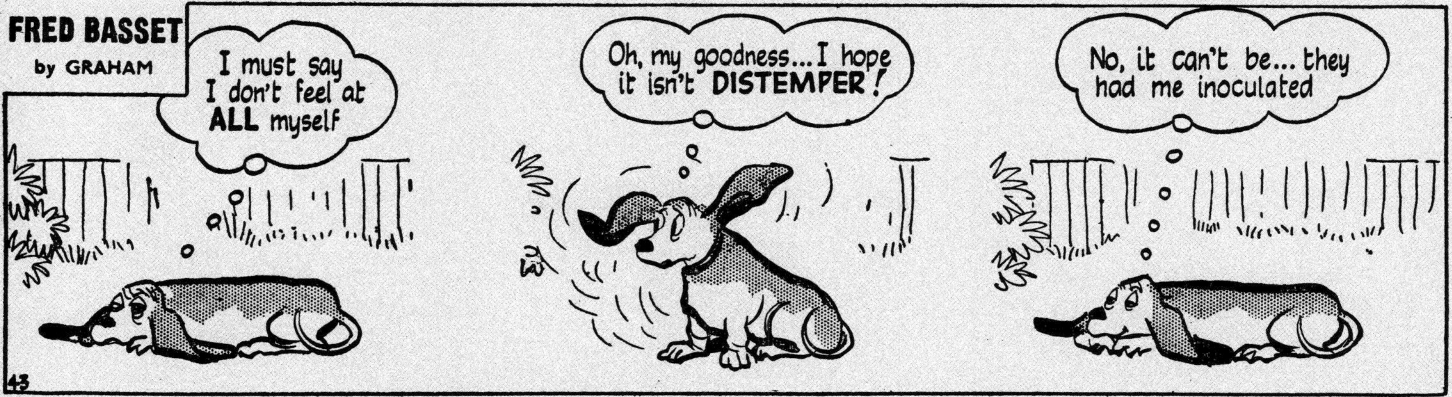
FRED BASSET
by GRAHAM
I must say I don't feel at ALL myself
Oh, my goodness... I hope it isn't DISTEMPER!
No, it can't be... they had me inoculated
43

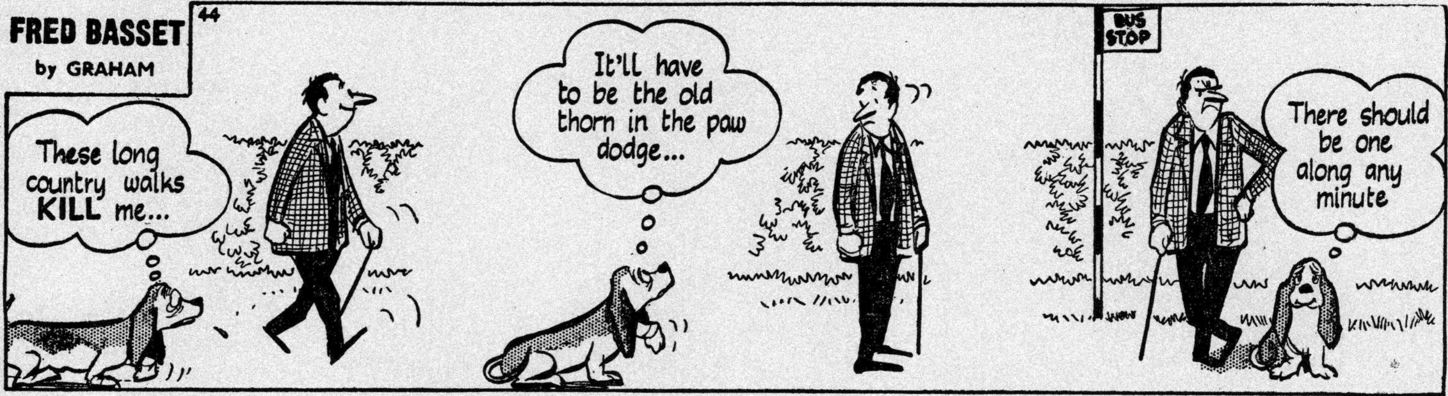
FRED BASSET
by GRAHAM
44
These long country walks KILL me...
It'll have to be the old thorn in the paw dodge...
BUS STOP
There should be one along any minute

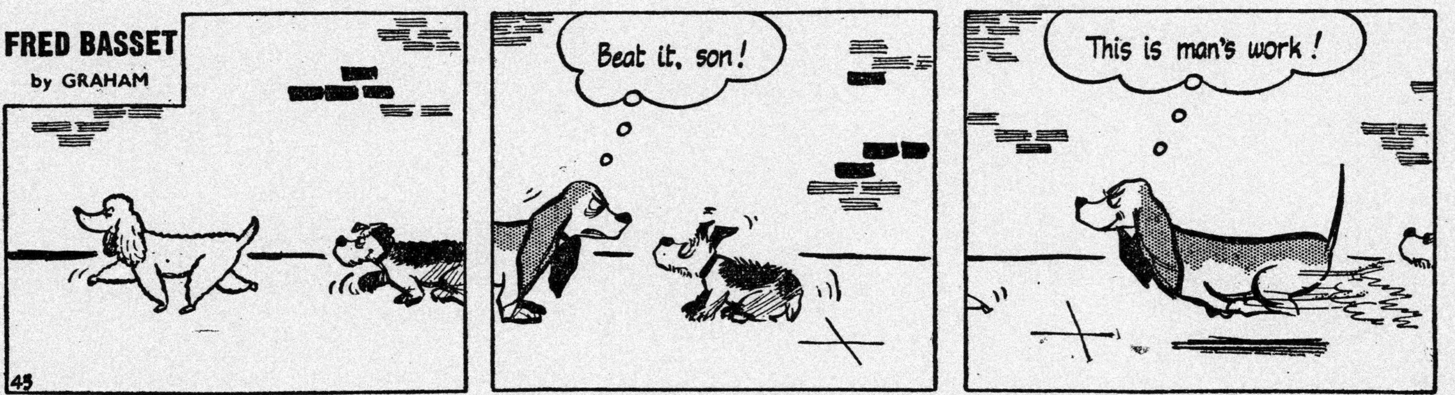
FRED BASSET
by GRAHAM
45
Beat it, son!
This is man's work!

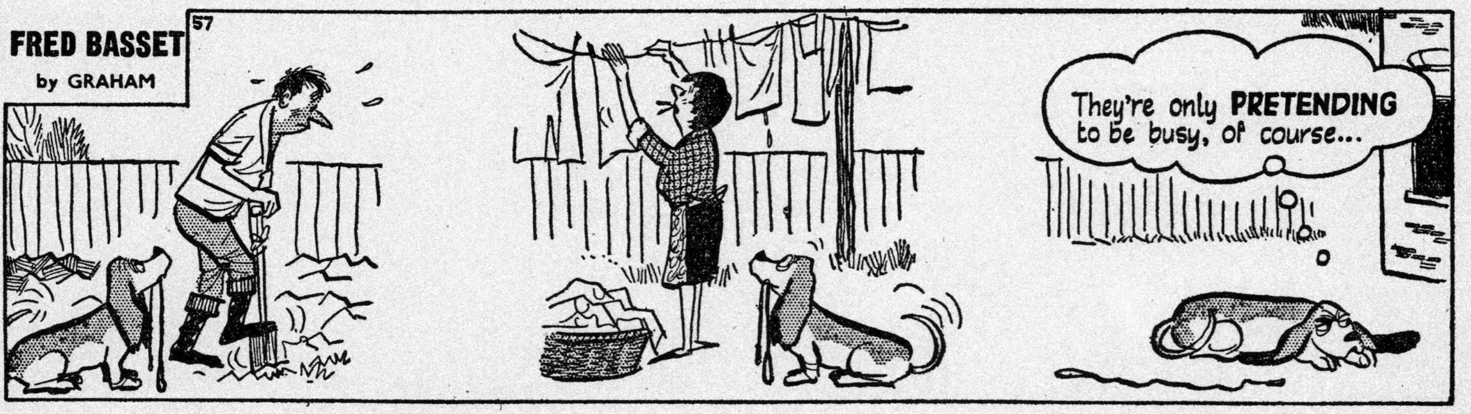
FRED BASSET
by GRAHAM
57
They're only PRETENDING to be busy, of course...

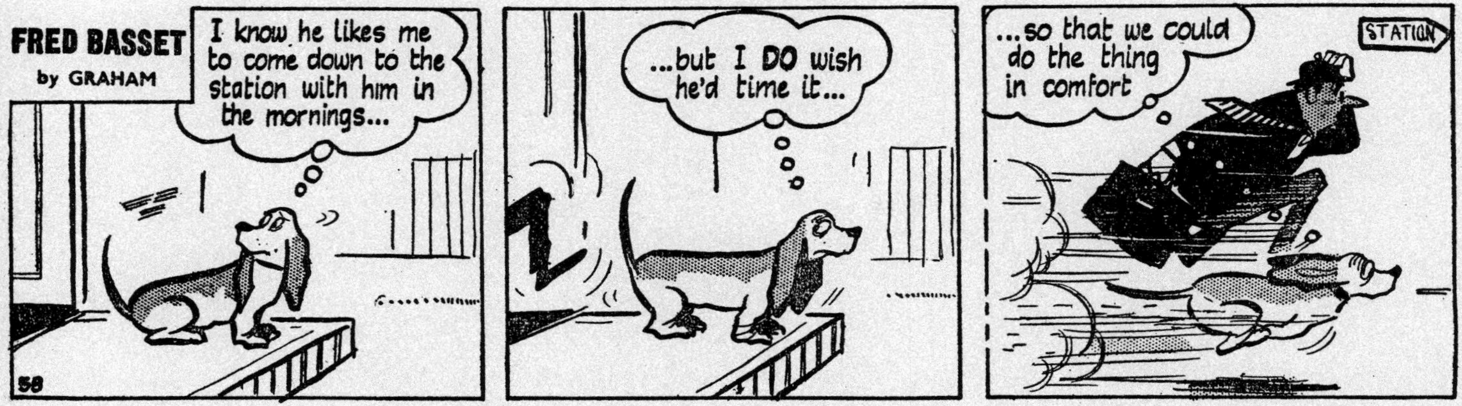
FRED BASSET
by GRAHAM
I know he likes me to come down to the station with him in the mornings...
...but I DO wish he'd time it...
...so that we could do the thing in comfort
STATION
58

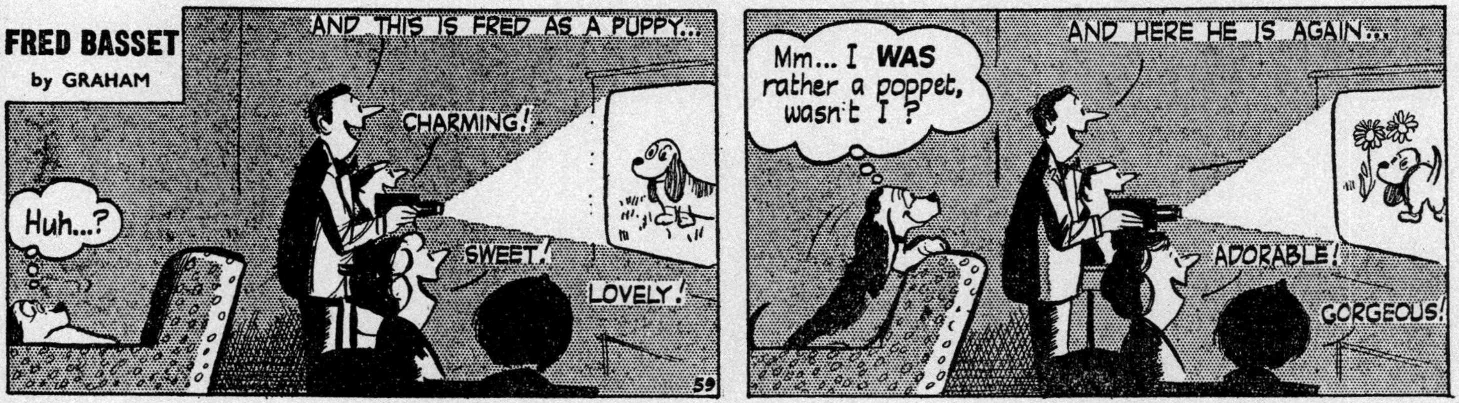
FRED BASSET
by GRAHAM
AND THIS IS FRED AS A PUPPY...
CHARMING!
Huh...?
SWEET!
LOVELY!
59
AND HERE HE IS AGAIN...
Mm... I WAS rather a poppet, wasn't I ?
ADORABLE!
GORGEOUS!

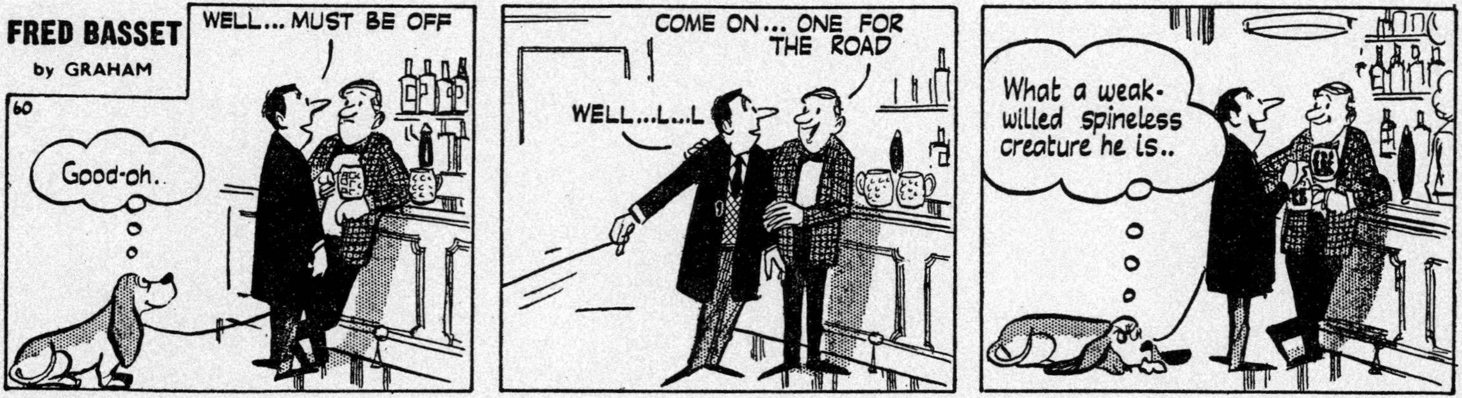
FRED BASSET
by GRAHAM
60
WELL... MUST BE OFF
Good-oh..
COME ON... ONE FOR THE ROAD
WELL...L...L
What a weak-willed spineless creature he is..

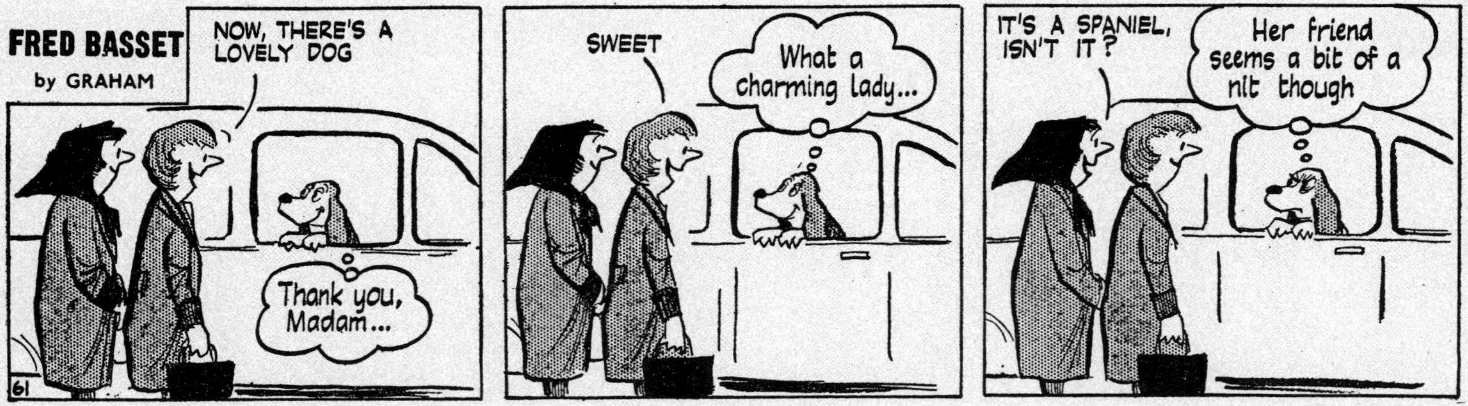
FRED BASSET
by GRAHAM
61
NOW, THERE'S A LOVELY DOG
Thank you, Madam...
SWEET
What a charming lady...
IT'S A SPANIEL, ISN'T IT ?
Her friend seems a bit of a nit though

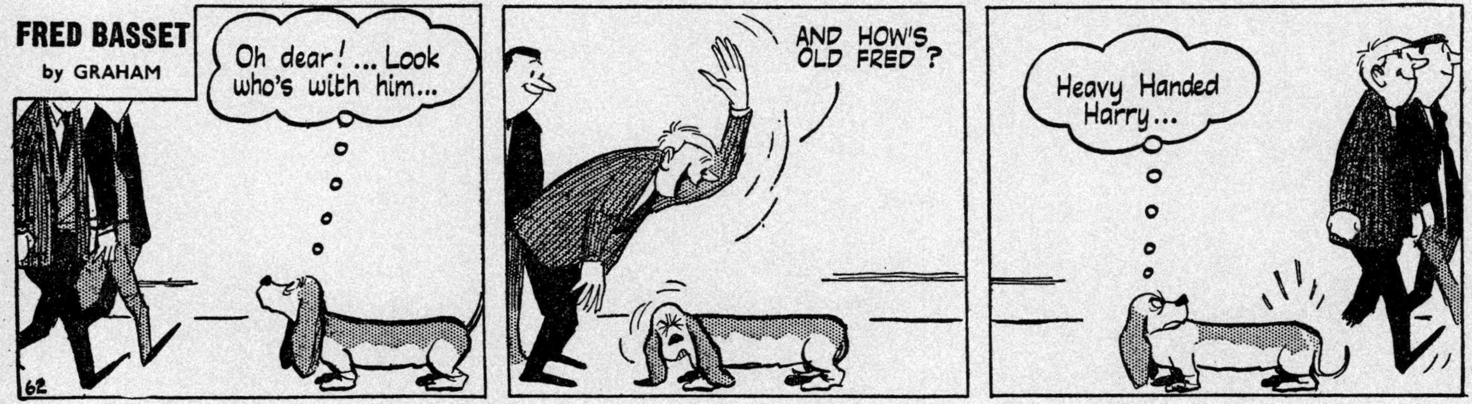
FRED BASSET
by GRAHAM
Oh dear! ... Look who's with him...
AND HOW'S OLD FRED ?
Heavy Handed Harry...
62

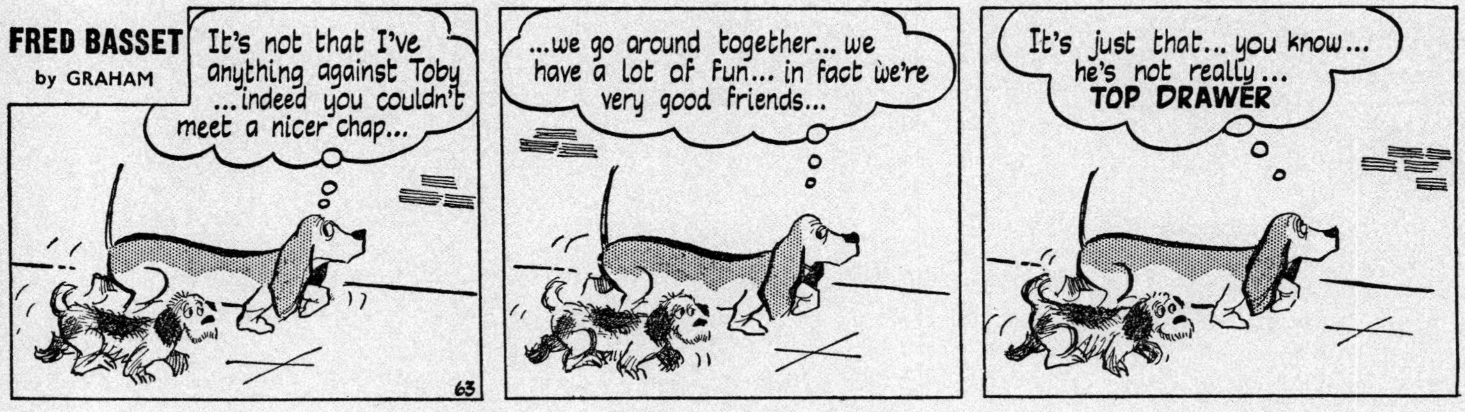
FRED BASSET
by GRAHAM
It's not that I've anything against Toby ...indeed you couldn't meet a nicer chap...
...we go around together... we have a lot of fun... in fact we're very good friends...
It's just that... you know... he's not really ... TOP DRAWER
63

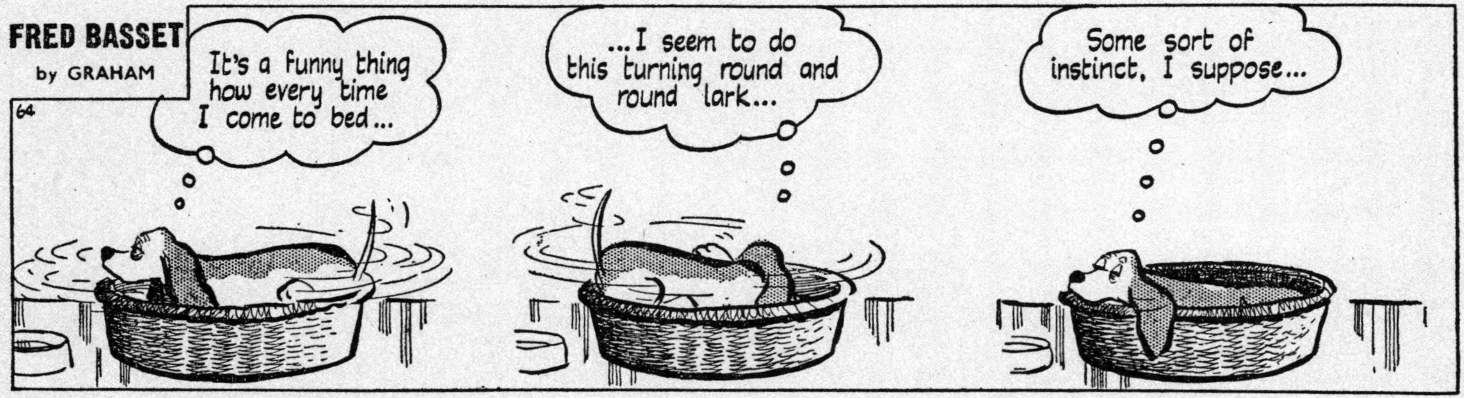
FRED BASSET
by GRAHAM
64
It's a funny thing how every time I come to bed...
...I seem to do this turning round and round lark...
Some sort of instinct, I suppose...

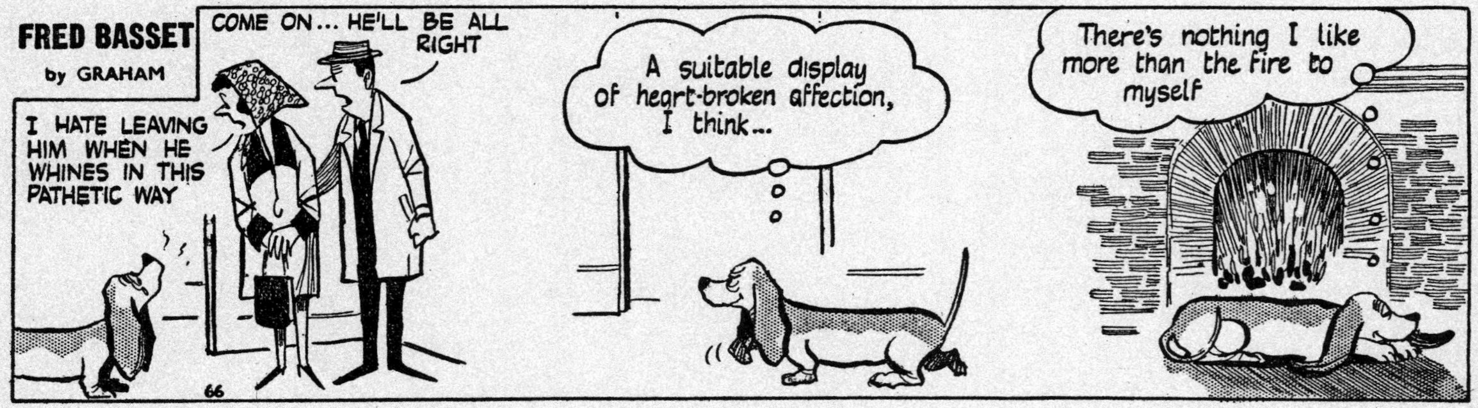
FRED BASSET
by GRAHAM
I HATE LEAVING HIM WHEN HE WHINES IN THIS PATHETIC WAY
COME ON... HE'LL BE ALL RIGHT
66
A suitable display of heart-broken affection, I think...
There's nothing I like more than the fire to myself

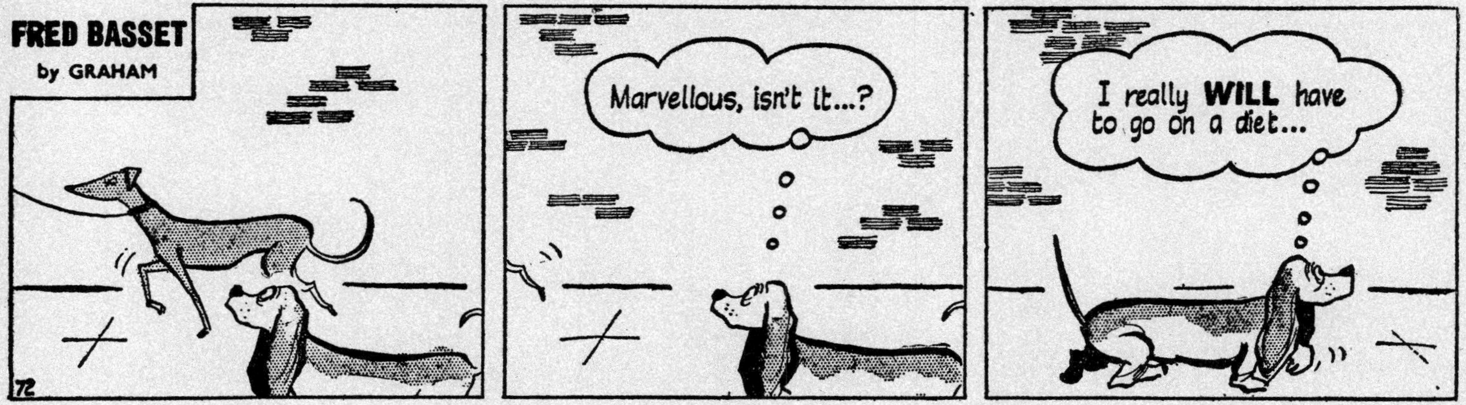
FRED BASSET
by GRAHAM
Marvellous, isn't it...?
I really WILL have to go on a diet...
72

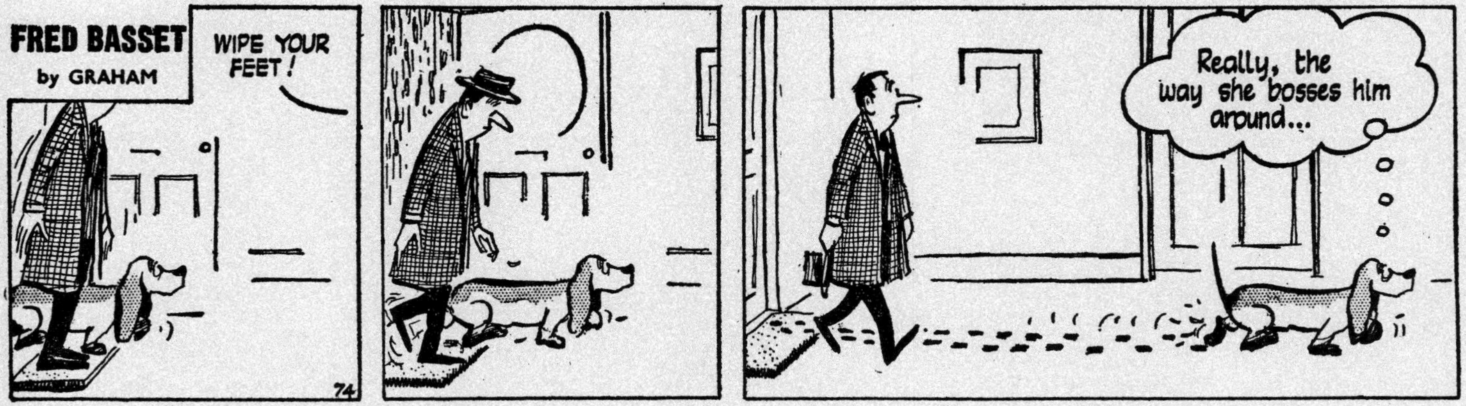
FRED BASSET
by GRAHAM
WIPE YOUR FEET!
Really, the way she bosses him around...
74

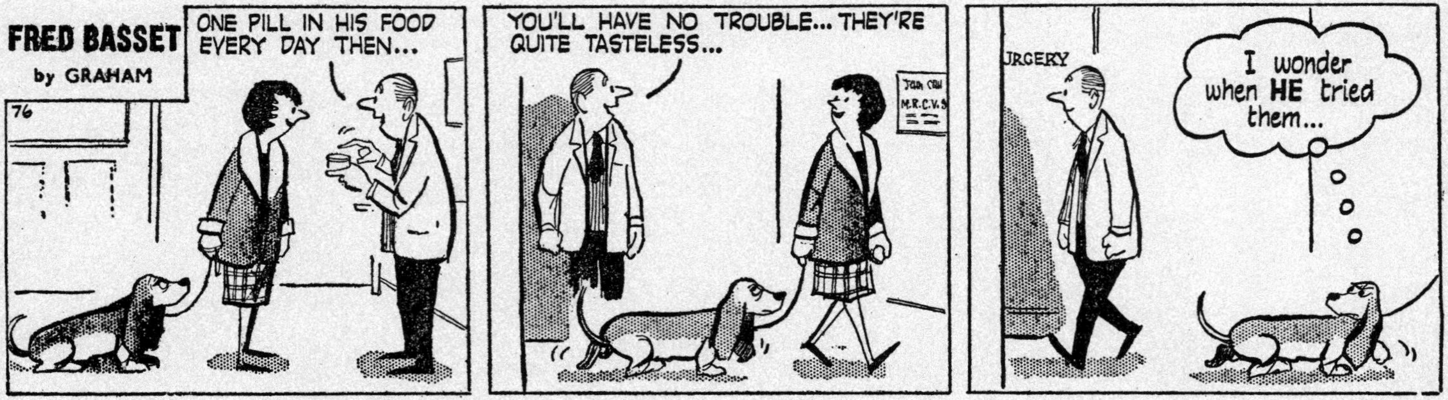
FRED BASSET
by GRAHAM
76
ONE PILL IN HIS FOOD EVERY DAY THEN...
YOU'LL HAVE NO TROUBLE... THEY'RE QUITE TASTELESS...
M.R.C.V.S
JRGERY
I wonder when HE tried them...

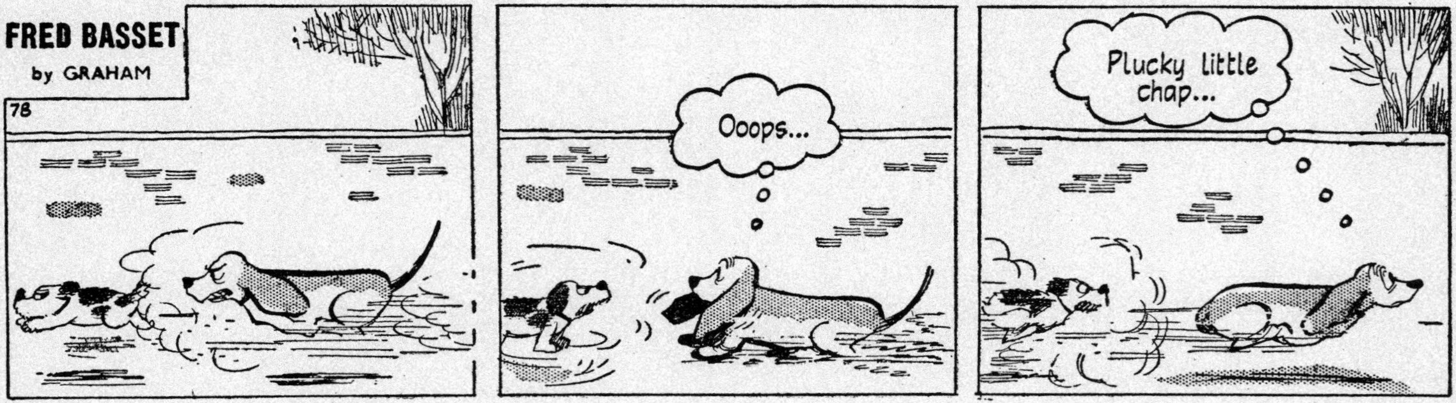
FRED BASSET
by GRAHAM
78
Ooops...
Plucky little chap...

FRED BASSET
by GRAHAM
79
MY PAPER!
... AND I HADN'T OPENED IT!
Oh, I say, steady...
I thought it was yesterday's...

FRED BASSET
by GRAHAM
80
They stand around in this smoke-filled room sloshing back gin...
...exchanging conversational inanities...
...and they call it a party!

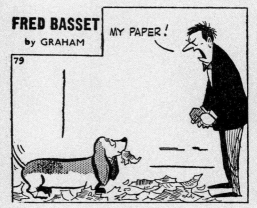

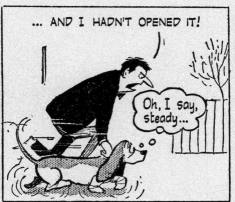

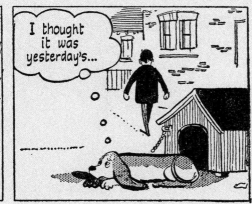

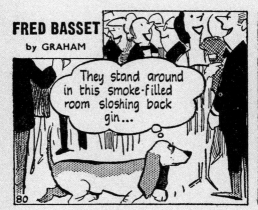

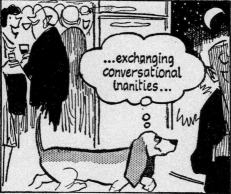

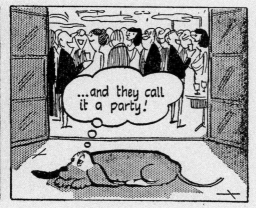

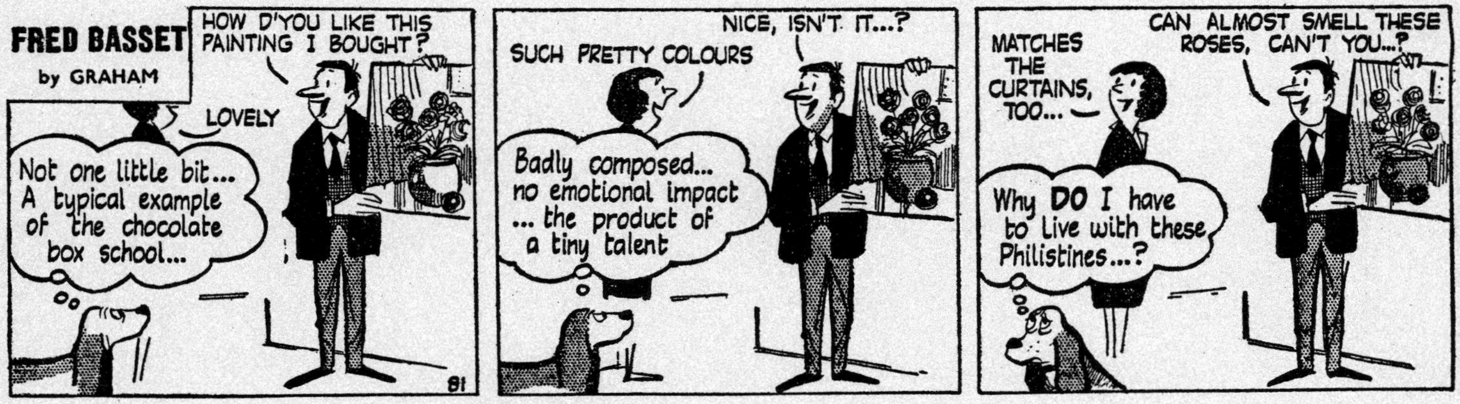
FRED BASSET
by GRAHAM
HOW D'YOU LIKE THIS PAINTING I BOUGHT?
LOVELY
Not one little bit... A typical example of the chocolate box school...
81
SUCH PRETTY COLOURS
NICE, ISN'T IT...?
Badly composed... no emotional impact ... the product of a tiny talent
MATCHES THE CURTAINS, TOO...
CAN ALMOST SMELL THESE ROSES, CAN'T YOU...?
Why DO I have to live with these Philistines...?

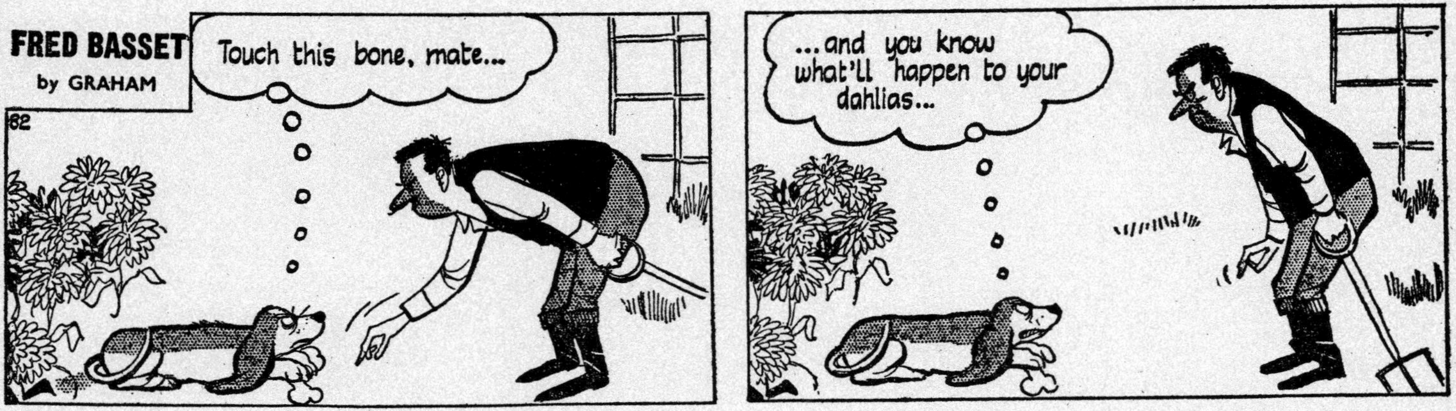
FRED BASSET
by GRAHAM
82
Touch this bone, mate...
...and you know what'll happen to your dahlias...

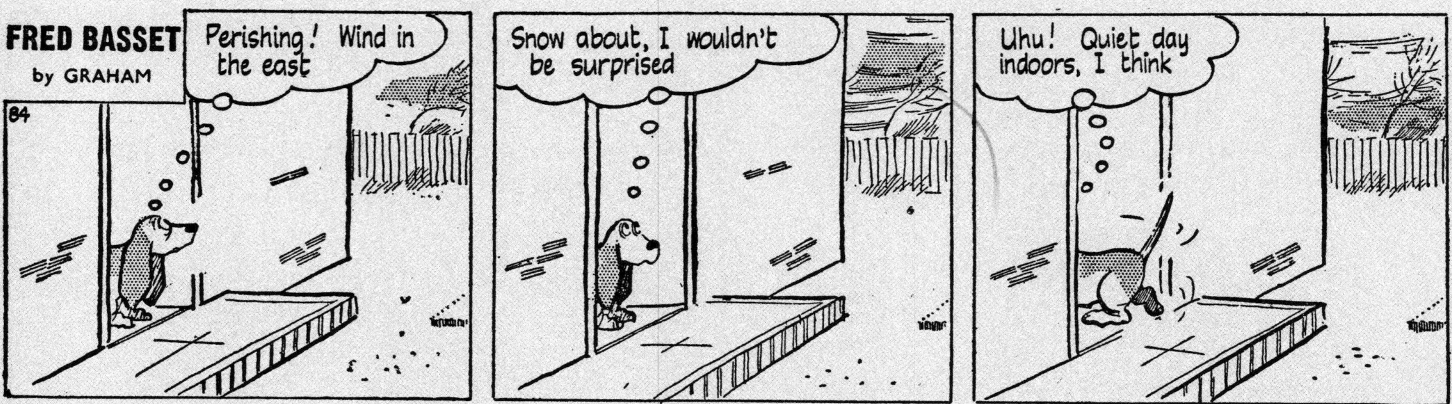
FRED BASSET
by GRAHAM
84
Perishing! Wind in the east
Snow about, I wouldn't be surprised
Uhu! Quiet day indoors, I think

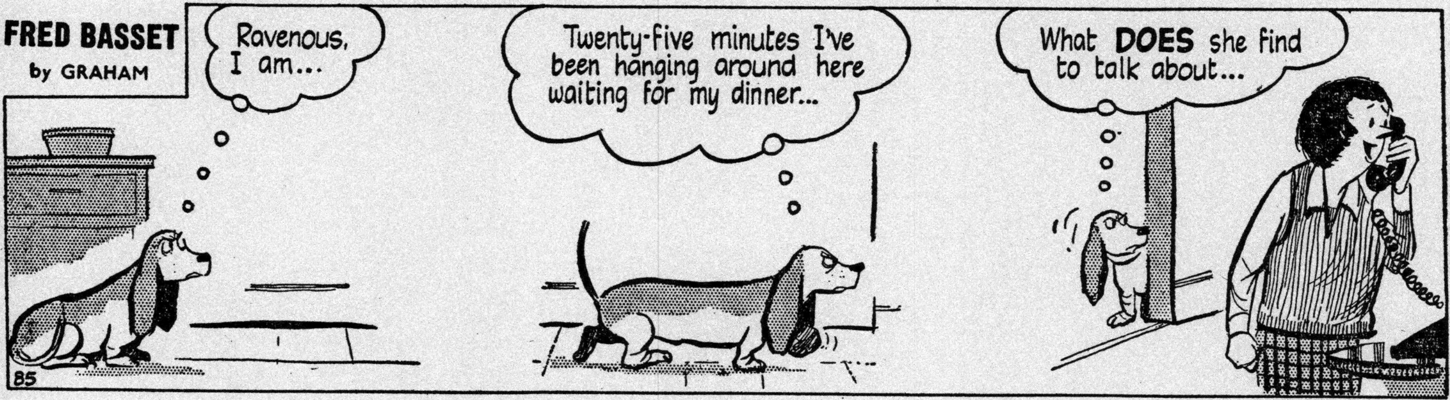
FRED BASSET
by GRAHAM
Ravenous, I am...
Twenty-five minutes I've been hanging around here waiting for my dinner...
What DOES she find to talk about...
85

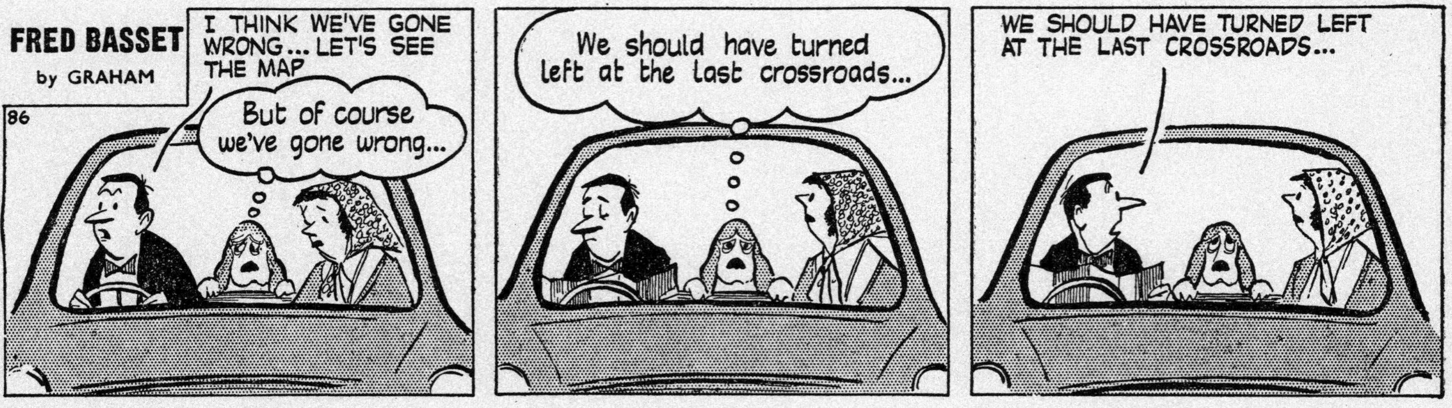
FRED BASSET
by GRAHAM
86
I THINK WE'VE GONE WRONG... LET'S SEE THE MAP
But of course we've gone wrong...
We should have turned left at the last crossroads...
WE SHOULD HAVE TURNED LEFT AT THE LAST CROSSROADS...

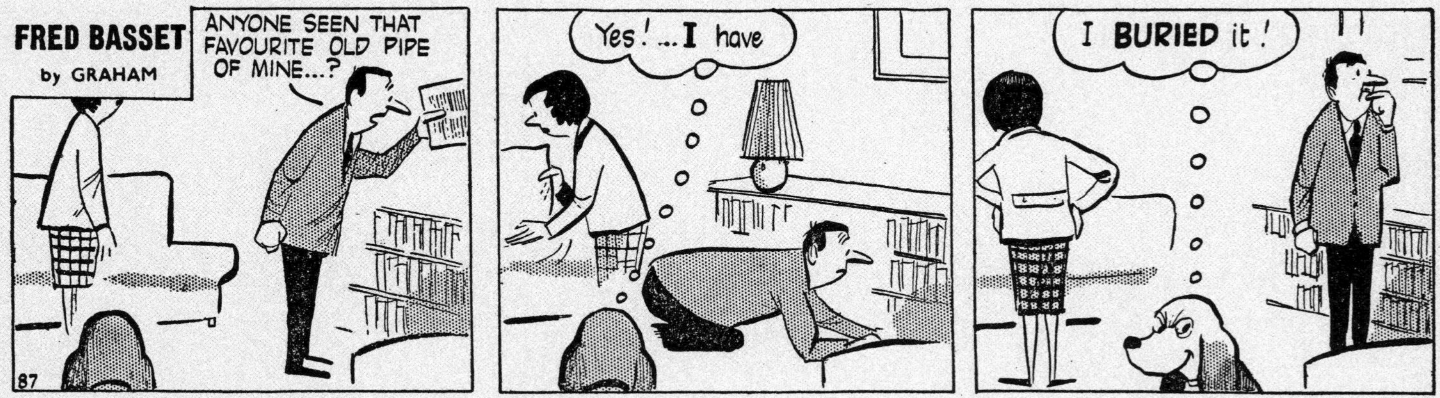
FRED BASSET
by GRAHAM
87
ANYONE SEEN THAT FAVOURITE OLD PIPE OF MINE...?
Yes! ... I have
I BURIED it!

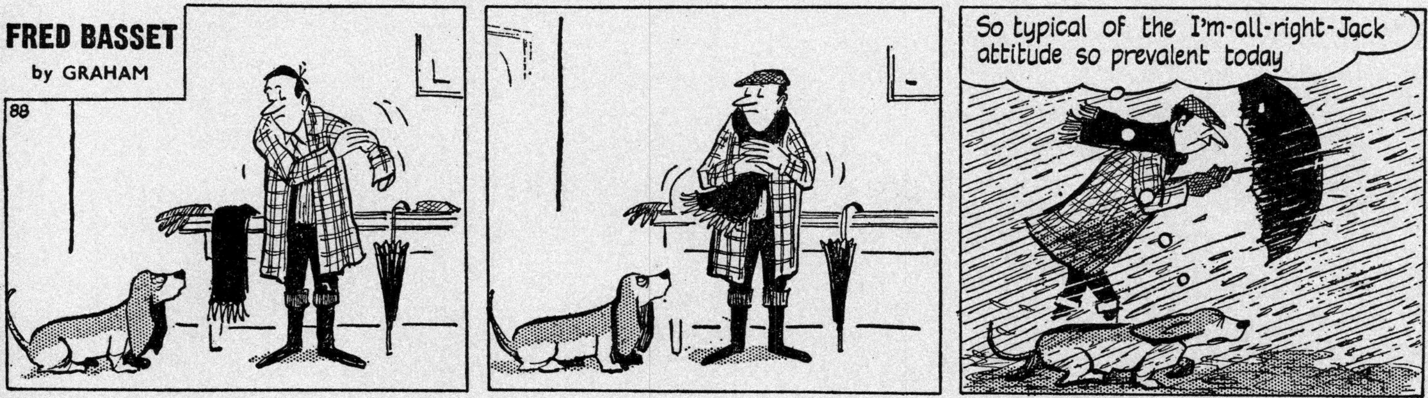
FRED BASSET
by GRAHAM
88
So typical of the I'm-all-right-Jack attitude so prevalent today

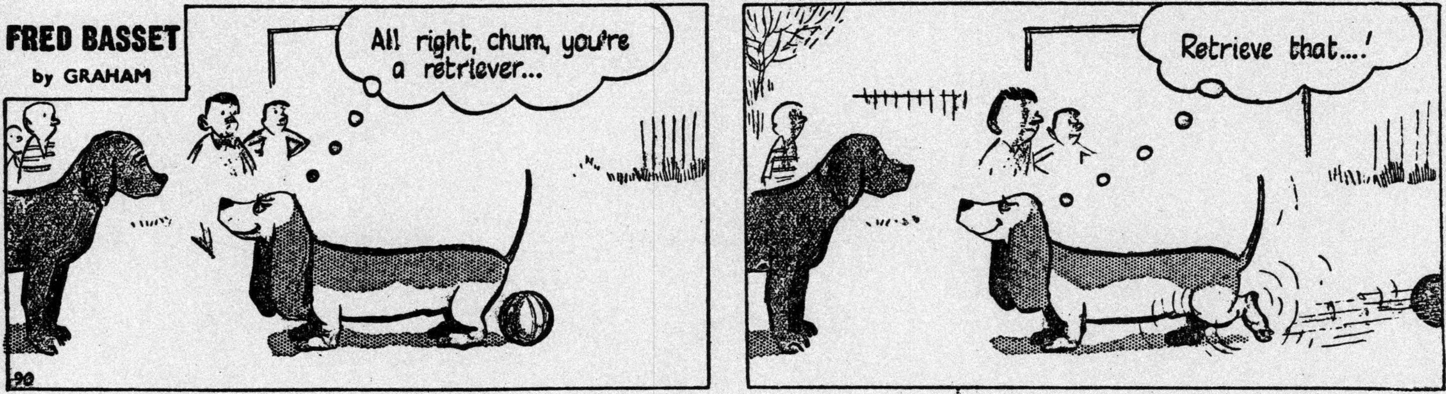
FRED BASSET
by GRAHAM
All right, chum, you're a retriever...
90
Retrieve that....!

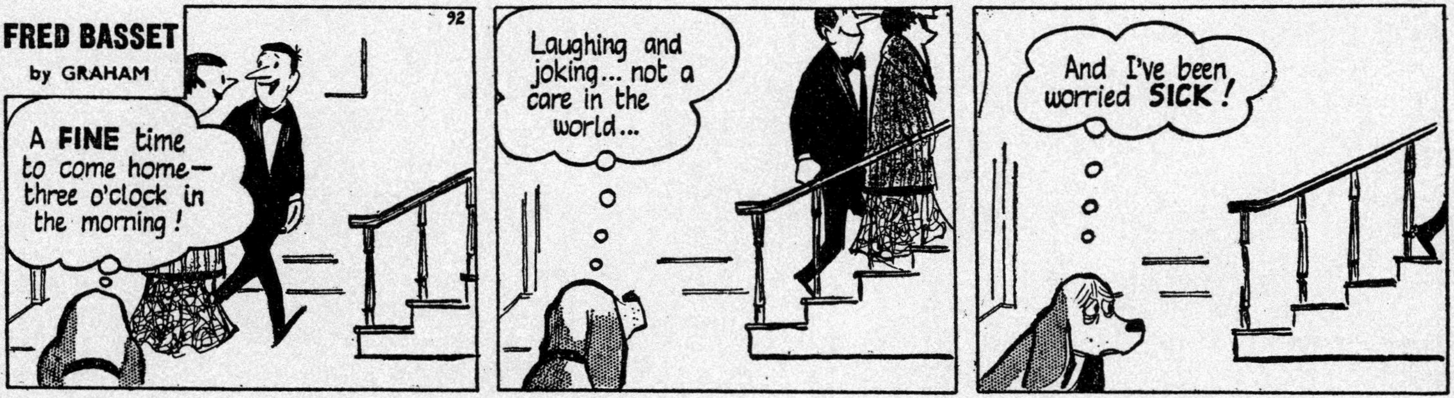
FRED BASSET
by GRAHAM
92
A FINE time to come home— three o'clock in the morning!
Laughing and joking... not a care in the world...
And I've been worried SICK!

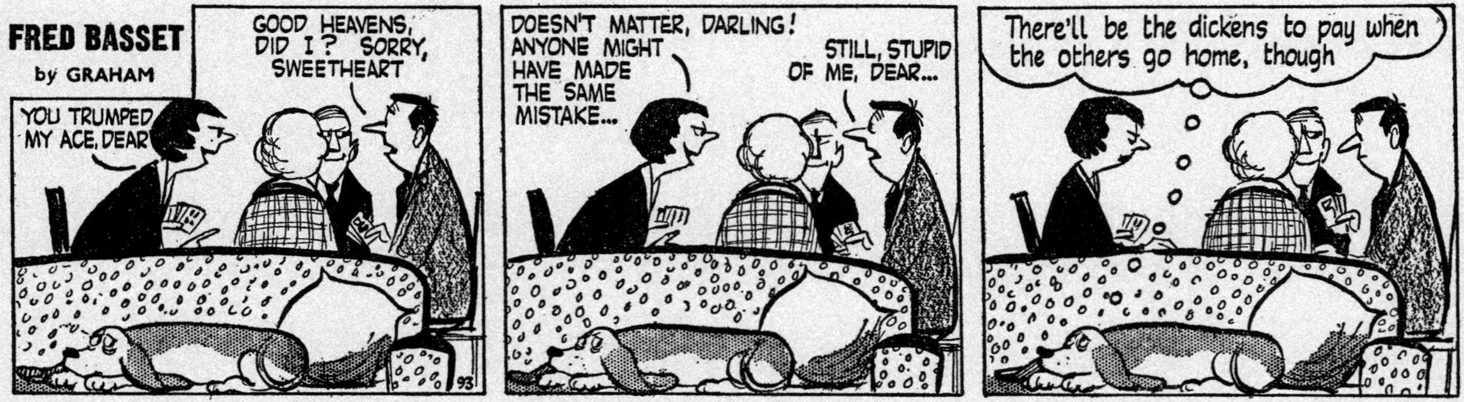
FRED BASSET
by GRAHAM
YOU TRUMPED MY ACE, DEAR
GOOD HEAVENS, DID I? SORRY, SWEETHEART
93
DOESN'T MATTER, DARLING! ANYONE MIGHT HAVE MADE THE SAME MISTAKE...
STILL, STUPID OF ME, DEAR...
There'll be the dickens to pay when the others go home, though

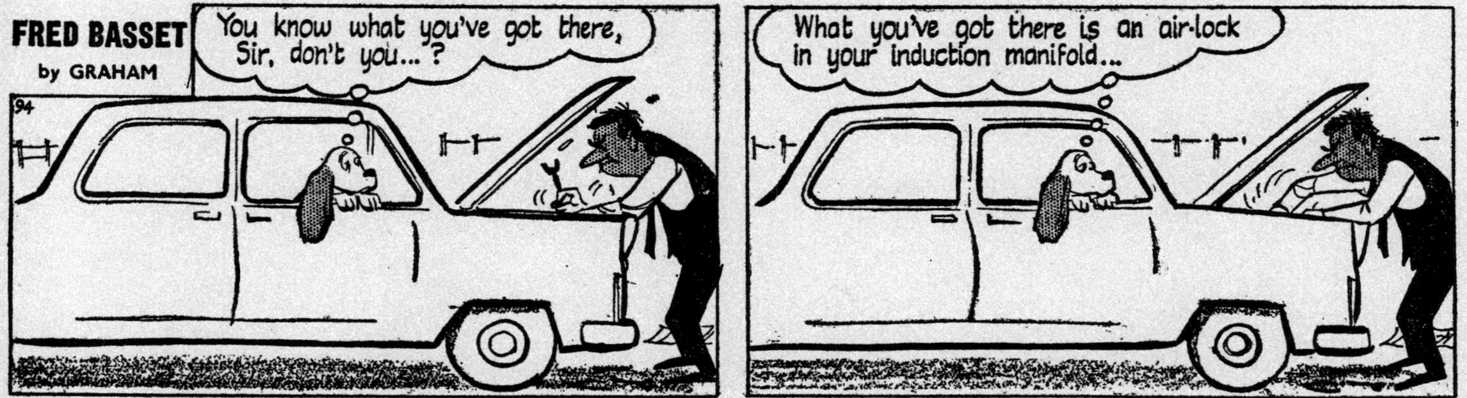

FRED BASSET
by GRAHAM
94
You know what you've got there, Sir, don't you...?
What you've got there is an air-lock in your induction manifold...

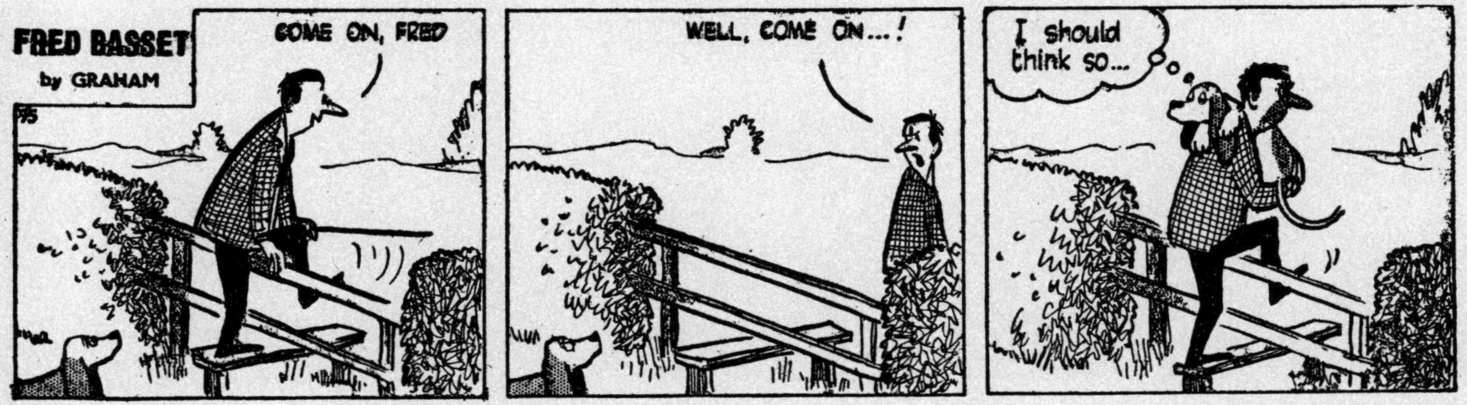

FRED BASSET
by GRAHAM
95
COME ON, FRED
WELL, COME ON...!
I should think so...

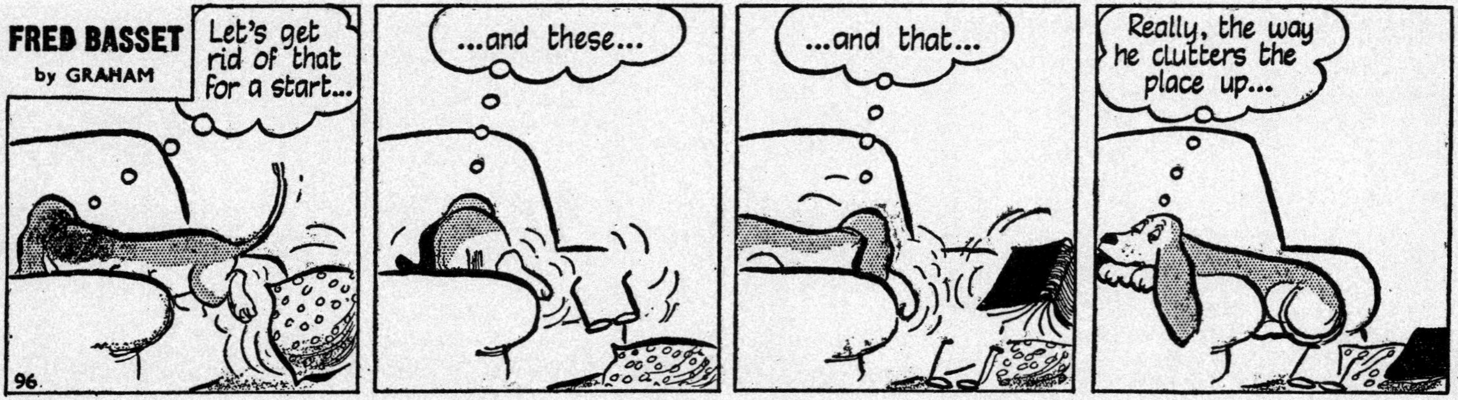
FRED BASSET
by GRAHAM
Let's get rid of that for a start...
...and these...
...and that...
Really, the way he clutters the place up...
96.

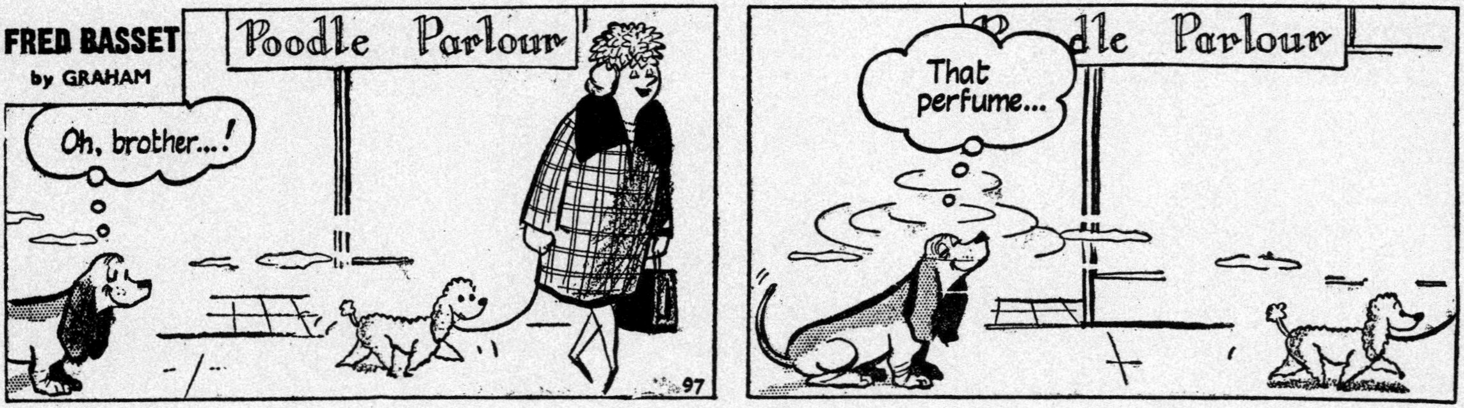
FRED BASSET
by GRAHAM
Poodle Parlour
Oh, brother...!
97
dle Parlour
That perfume...

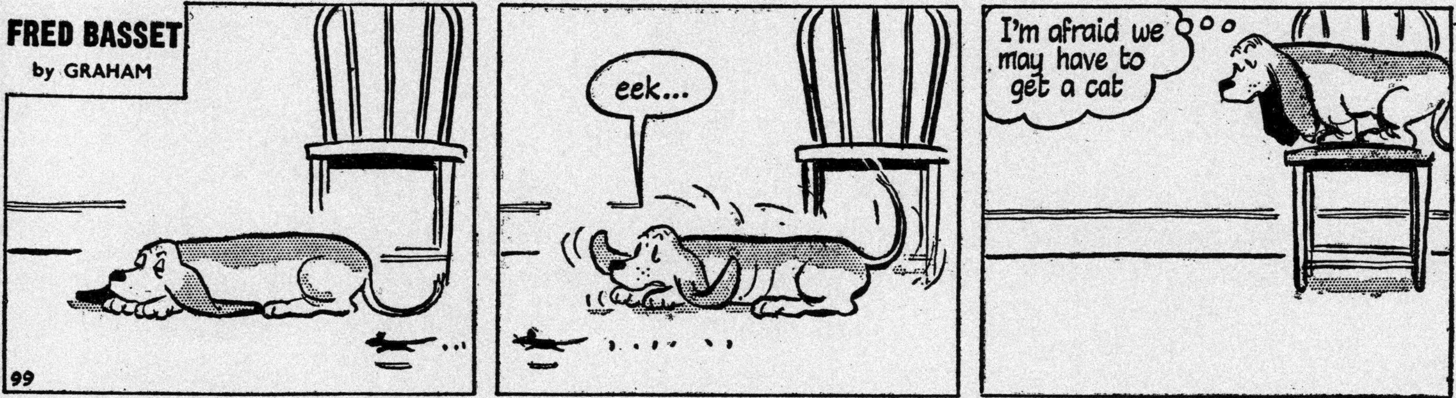
FRED BASSET
by GRAHAM
eek...
I'm afraid we may have to get a cat
99

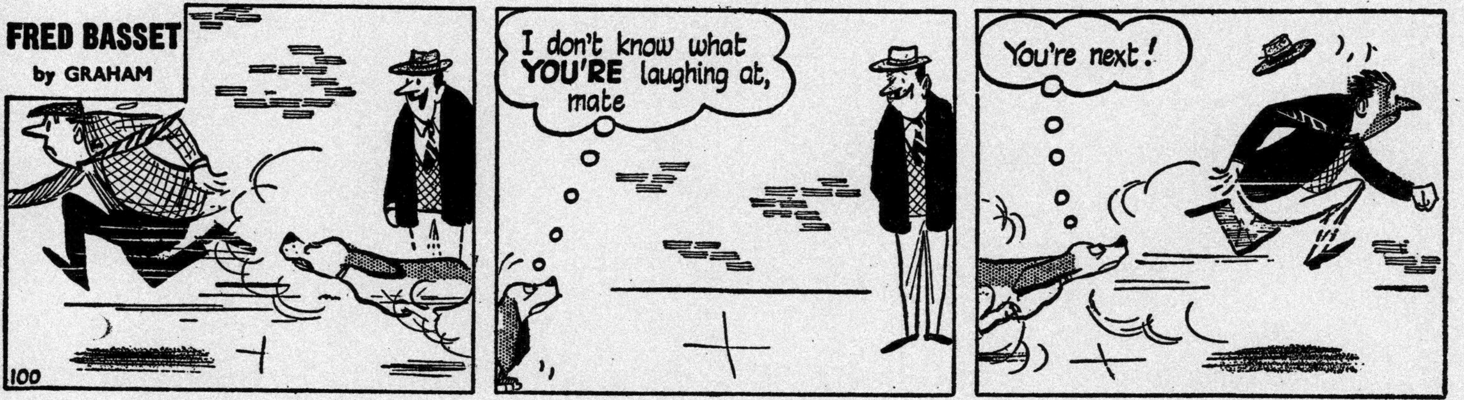
FRED BASSET
by GRAHAM
I don't know what YOU'RE laughing at, mate
You're next!
100

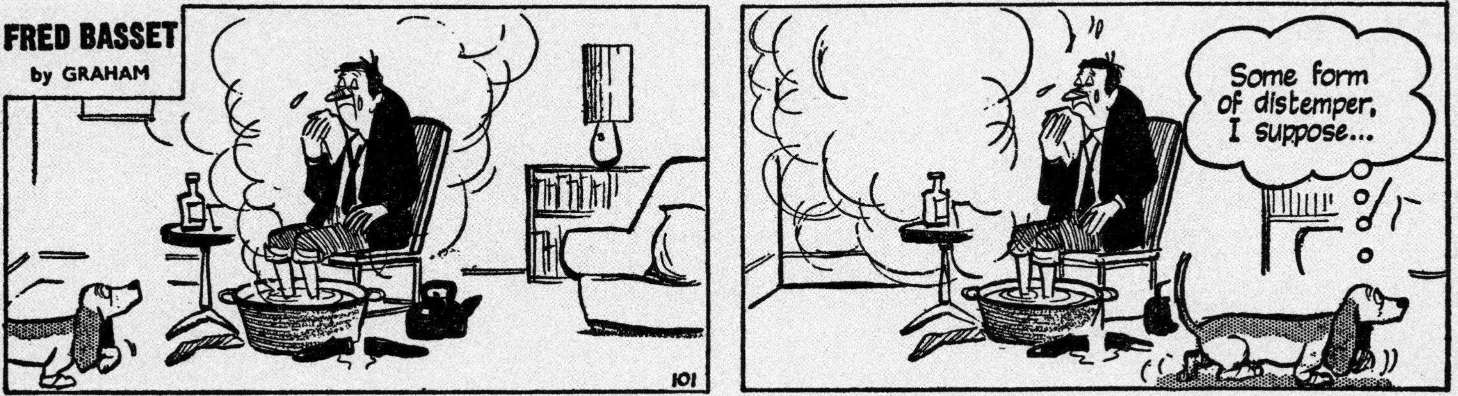
FRED BASSET
by GRAHAM
101
Some form of distemper, I suppose...

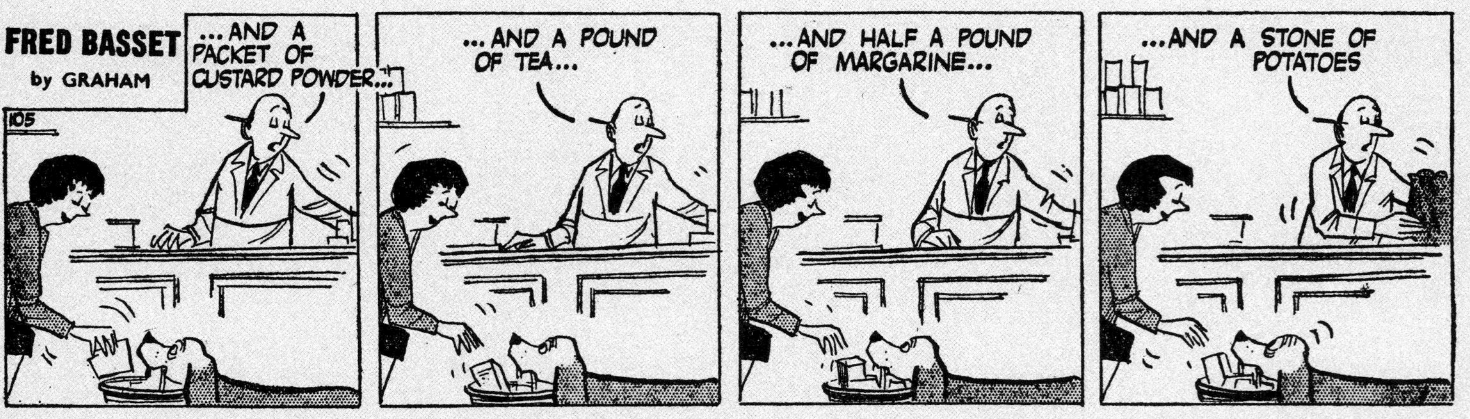
FRED BASSET
by GRAHAM
105
...AND A PACKET OF CUSTARD POWDER...
...AND A POUND OF TEA...
...AND HALF A POUND OF MARGARINE...
...AND A STONE OF POTATOES

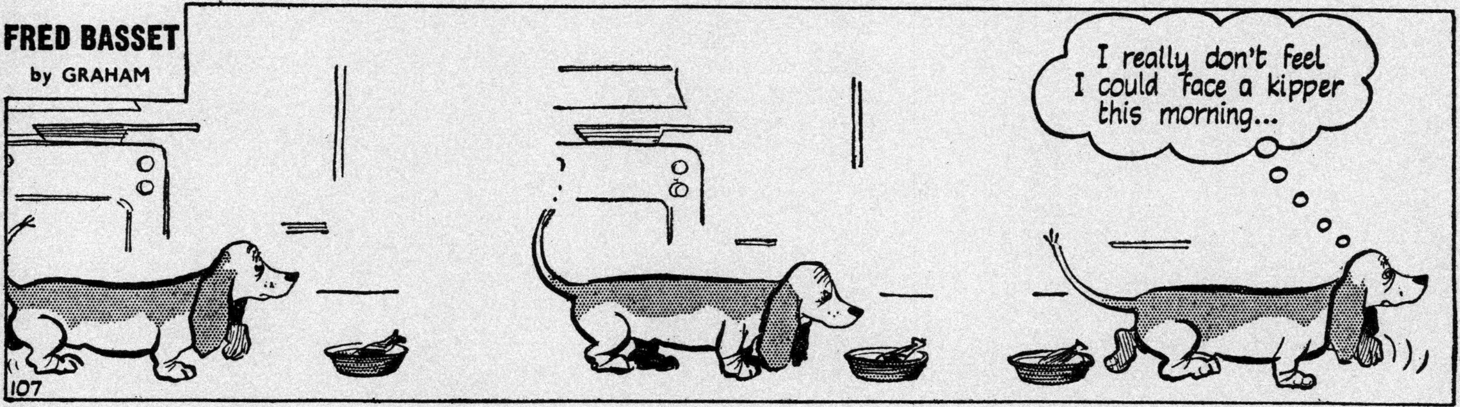
FRED BASSET
by GRAHAM
I really don't feel I could face a kipper this morning...
107

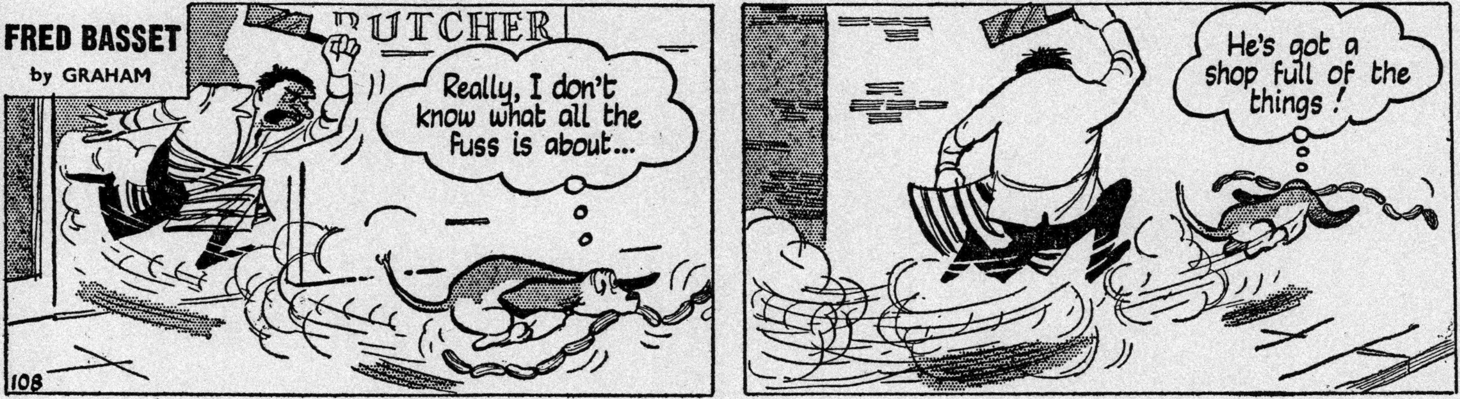
FRED BASSET
by GRAHAM
BUTCHER
Really, I don't know what all the fuss is about...
He's got a shop full of the things!
108

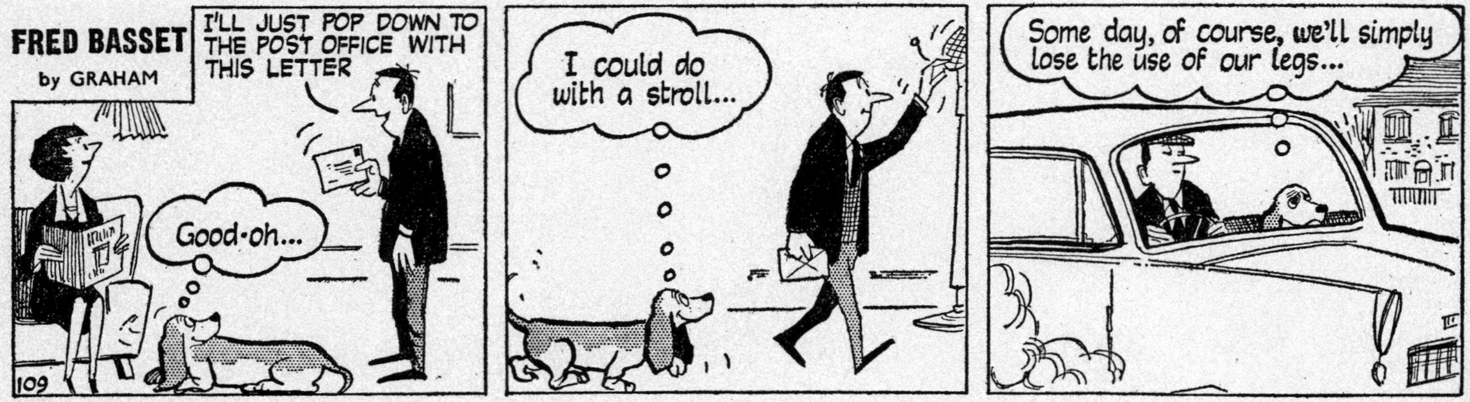
FRED BASSET
by GRAHAM
I'LL JUST POP DOWN TO THE POST OFFICE WITH THIS LETTER
Good-oh...
109
I could do with a stroll...
Some day, of course, we'll simply lose the use of our legs...

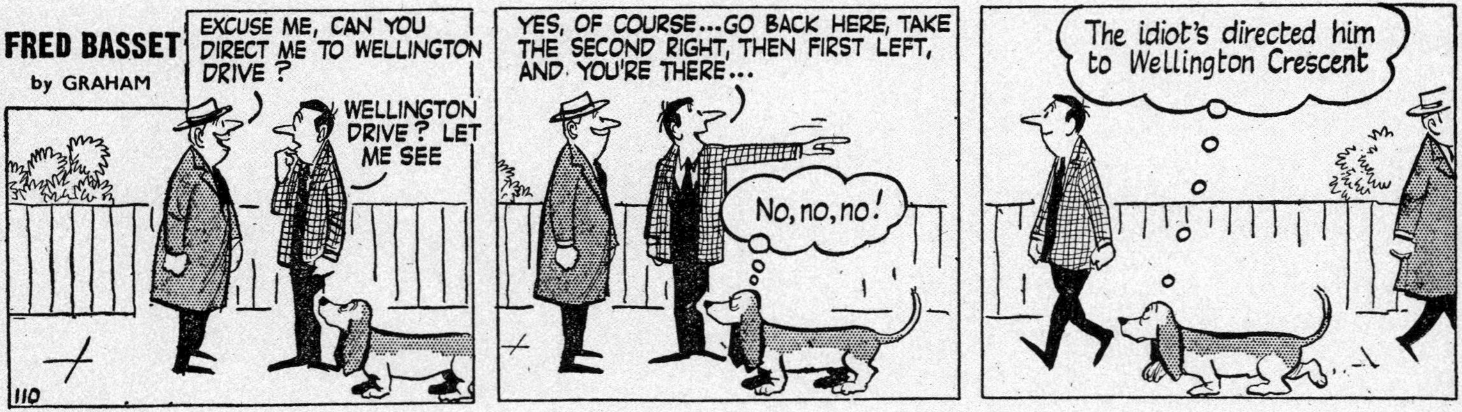
FRED BASSET
by GRAHAM
EXCUSE ME, CAN YOU DIRECT ME TO WELLINGTON DRIVE ?
WELLINGTON DRIVE ? LET ME SEE
110
YES, OF COURSE...GO BACK HERE, TAKE THE SECOND RIGHT, THEN FIRST LEFT, AND YOU'RE THERE...
No, no, no!
The idiot's directed him to Wellington Crescent

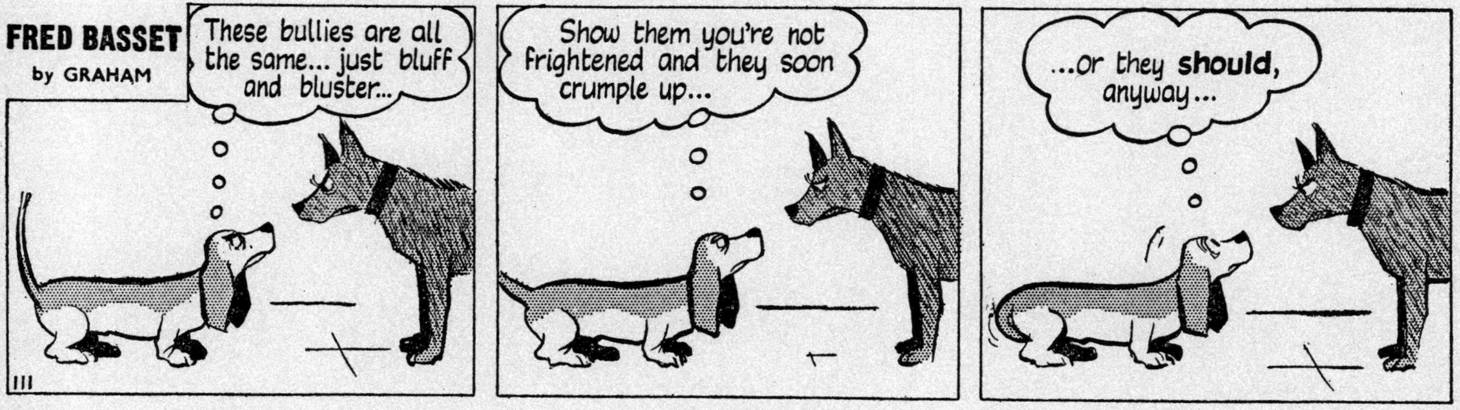
FRED BASSET
by GRAHAM
These bullies are all the same... just bluff and bluster...
Show them you're not frightened and they soon crumple up...
...or they **should**, anyway...
111

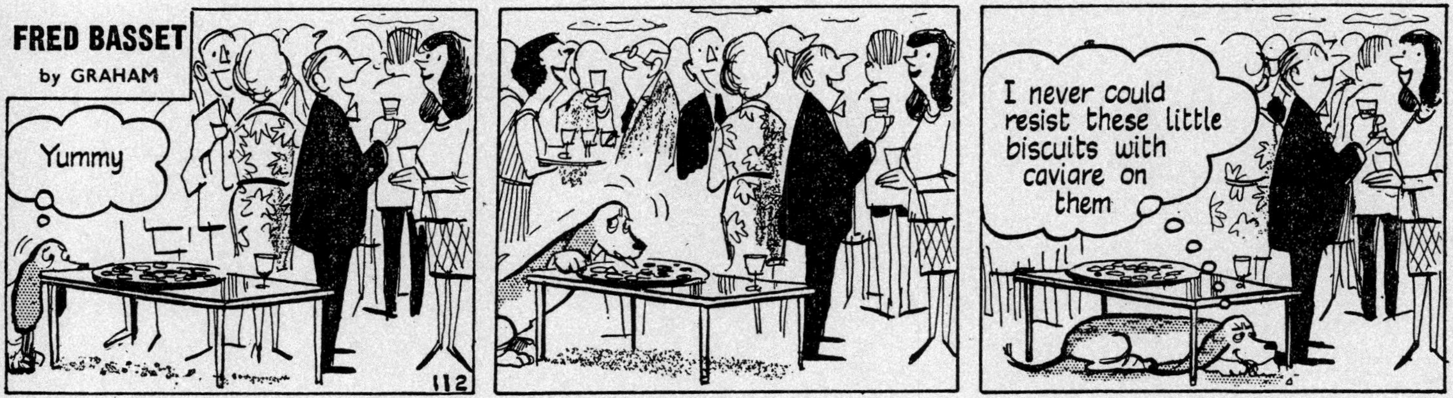
FRED BASSET
by GRAHAM
Yummy
I never could resist these little biscuits with caviare on them
112

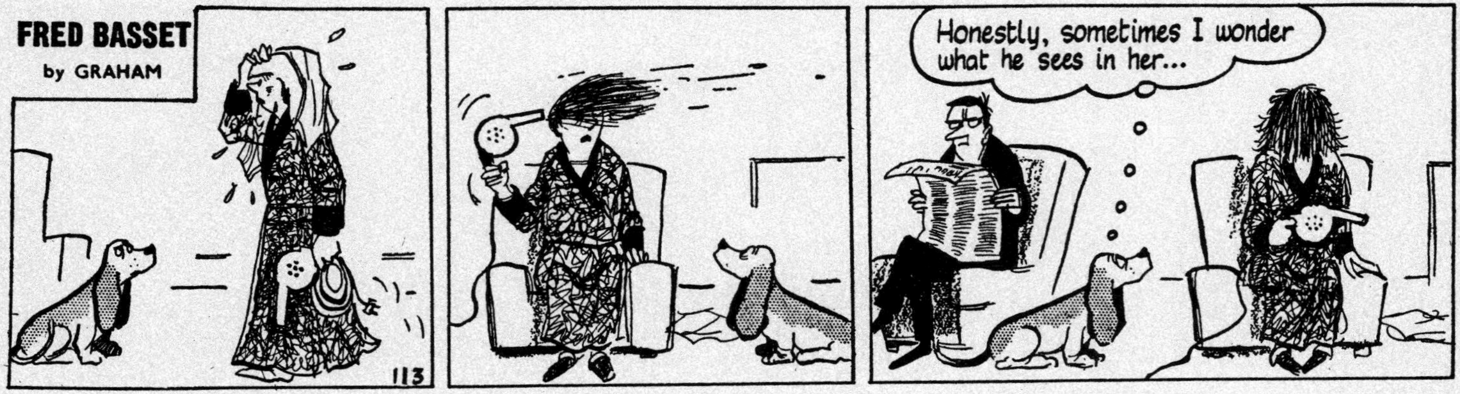
FRED BASSET
by GRAHAM
113
Honestly, sometimes I wonder what he sees in her...

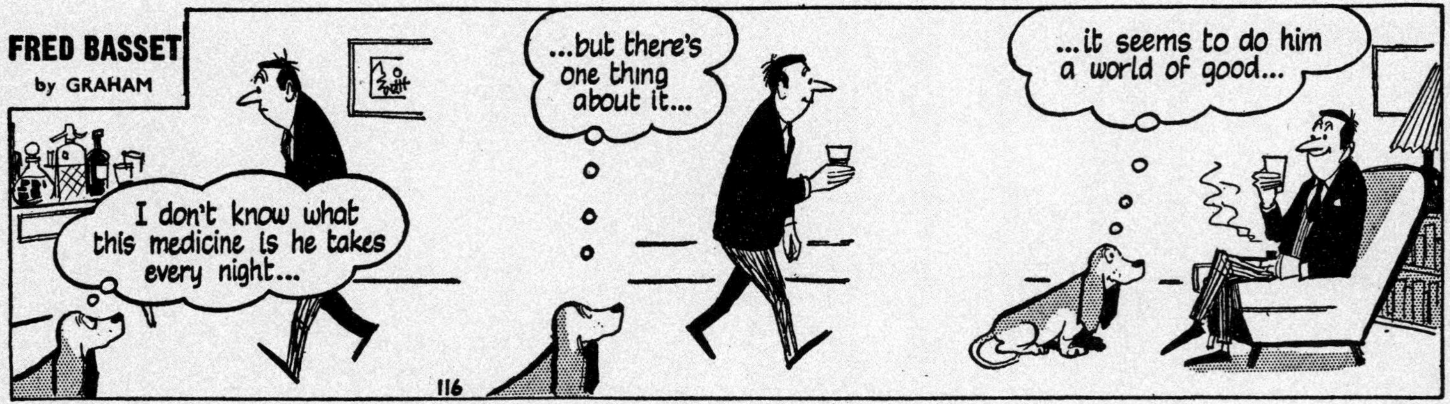
FRED BASSET
by GRAHAM
I don't know what this medicine is he takes every night...
116
...but there's one thing about it...
...it seems to do him a world of good...

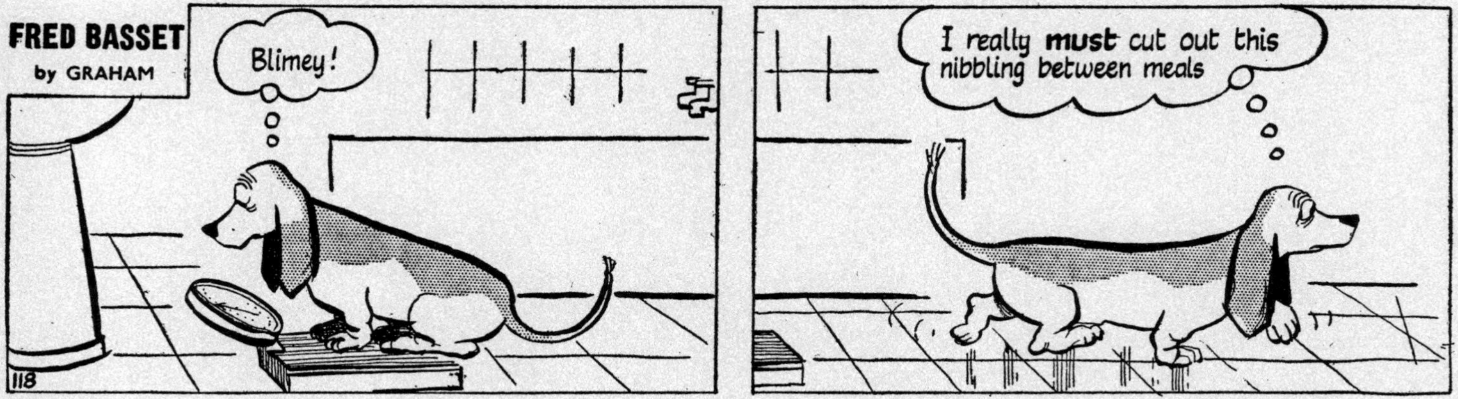
FRED BASSET
by GRAHAM
Blimey!
I really **must** cut out this nibbling between meals
118

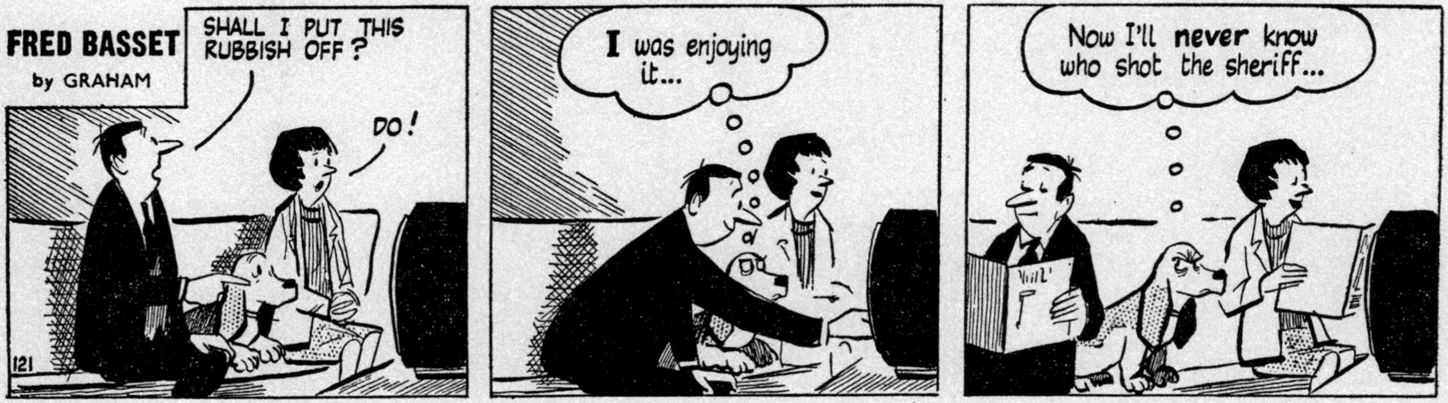
FRED BASSET
by GRAHAM
SHALL I PUT THIS RUBBISH OFF?
DO!
I was enjoying it...
Now I'll **never** know who shot the sheriff...
121

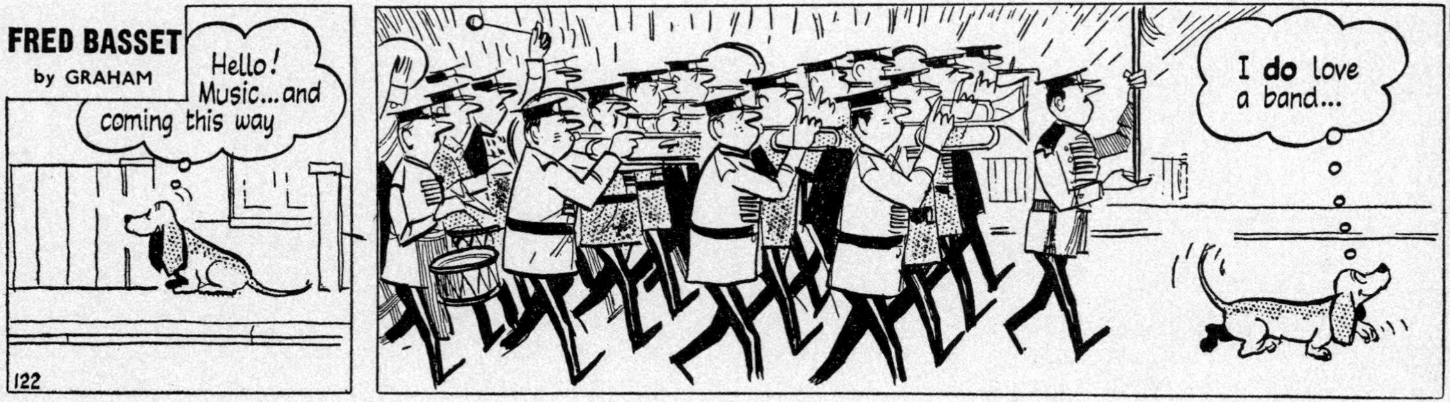
FRED BASSET
by GRAHAM
Hello! Music...and coming this way
I do love a band...
122

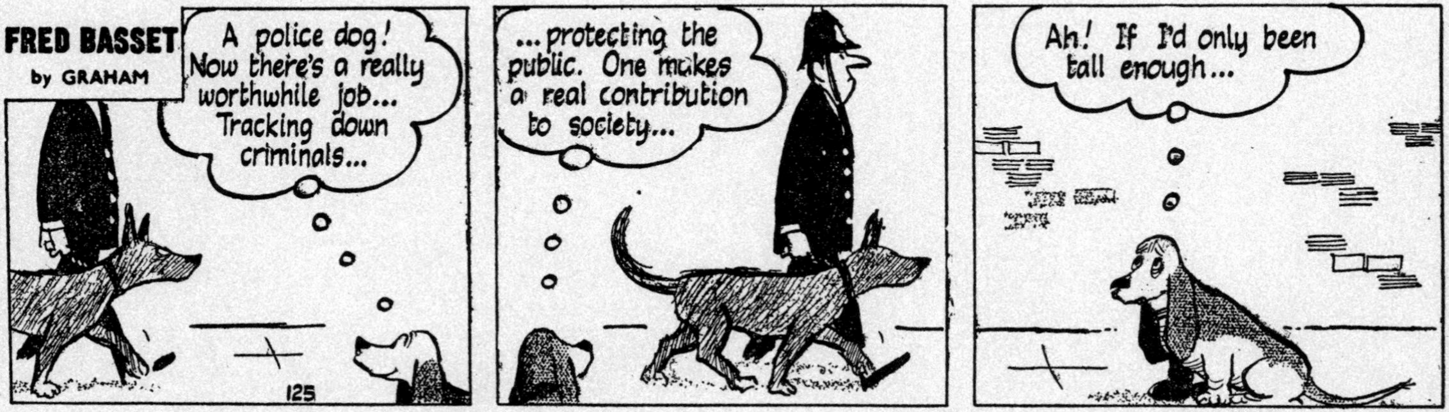
FRED BASSET
by GRAHAM
A police dog! Now there's a really worthwhile job... Tracking down criminals...
125
...protecting the public. One makes a real contribution to society...
Ah! If I'd only been tall enough...

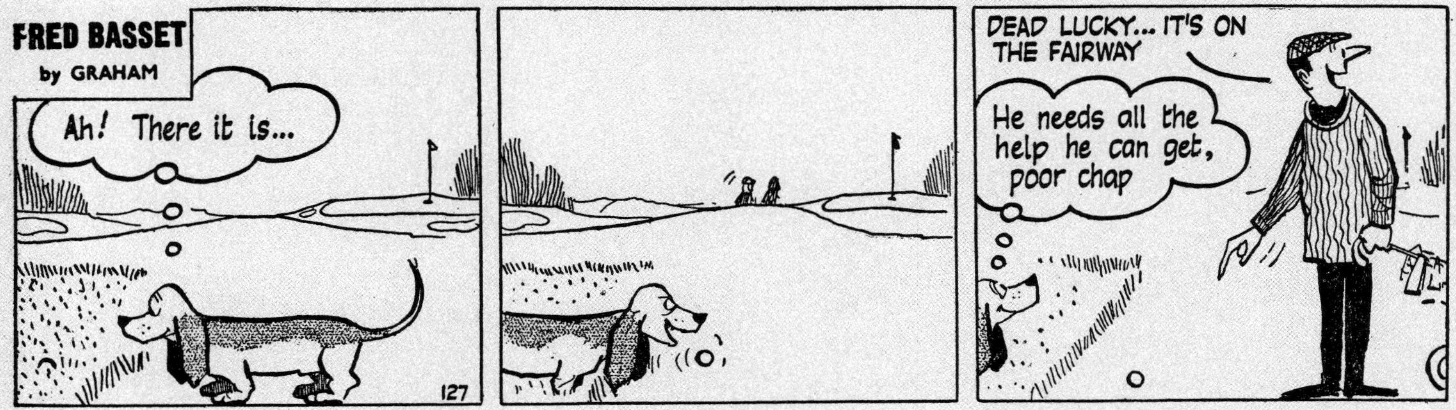
FRED BASSET
by GRAHAM
Ah! There it is...
127
DEAD LUCKY... IT'S ON THE FAIRWAY
He needs all the help he can get, poor chap

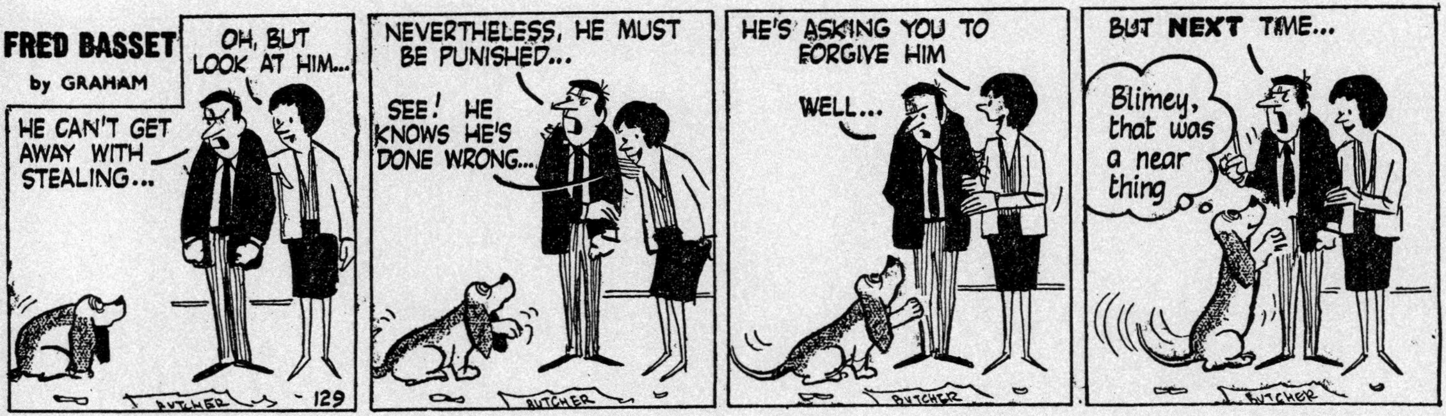
FRED BASSET
by GRAHAM
HE CAN'T GET AWAY WITH STEALING...
OH, BUT LOOK AT HIM...
129
NEVERTHELESS, HE MUST BE PUNISHED...
SEE! HE KNOWS HE'S DONE WRONG...
HE'S ASKING YOU TO FORGIVE HIM
WELL...
BUT NEXT TIME...
Blimey, that was a near thing

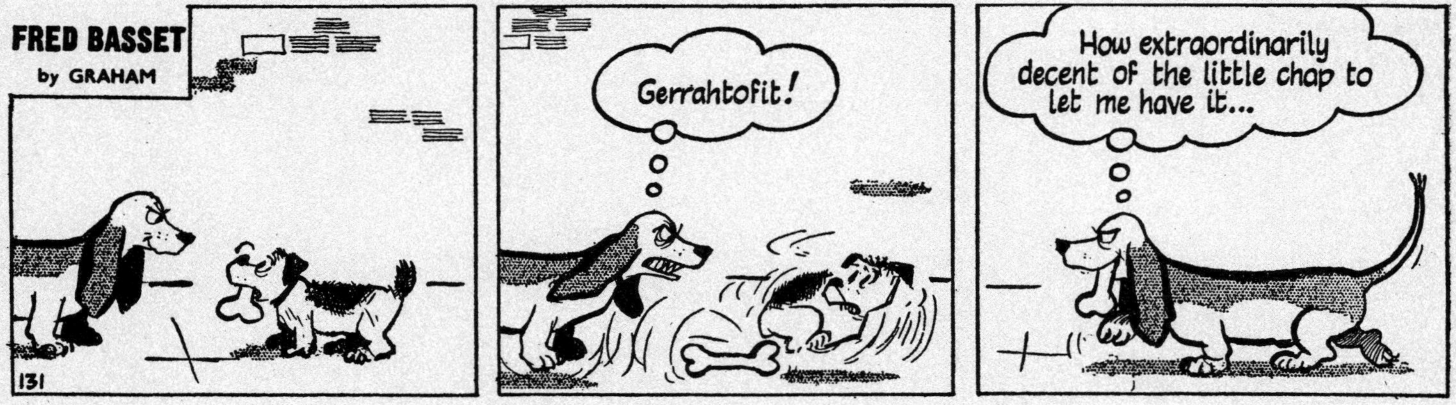
FRED BASSET
by GRAHAM
131
Gerrahtofit!
How extraordinarily decent of the little chap to let me have it...

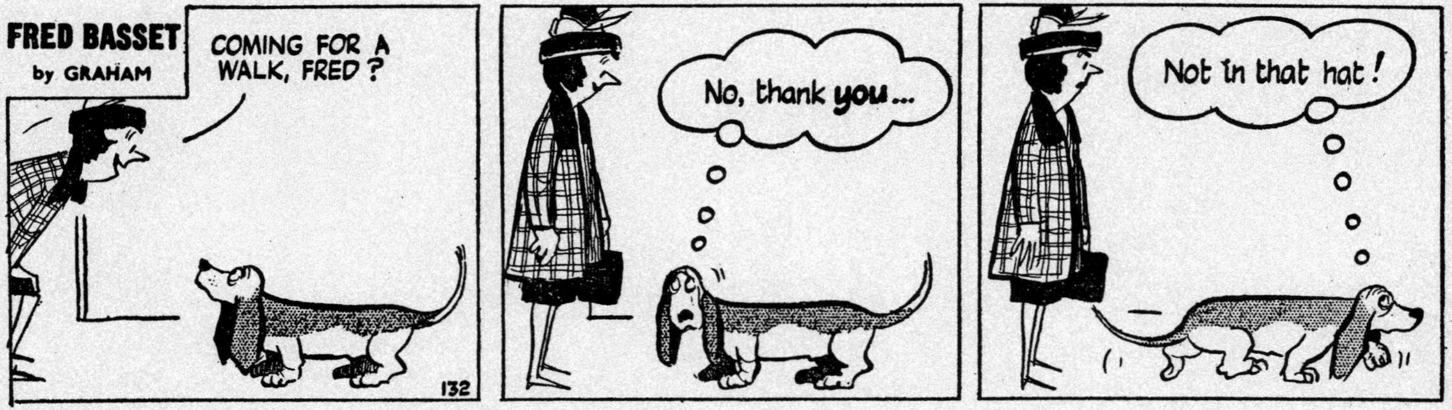
FRED BASSET
by GRAHAM
COMING FOR A WALK, FRED?
132
No, thank you...
Not in that hat!

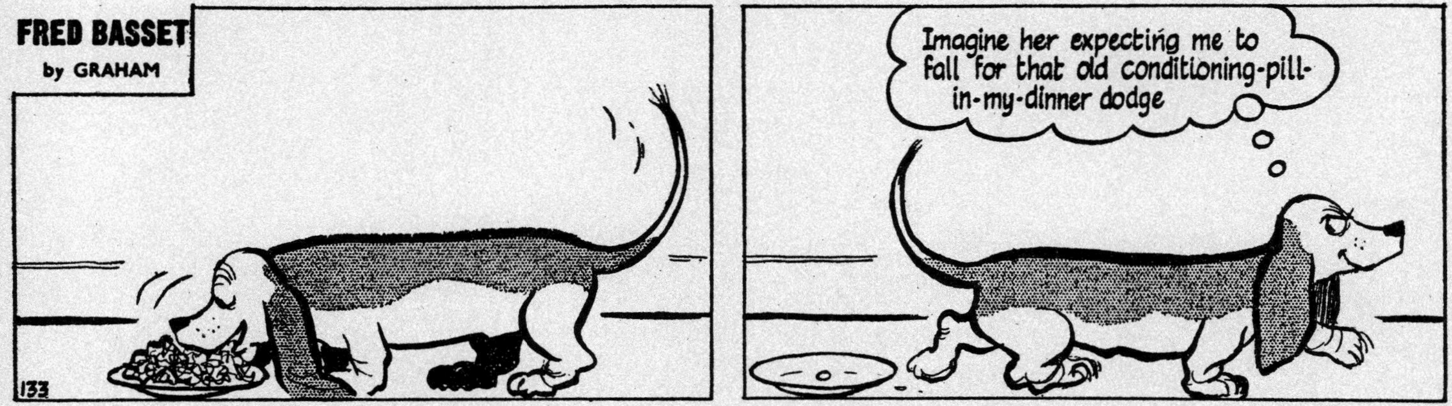
FRED BASSET
by GRAHAM
133
Imagine her expecting me to fall for that old conditioning-pill-in-my-dinner dodge

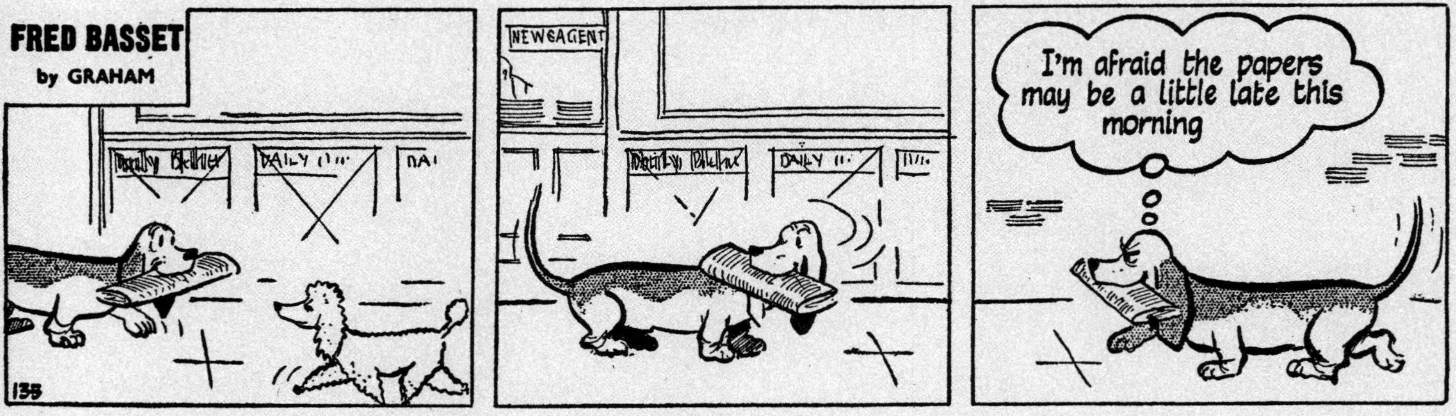
FRED BASSET
by GRAHAM
135
NEWSAGENT
I'm afraid the papers may be a little late this morning

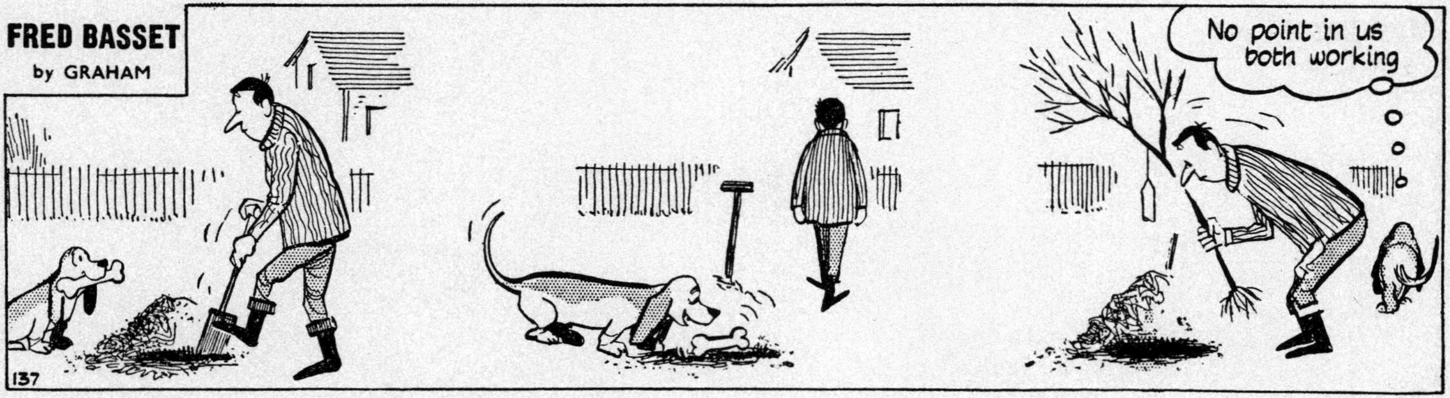
FRED BASSET
by GRAHAM
No point in us both working
137

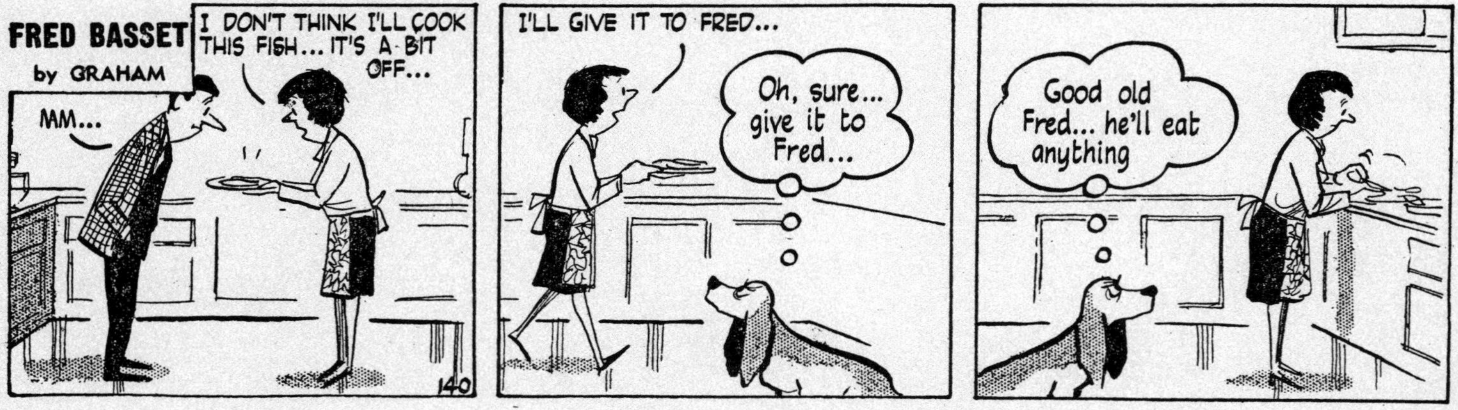
FRED BASSET
by GRAHAM
I DON'T THINK I'LL COOK THIS FISH... IT'S A BIT OFF...
MM...
140
I'LL GIVE IT TO FRED...
Oh, sure... give it to Fred...
Good old Fred... he'll eat anything

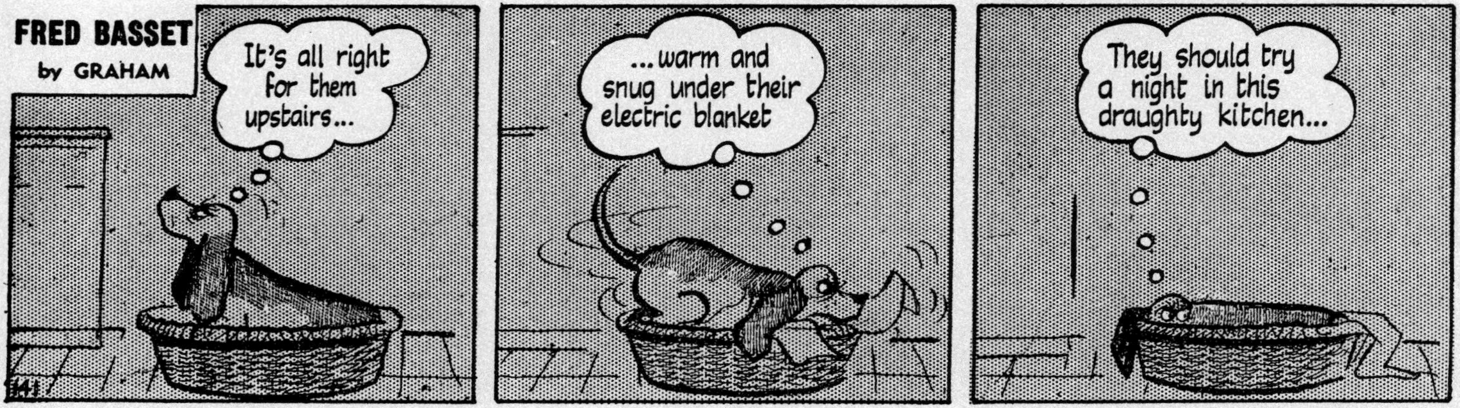
FRED BASSET
by GRAHAM
141
It's all right for them upstairs...
...warm and snug under their electric blanket
They should try a night in this draughty kitchen...

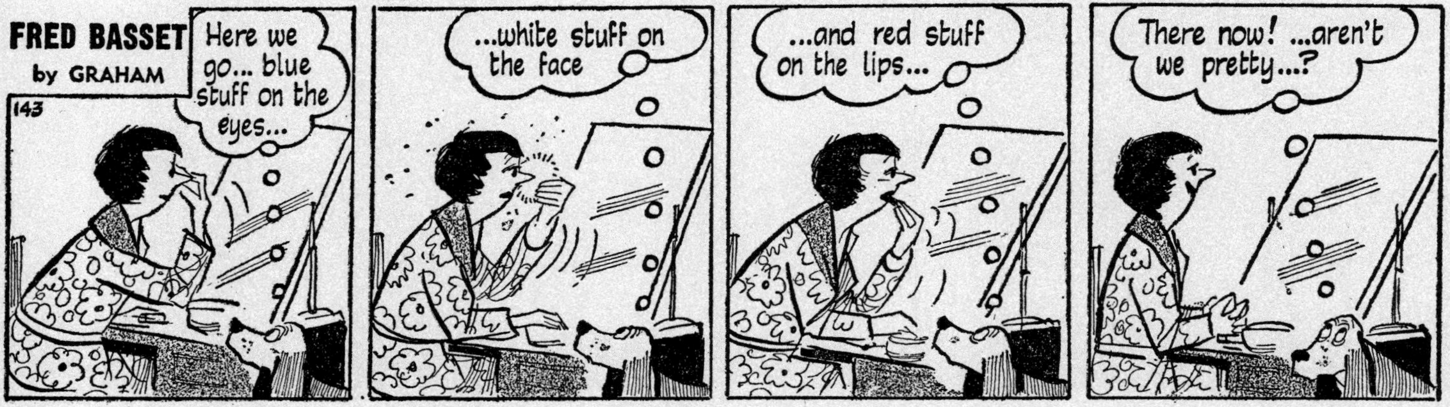
FRED BASSET
by GRAHAM
143
Here we go... blue stuff on the eyes...
...white stuff on the face
...and red stuff on the lips...
There now! ...aren't we pretty...?

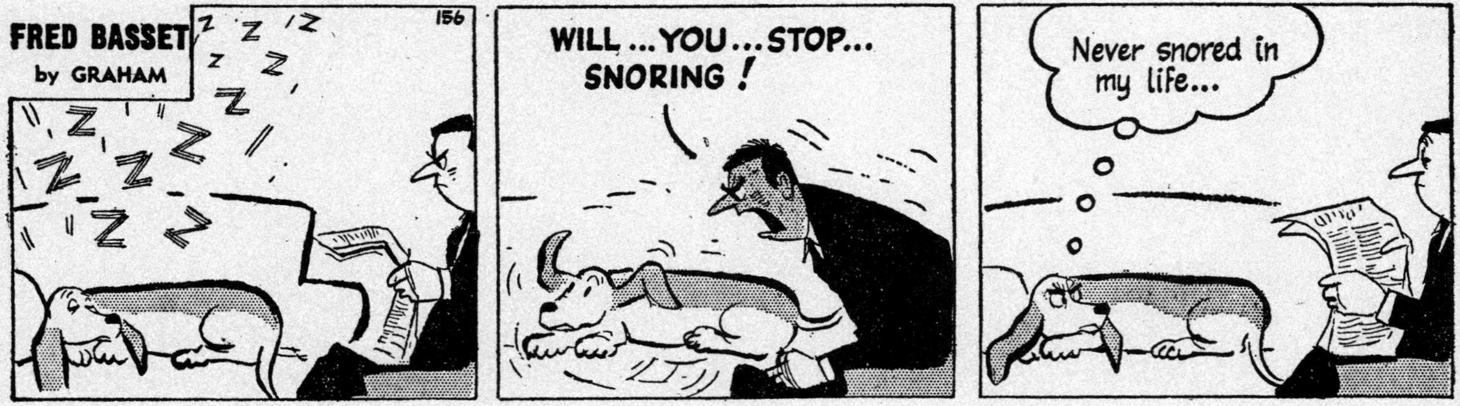
FRED BASSET
by GRAHAM
156
Z Z Z Z Z Z Z Z Z Z Z
WILL ... YOU ... STOP... SNORING !
Never snored in my life...

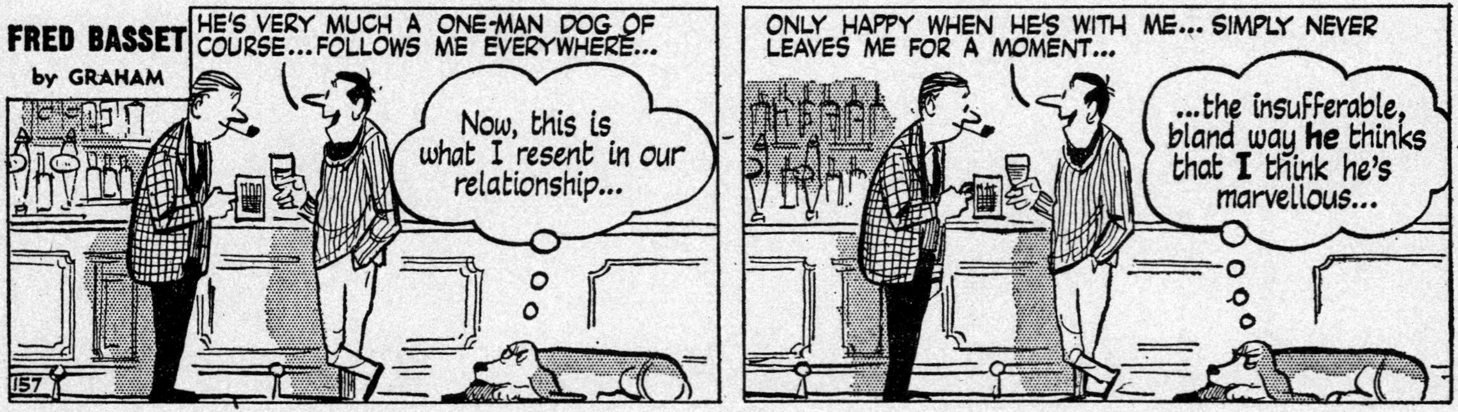
FRED BASSET
by GRAHAM
HE'S VERY MUCH A ONE-MAN DOG OF COURSE... FOLLOWS ME EVERYWHERE...
Now, this is what I resent in our relationship...
157
ONLY HAPPY WHEN HE'S WITH ME... SIMPLY NEVER LEAVES ME FOR A MOMENT...
...the insufferable, bland way **he** thinks that **I** think he's marvellous...

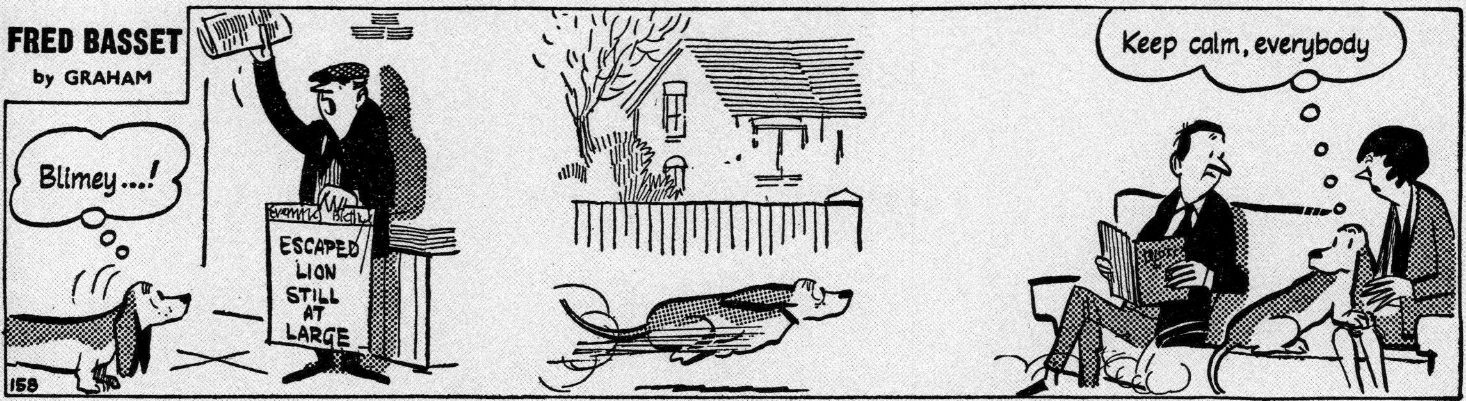
FRED BASSET
by GRAHAM
Blimey...!
ESCAPED LION STILL AT LARGE
Keep calm, everybody
158

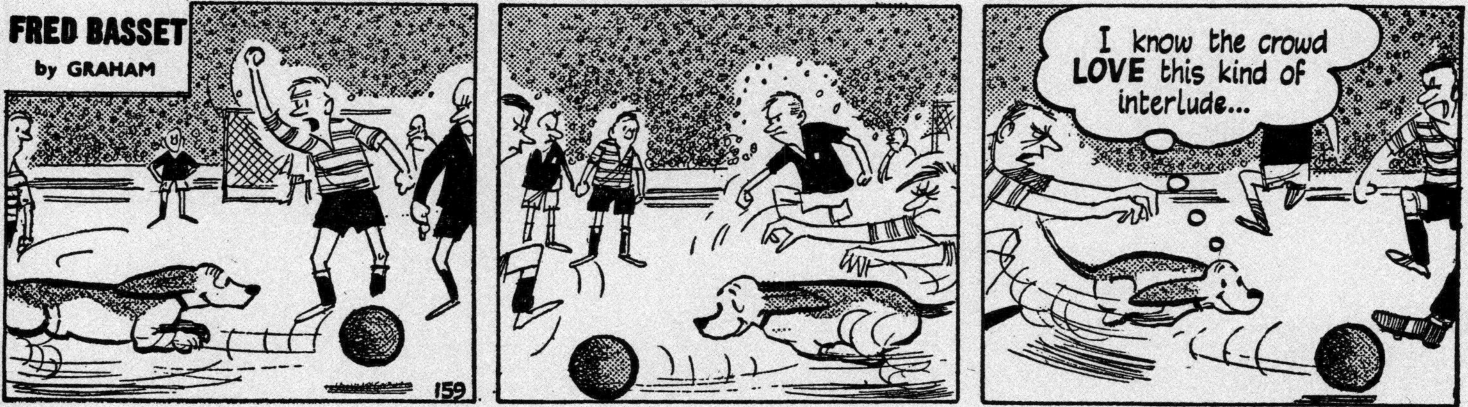
FRED BASSET
by GRAHAM
159
I know the crowd LOVE this kind of interlude...

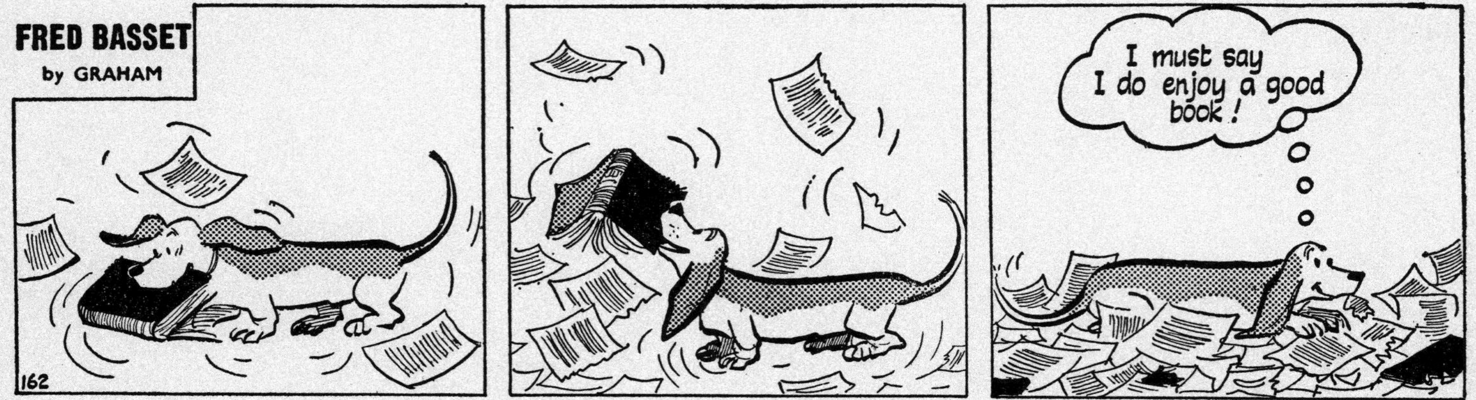
FRED BASSET
by GRAHAM
162
I must say I do enjoy a good book!

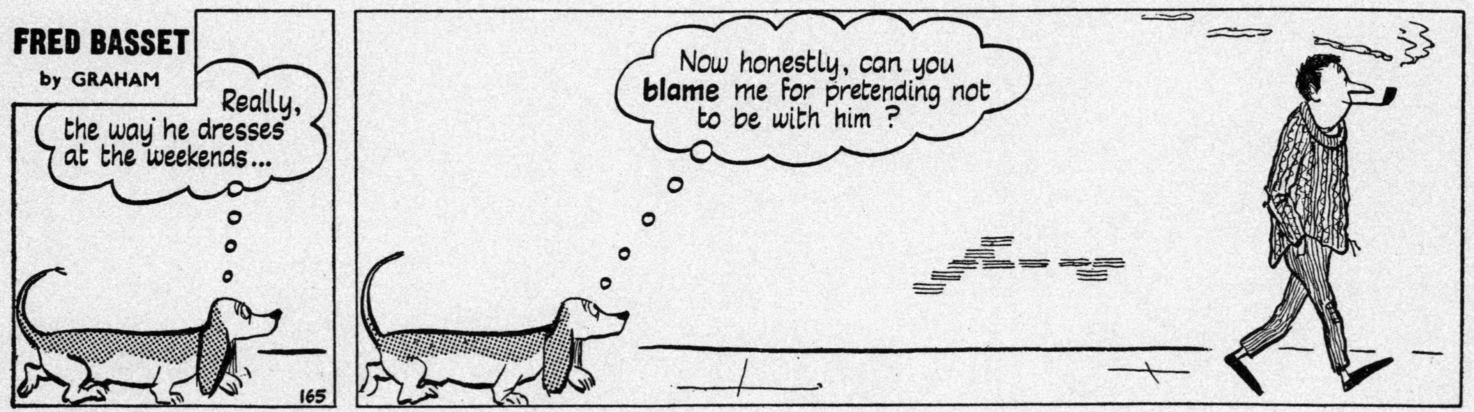
FRED BASSET
by GRAHAM
Really, the way he dresses at the weekends...
165
Now honestly, can you **blame** me for pretending not to be with him ?

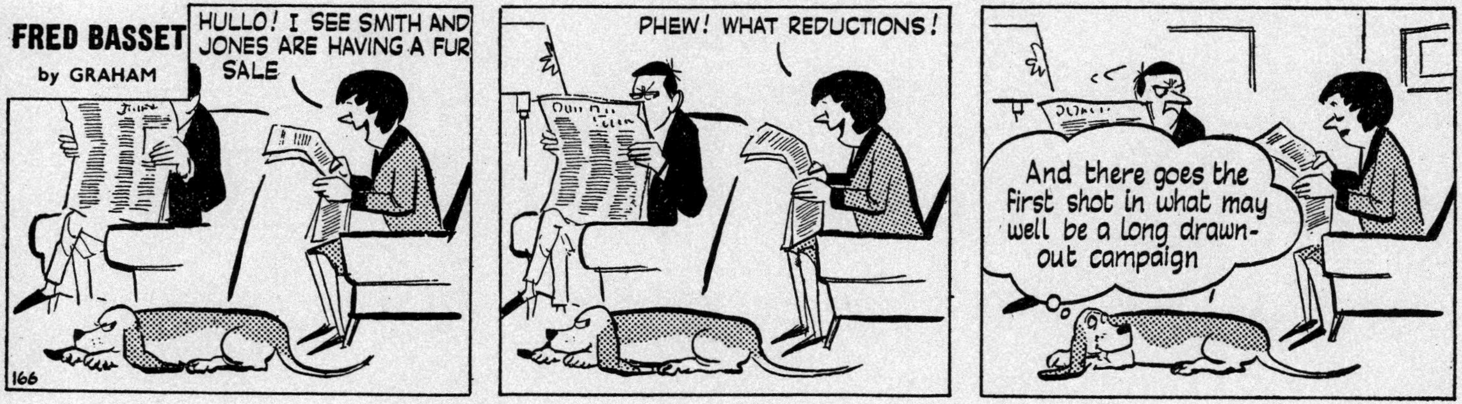
FRED BASSET
by GRAHAM
HULLO! I SEE SMITH AND JONES ARE HAVING A FUR SALE
166
PHEW! WHAT REDUCTIONS!
And there goes the first shot in what may well be a long drawn-out campaign

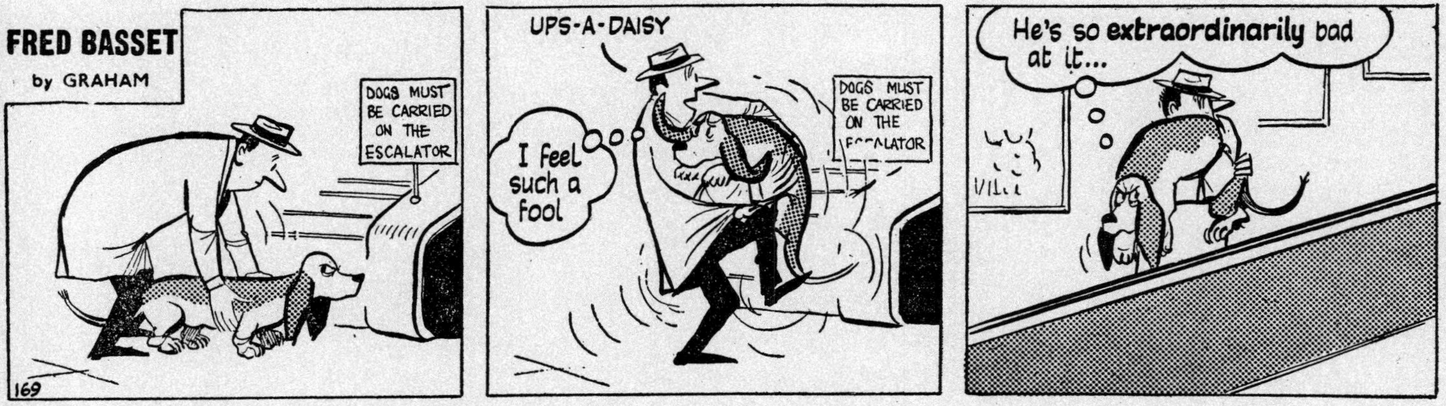
FRED BASSET
by GRAHAM
DOGS MUST BE CARRIED ON THE ESCALATOR
169
UPS-A-DAISY
I feel such a fool
DOGS MUST BE CARRIED ON THE
He's so **extraordinarily** bad at it...

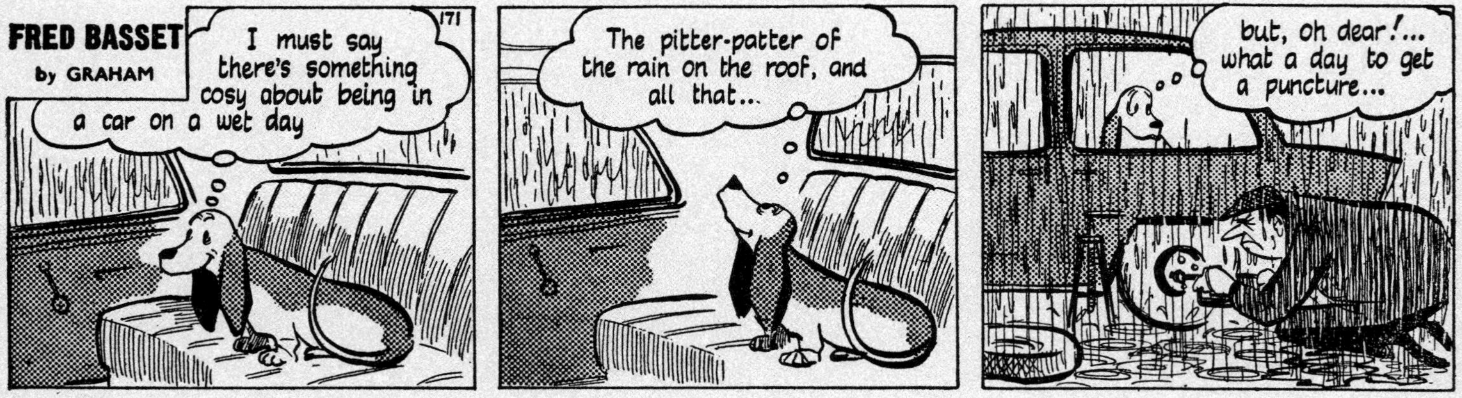
FRED BASSET
by GRAHAM
171
I must say there's something cosy about being in a car on a wet day
The pitter-patter of the rain on the roof, and all that...
but, oh dear!... what a day to get a puncture...

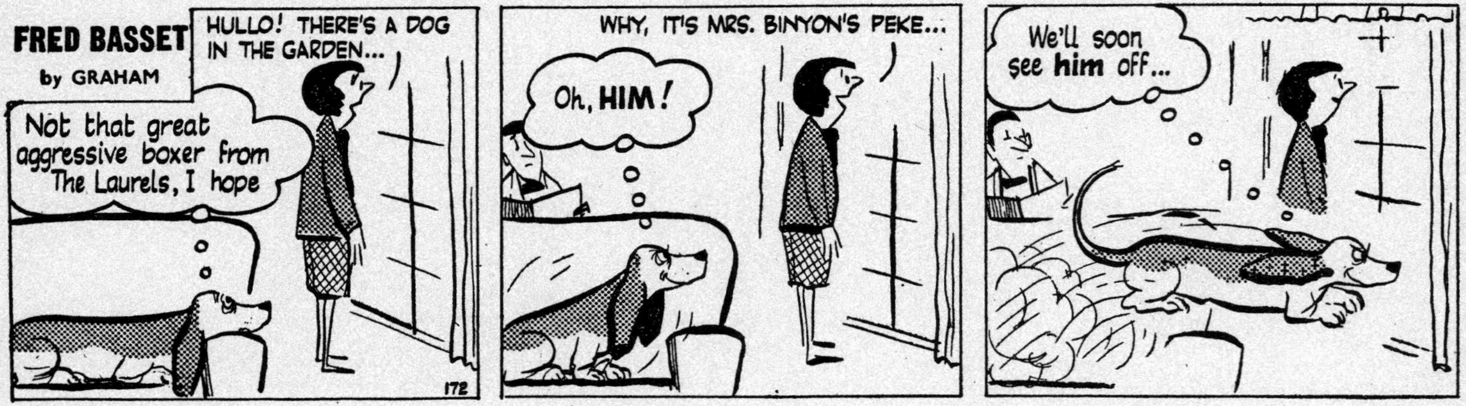
FRED BASSET
by GRAHAM
HULLO! THERE'S A DOG IN THE GARDEN...
Not that great aggressive boxer from The Laurels, I hope
172
WHY, IT'S MRS. BINYON'S PEKE...
Oh, HIM!
We'll soon see him off...

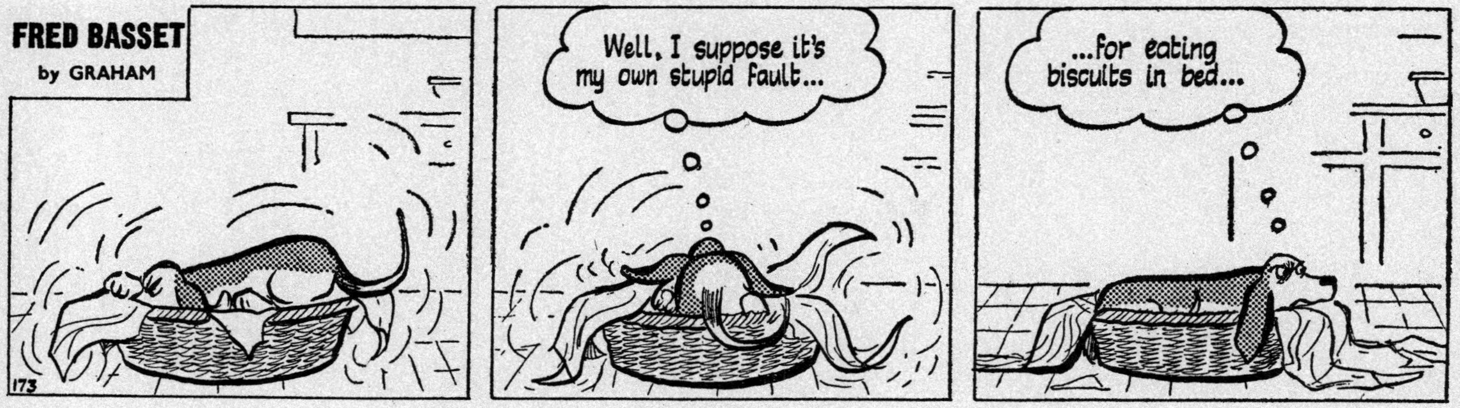
FRED BASSET
by GRAHAM
173
Well, I suppose it's my own stupid fault...
...for eating biscuits in bed...

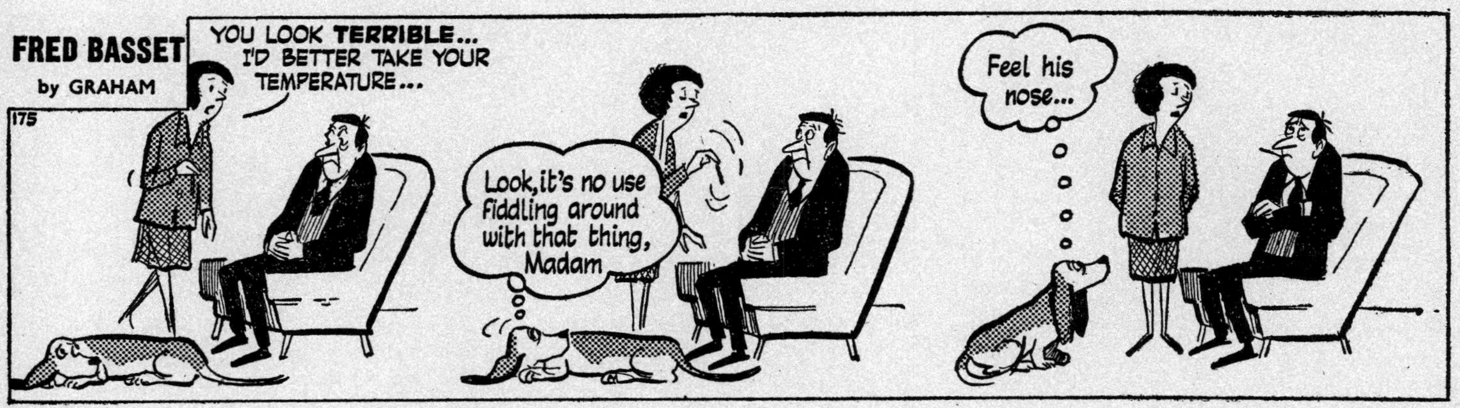
FRED BASSET
by GRAHAM
175
YOU LOOK TERRIBLE... I'D BETTER TAKE YOUR TEMPERATURE...
Look, it's no use fiddling around with that thing, Madam
Feel his nose...

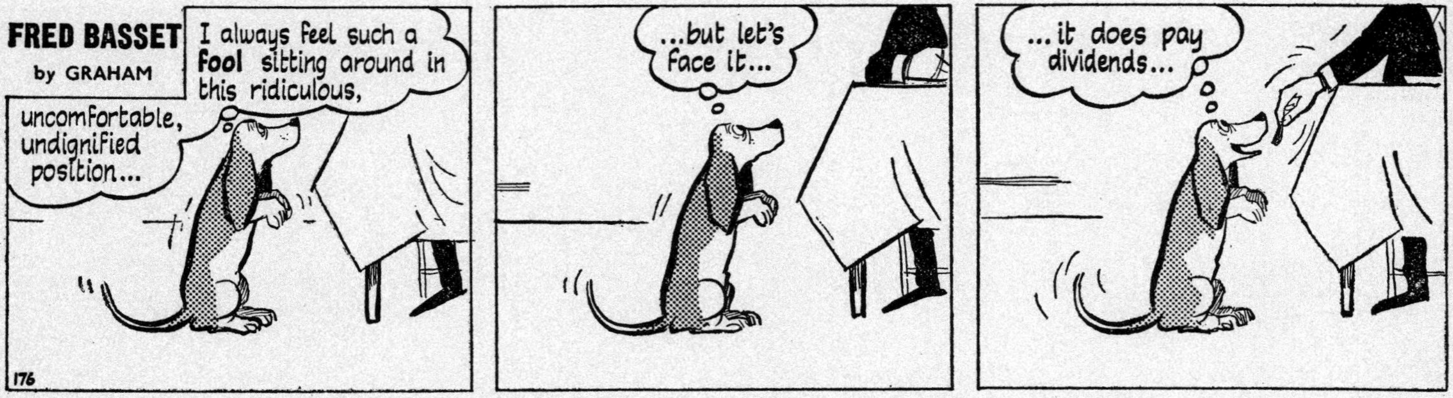
FRED BASSET
by GRAHAM
I always feel such a **fool** sitting around in this ridiculous,
uncomfortable, undignified position...
...but let's face it...
...it does pay dividends...
176

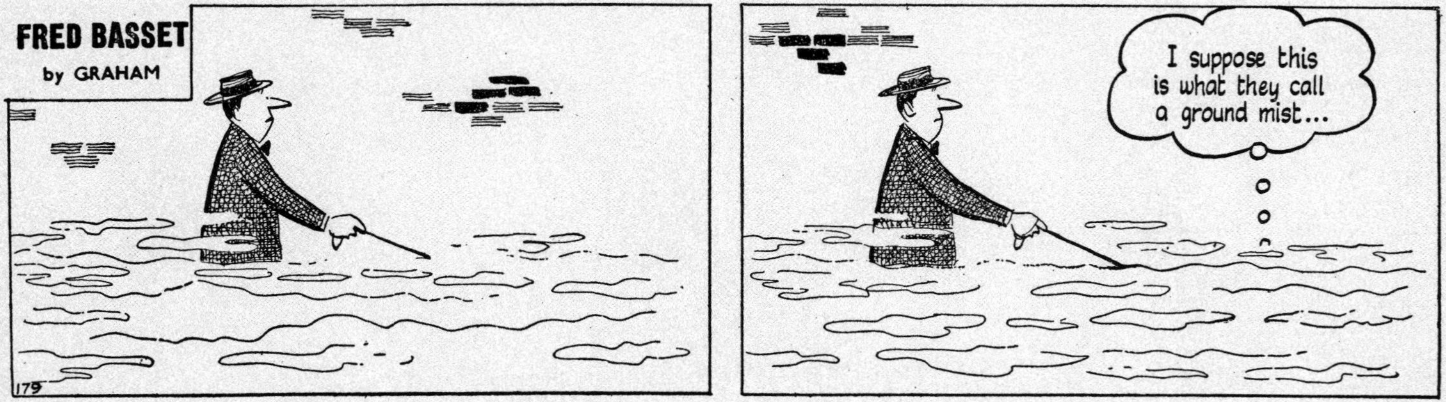
FRED BASSET
by GRAHAM
I suppose this is what they call a ground mist...
179

FRED BASSET
by GRAHAM
SIT!
NOW HE'LL SIT THERE UNTIL I CALL HIM...
MARVELLOUS
...NO MATTER HOW FAR I GO...
WONDERFUL
Frankly, I don't trust his memory these days
181

FRED BASSET
by GRAHAM
DOG SHOW
TODAY
RING
Best of breed, maybe...
...or even — dare I say it — SUPREME CHAMPION!
I think somebody's taking the mickey out of old Fred
CLASS 4
MOST COMICAL DOG
183

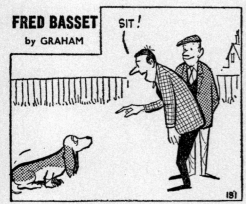

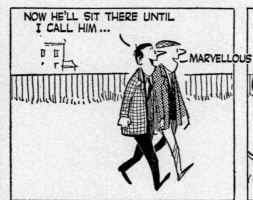

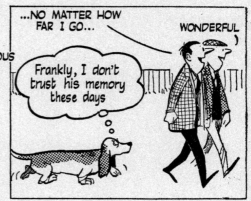

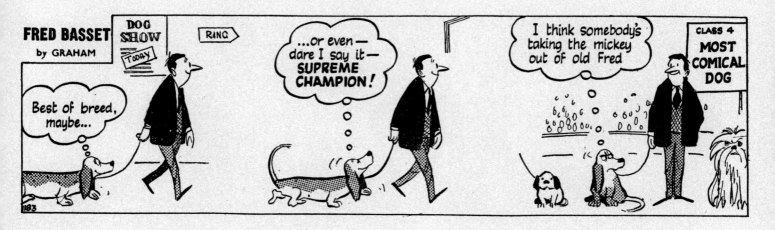

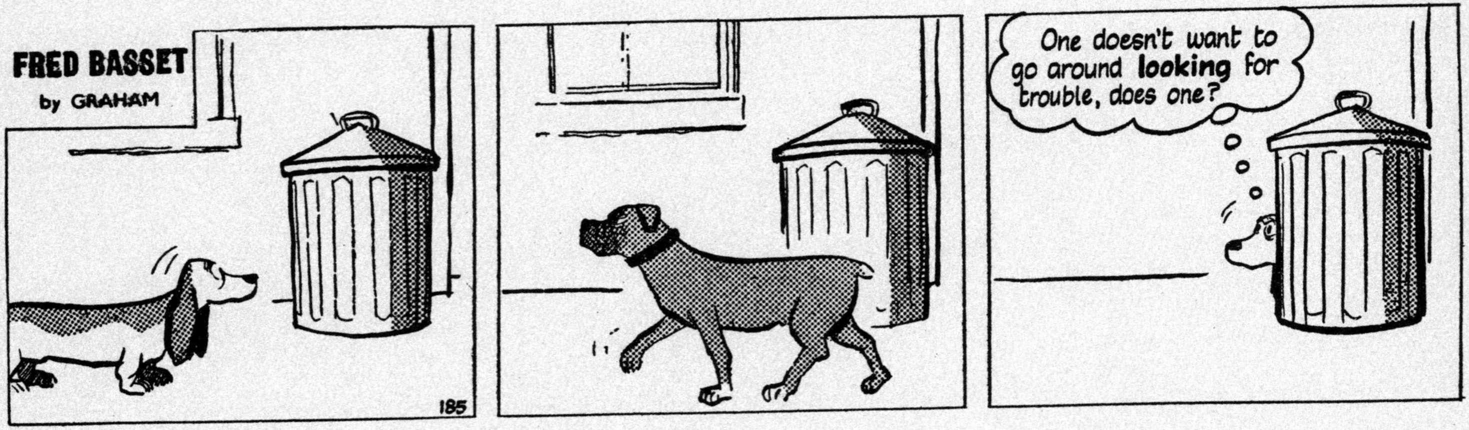
FRED BASSET
by GRAHAM
185
One doesn't want to go around **looking** for trouble, does one?

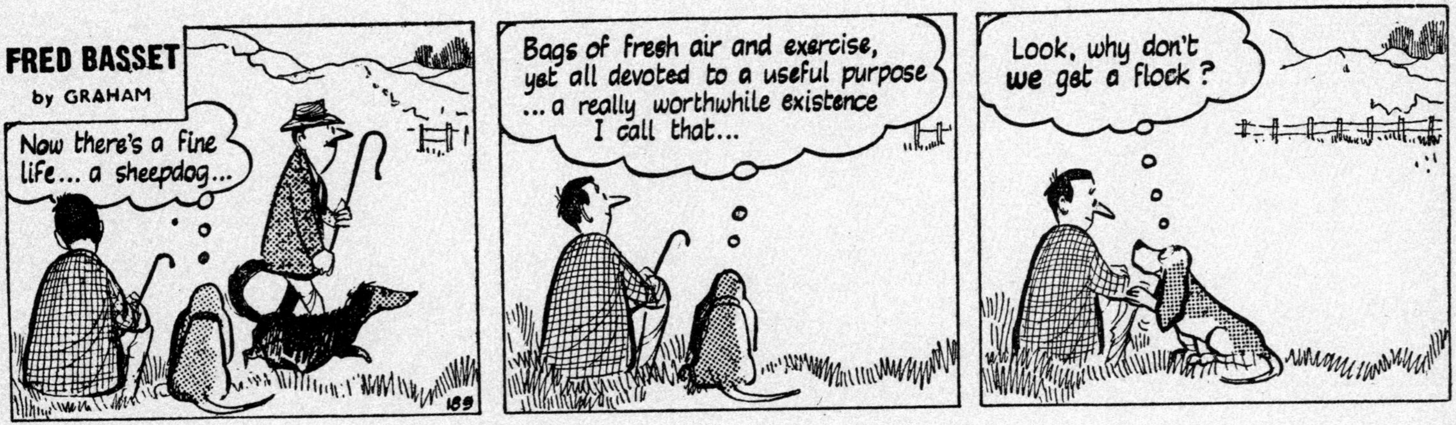
FRED BASSET
by GRAHAM
Now there's a fine life... a sheepdog...
189
Bags of fresh air and exercise, yet all devoted to a useful purpose ... a really worthwhile existence I call that...
Look, why don't **we** get a flock ?

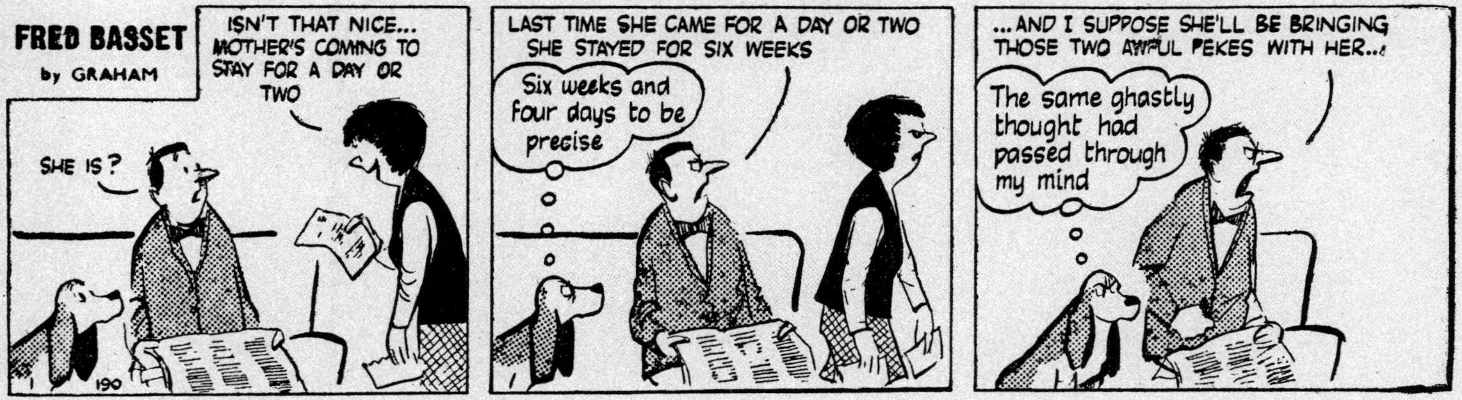
FRED BASSET
by GRAHAM
ISN'T THAT NICE... MOTHER'S COMING TO STAY FOR A DAY OR TWO
SHE IS?
190
LAST TIME SHE CAME FOR A DAY OR TWO SHE STAYED FOR SIX WEEKS
Six weeks and four days to be precise
...AND I SUPPOSE SHE'LL BE BRINGING THOSE TWO AWFUL PEKES WITH HER...!
The same ghastly thought had passed through my mind

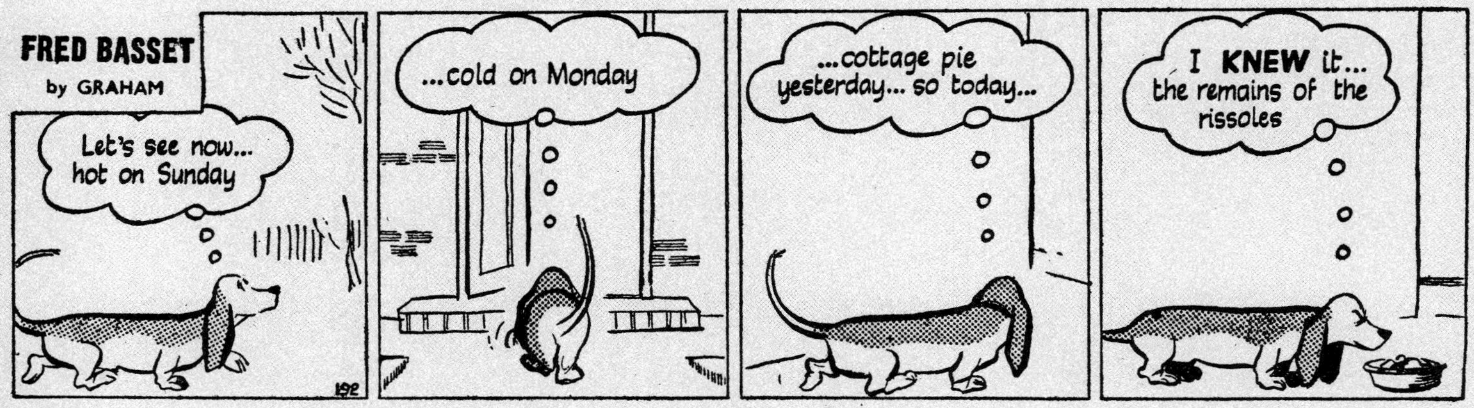
FRED BASSET
by GRAHAM
Let's see now... hot on Sunday
192
...cold on Monday
...cottage pie yesterday... so today...
I **KNEW** it... the remains of the rissoles

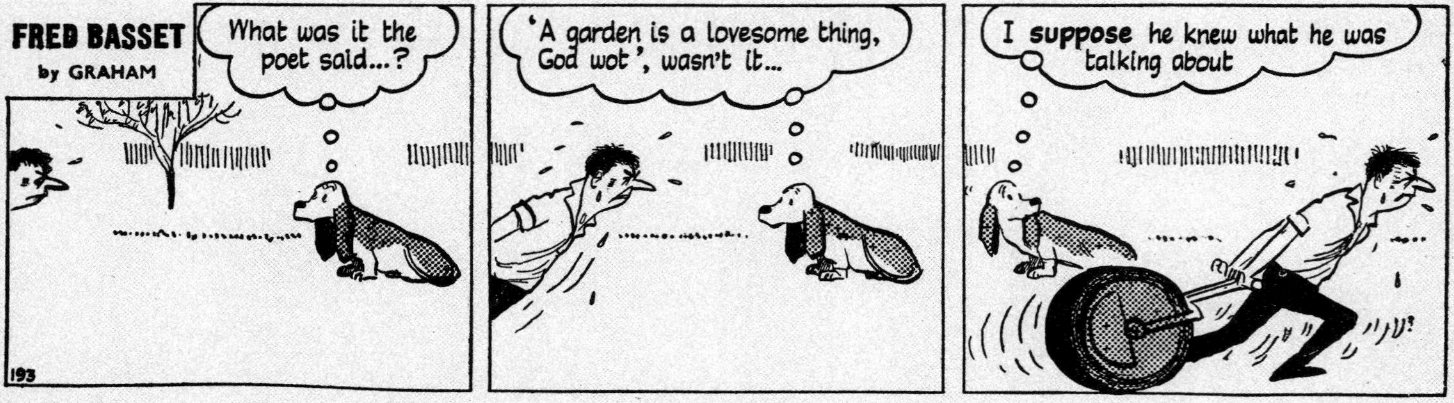
FRED BASSET
by GRAHAM
What was it the poet said...?
193
'A garden is a lovesome thing, God wot', wasn't it...
I suppose he knew what he was talking about

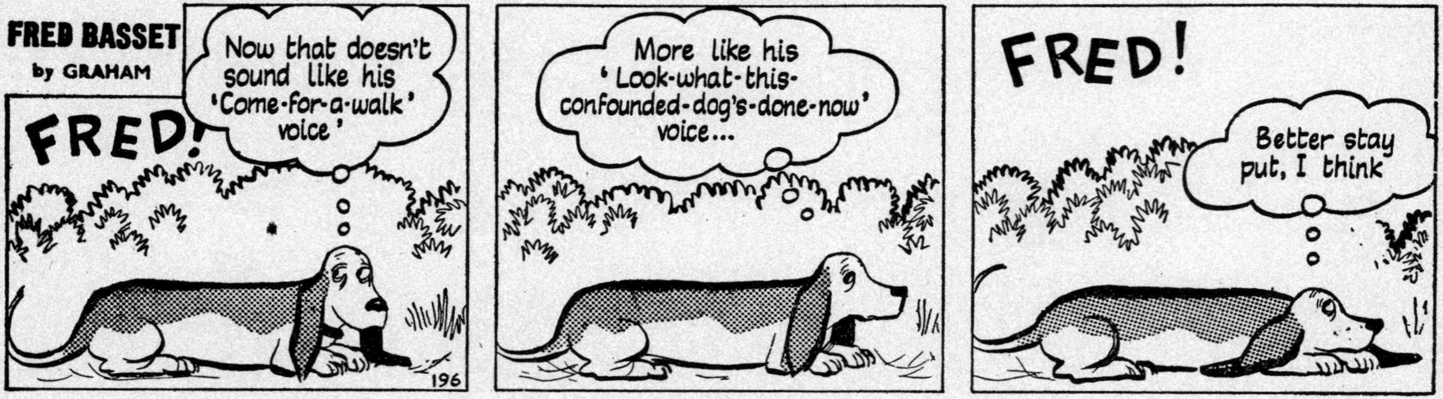
FRED BASSET
by GRAHAM
FRED!
Now that doesn't sound like his 'Come-for-a-walk' voice'
196
More like his 'Look-what-this-confounded-dog's-done-now' voice...
FRED!
Better stay put, I think

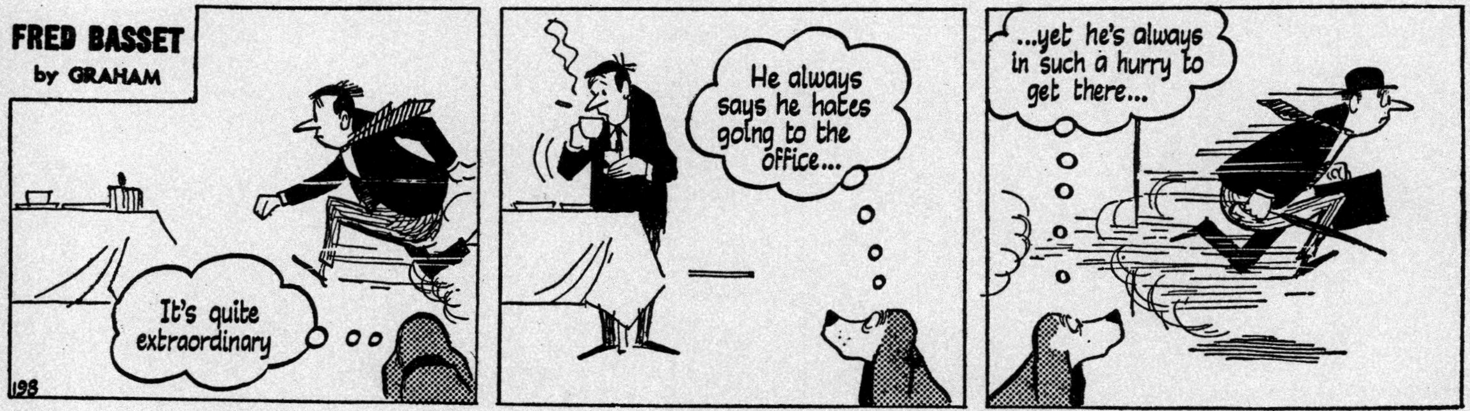
FRED BASSET
by GRAHAM
It's quite extraordinary
198
He always says he hates going to the office...
...yet he's always in such a hurry to get there...

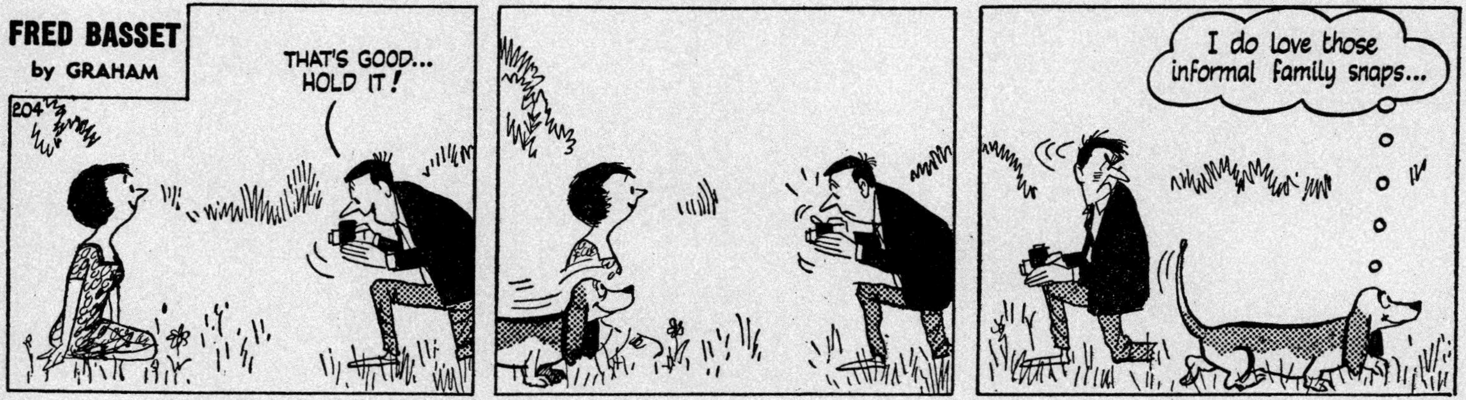
FRED BASSET
by GRAHAM
204
THAT'S GOOD... HOLD IT!
I do love those informal family snaps...

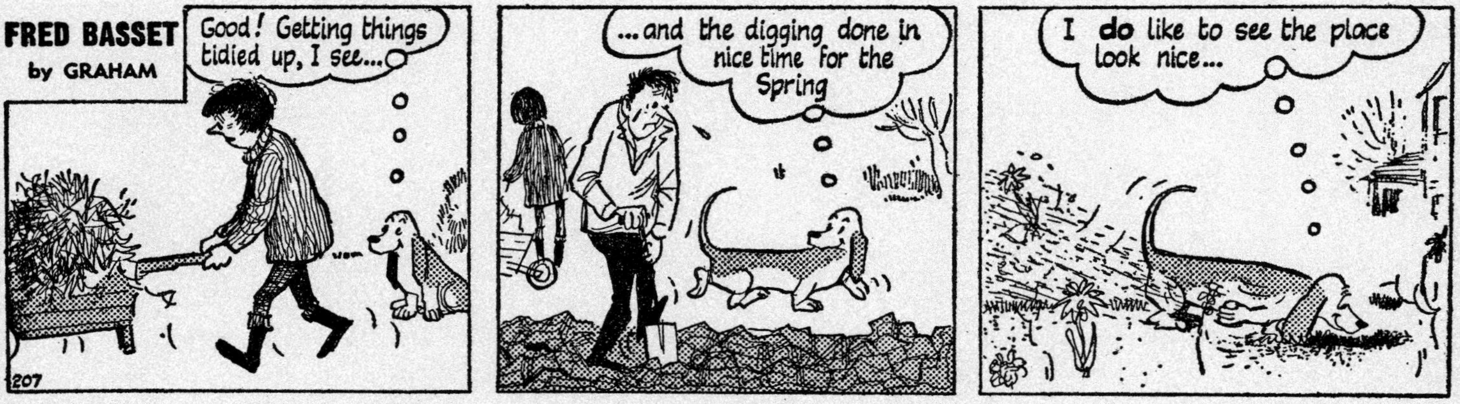
FRED BASSET
by GRAHAM
Good! Getting things tidied up, I see...
...and the digging done in nice time for the Spring
I do like to see the place look nice...
207

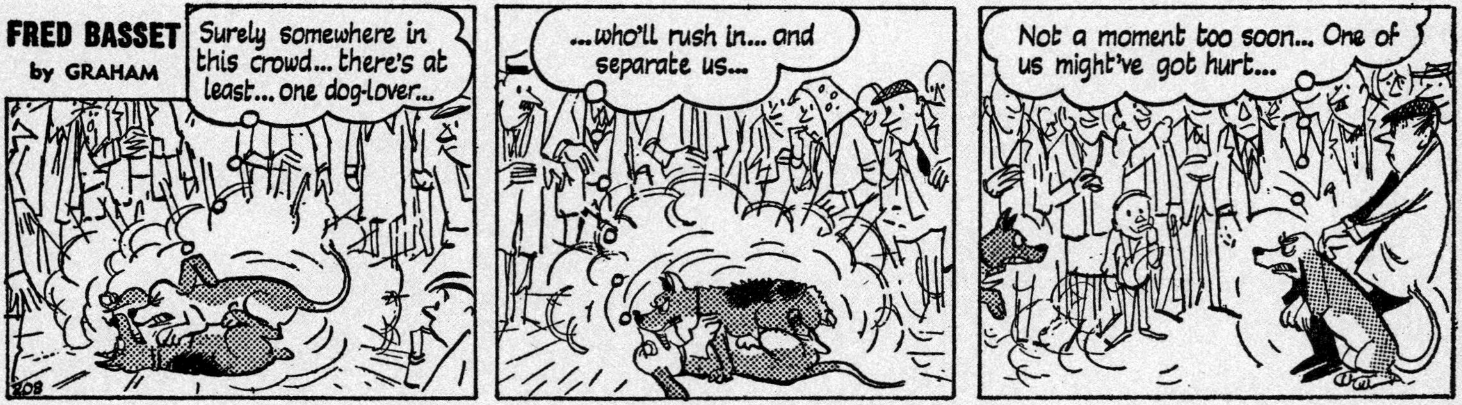
FRED BASSET
by GRAHAM
Surely somewhere in this crowd... there's at least... one dog-lover...
...who'll rush in... and separate us...
Not a moment too soon... One of us might've got hurt...
208

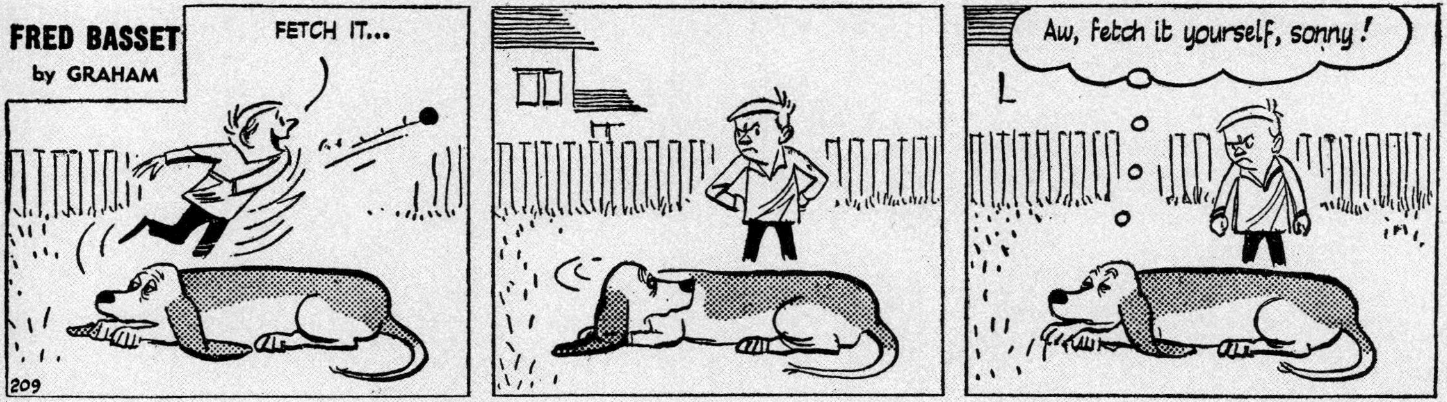
FRED BASSET
by GRAHAM
FETCH IT...
Aw, fetch it yourself, sonny!
209

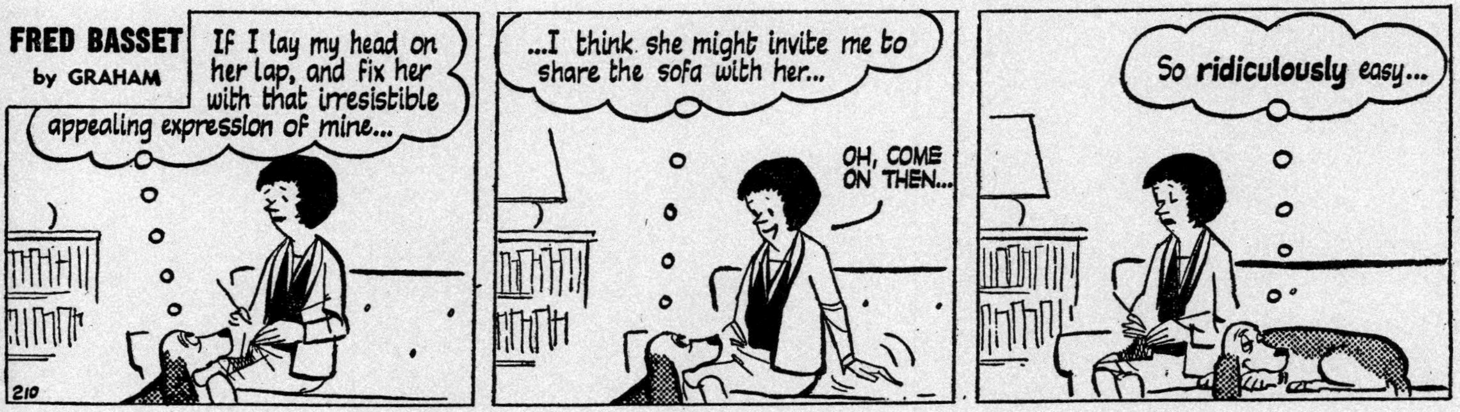
FRED BASSET
by GRAHAM
If I lay my head on her lap, and fix her with that irresistible appealing expression of mine...
...I think she might invite me to share the sofa with her...
OH, COME ON THEN...
So **ridiculously** easy...
210

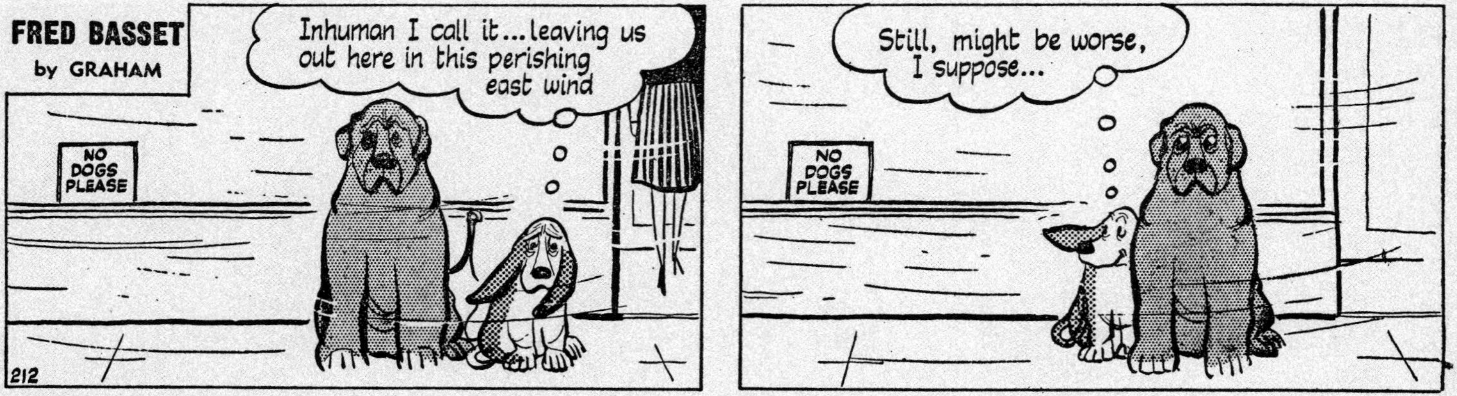
FRED BASSET
by GRAHAM
Inhuman I call it...leaving us out here in this perishing east wind
NO DOGS PLEASE
212
Still, might be worse, I suppose...
NO DOGS PLEASE

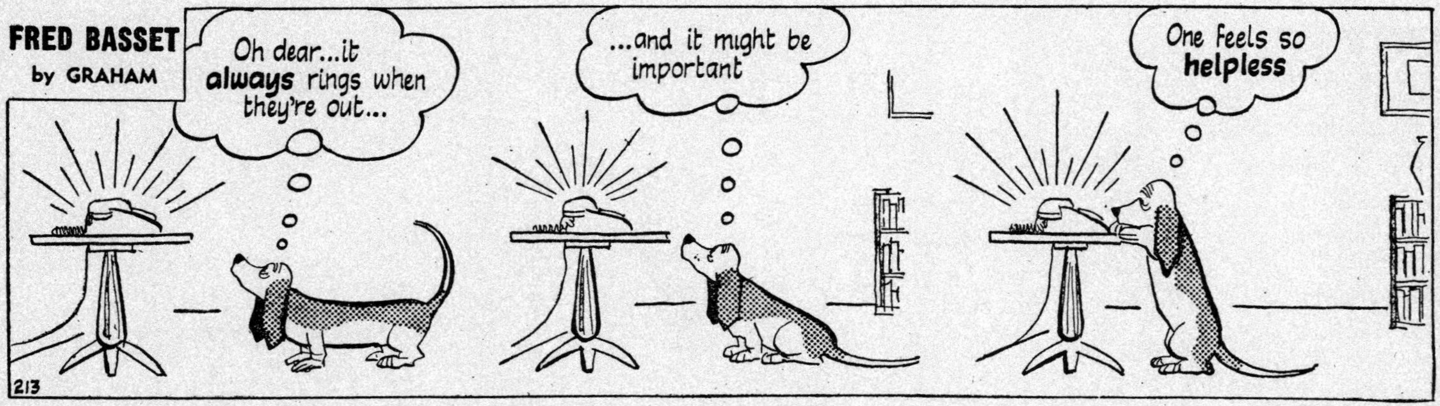
FRED BASSET
by GRAHAM
Oh dear...it **always** rings when they're out...
...and it might be important
One feels so **helpless**
213

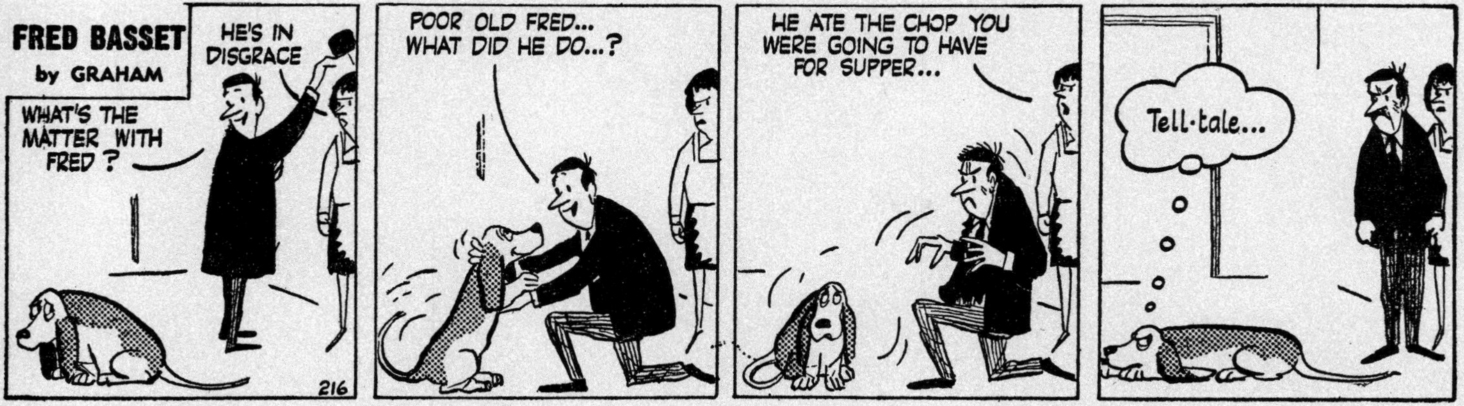
FRED BASSET
by GRAHAM
WHAT'S THE MATTER WITH FRED ?
HE'S IN DISGRACE
216
POOR OLD FRED... WHAT DID HE DO...?
HE ATE THE CHOP YOU WERE GOING TO HAVE FOR SUPPER...
Tell·tale...

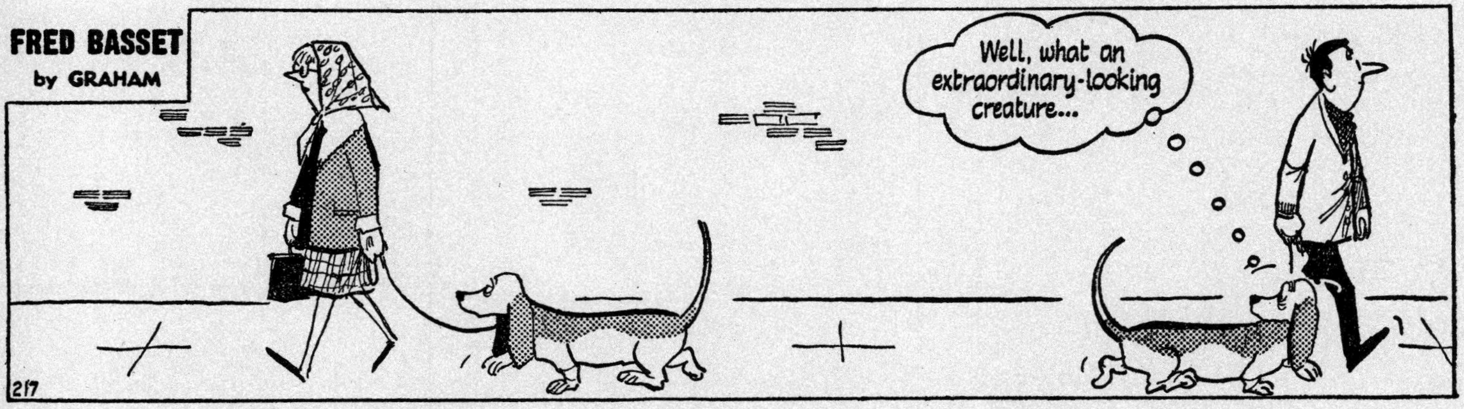
FRED BASSET
by GRAHAM
Well, what an extraordinary-looking creature...
217

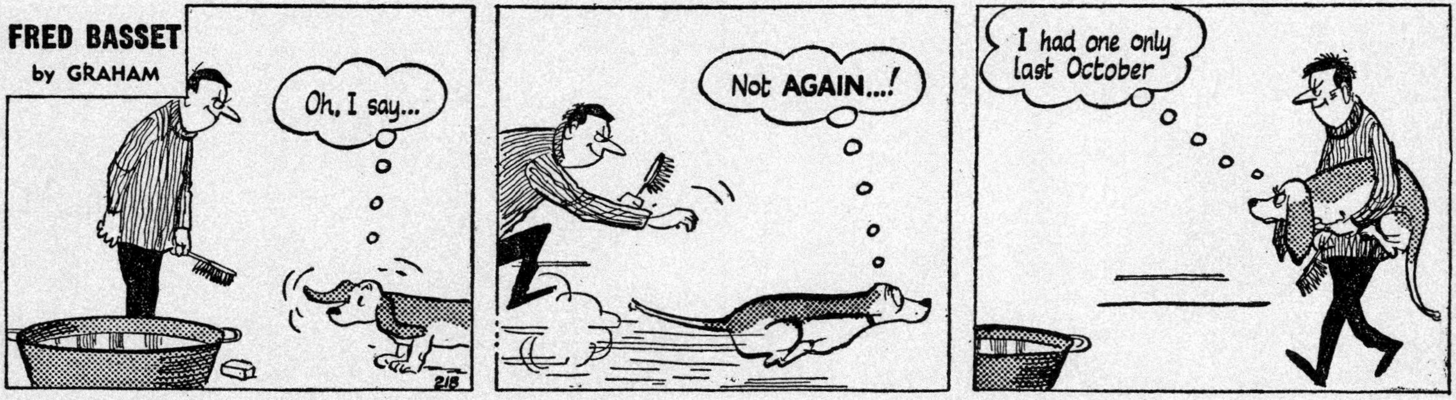

FRED BASSET
by GRAHAM
Oh, I say...
218
Not AGAIN...!
I had one only last October

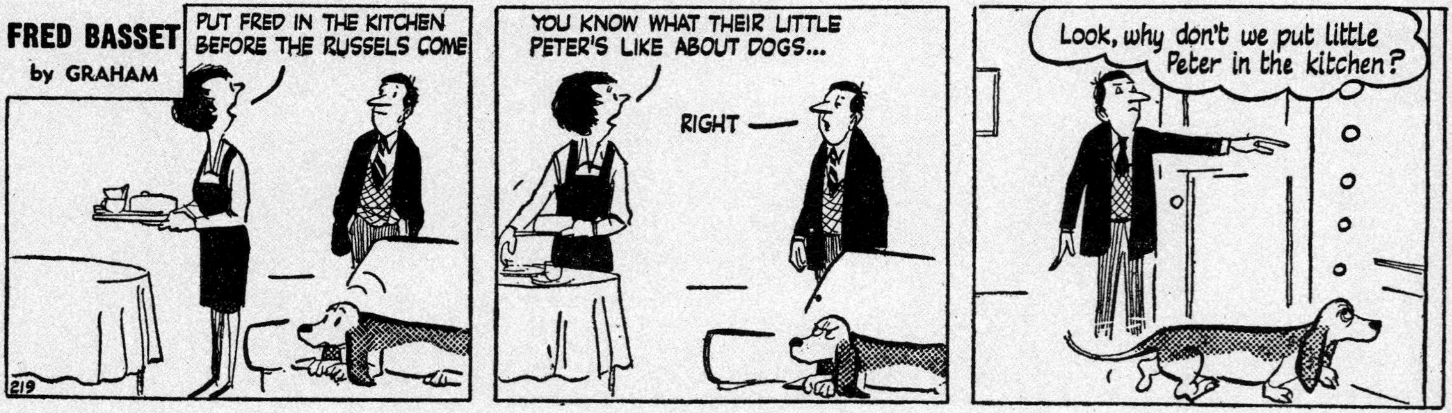

FRED BASSET
by GRAHAM
PUT FRED IN THE KITCHEN BEFORE THE RUSSELS COME
219
YOU KNOW WHAT THEIR LITTLE PETER'S LIKE ABOUT DOGS...
RIGHT —
Look, why don't we put little Peter in the kitchen?

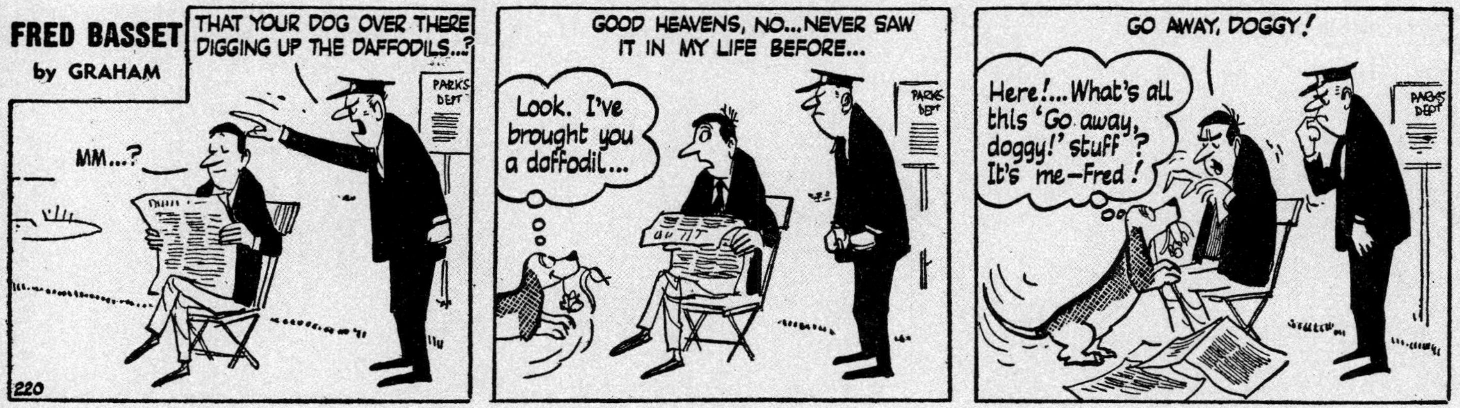
FRED BASSET
by GRAHAM
THAT YOUR DOG OVER THERE DIGGING UP THE DAFFODILS...?
MM...?
220
GOOD HEAVENS, NO...NEVER SAW IT IN MY LIFE BEFORE...
Look. I've brought you a daffodil...
PARKS DEPT
GO AWAY, DOGGY!
Here!...What's all this 'Go away, doggy!' stuff? It's me—Fred!
PARKS DEPT

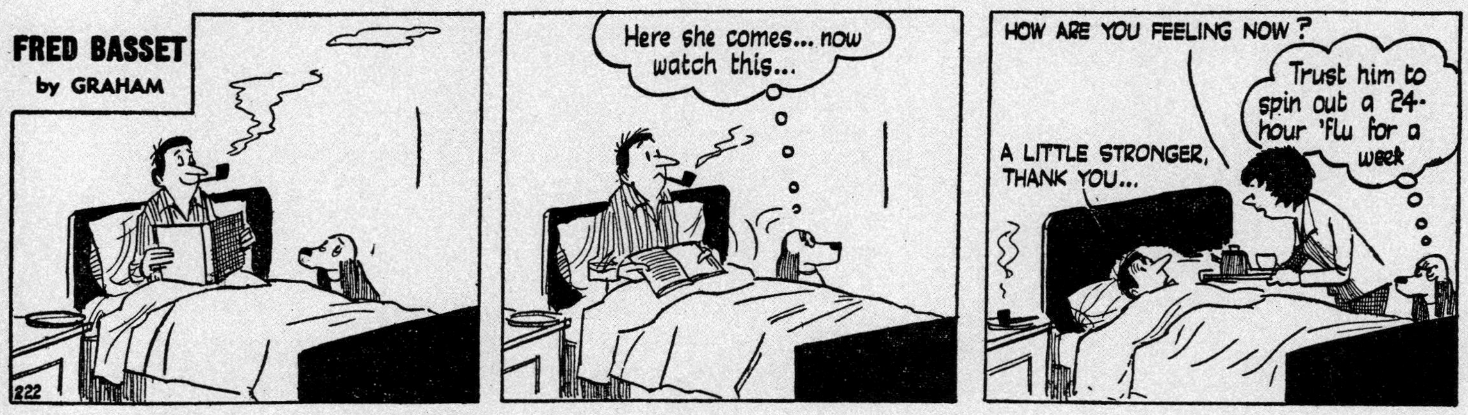
FRED BASSET
by GRAHAM
222
Here she comes... now watch this...
HOW ARE YOU FEELING NOW?
A LITTLE STRONGER, THANK YOU...
Trust him to spin out a 24-hour 'flu for a week

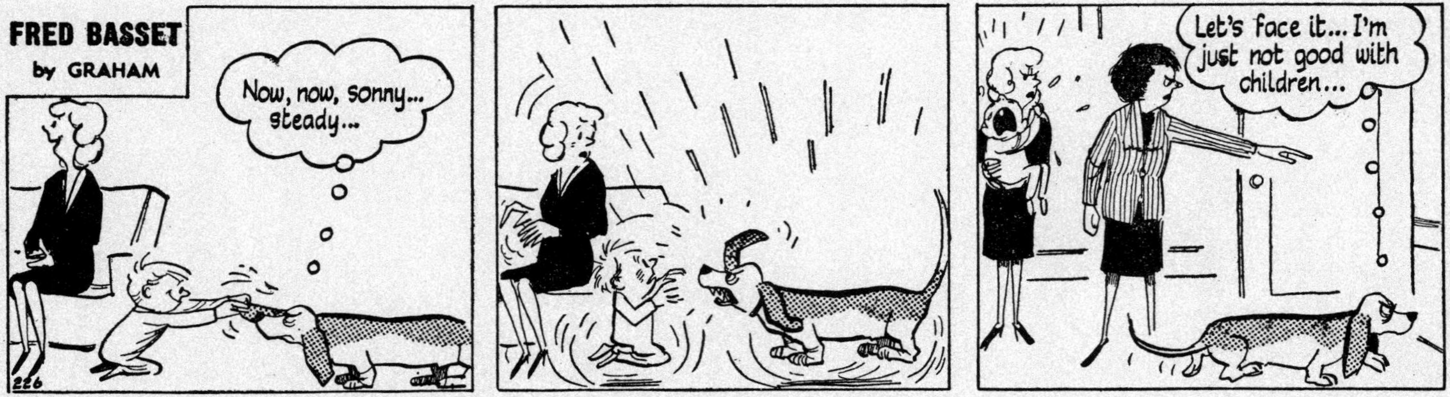
FRED BASSET
by GRAHAM
Now, now, sonny... steady...
Let's face it... I'm just not good with children...
226

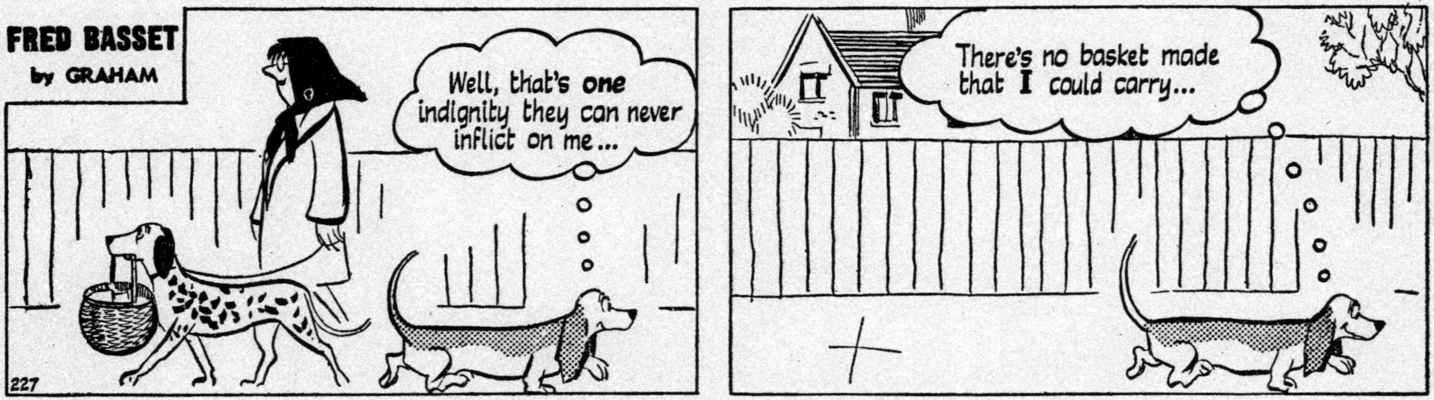
FRED BASSET
by GRAHAM
Well, that's **one** indignity they can never inflict on me...
There's no basket made that **I** could carry...
227

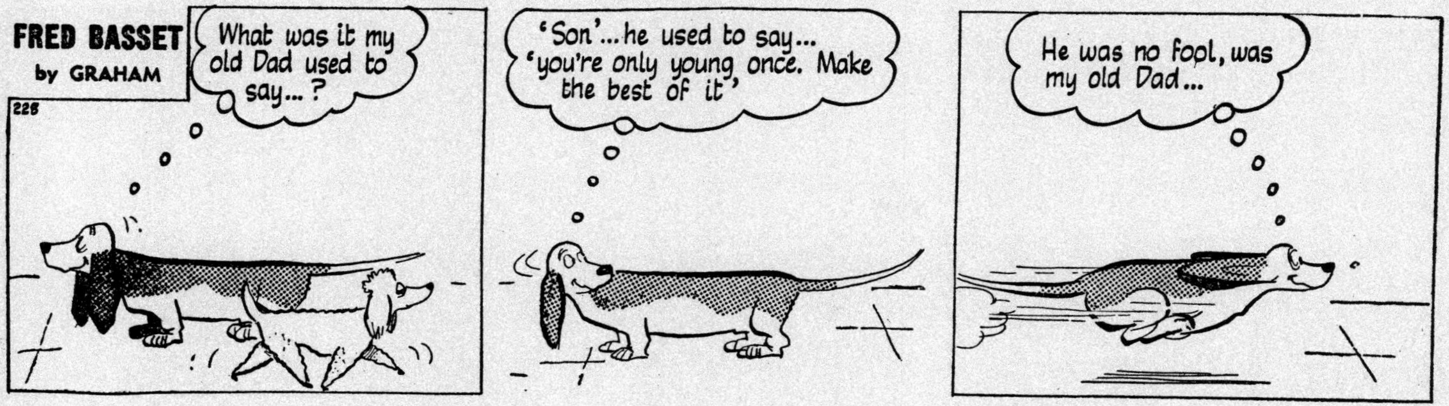
FRED BASSET
by GRAHAM
228
What was it my old Dad used to say...?
'Son'...he used to say... 'you're only young once. Make the best of it'
He was no fool, was my old Dad...

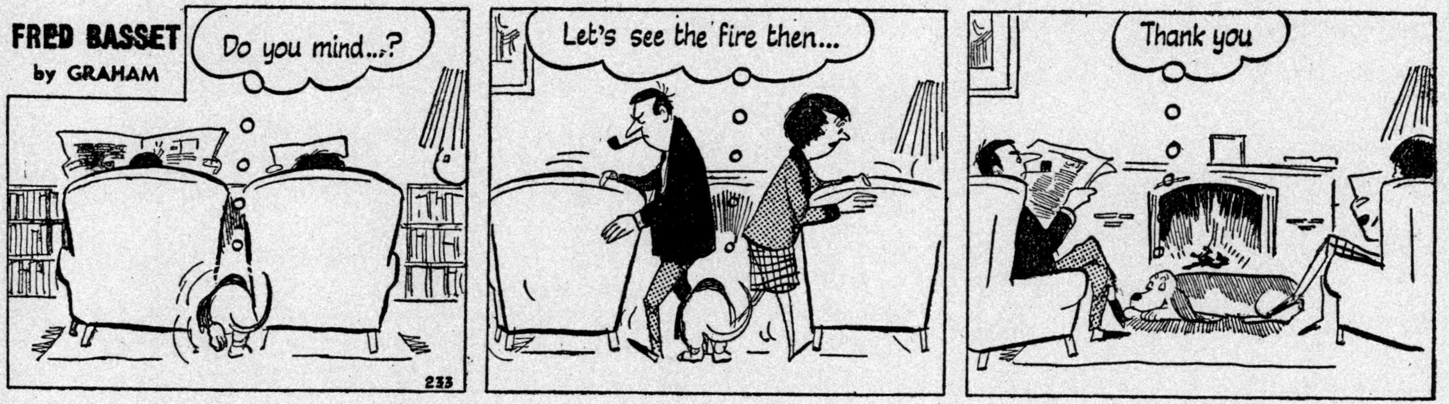
FRED BASSET
by GRAHAM
Do you mind...?
233
Let's see the fire then...
Thank you

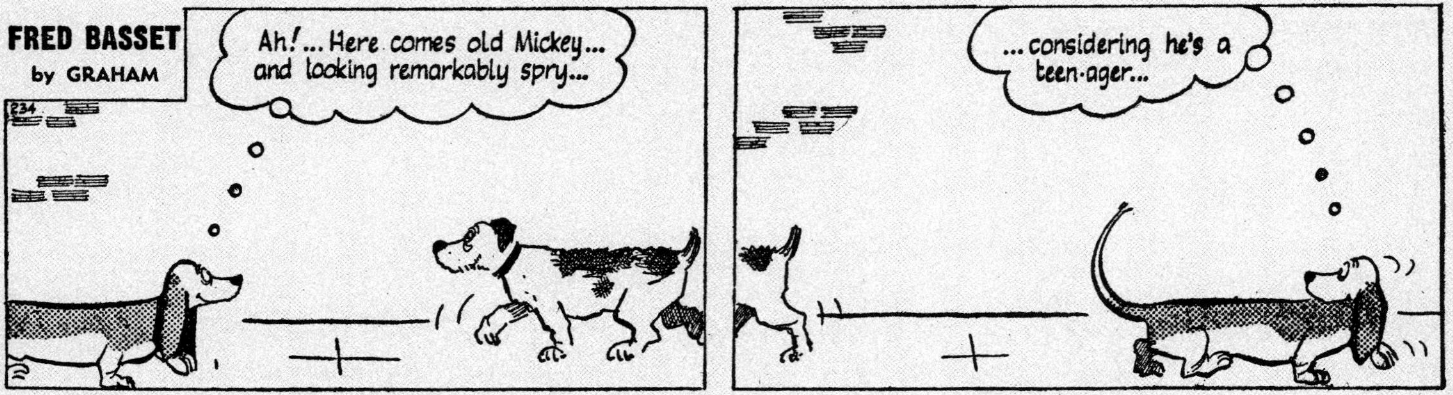
FRED BASSET
by GRAHAM
234
Ah! ... Here comes old Mickey... and looking remarkably spry...
... considering he's a teen-ager...

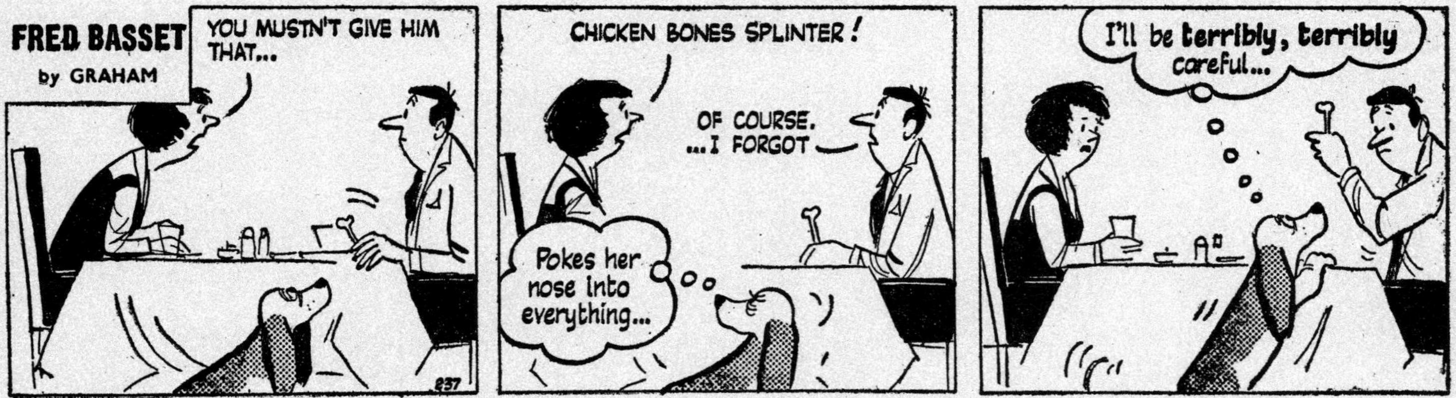
FRED BASSET
by GRAHAM
YOU MUSTN'T GIVE HIM THAT...
237
CHICKEN BONES SPLINTER!
OF COURSE. ...I FORGOT
Pokes her nose into everything...
I'll be terribly, terribly careful...

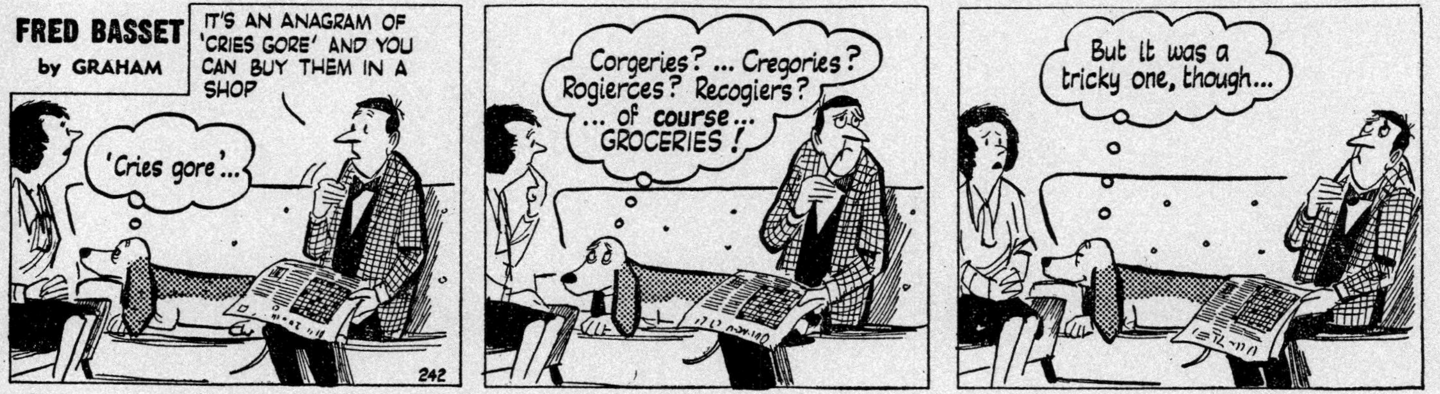
FRED BASSET
by GRAHAM
IT'S AN ANAGRAM OF 'CRIES GORE' AND YOU CAN BUY THEM IN A SHOP
'Cries gore'...
Corgeries? ... Cregories? Rogierces? Recogiers? ... of course... GROCERIES!
But it was a tricky one, though...
242

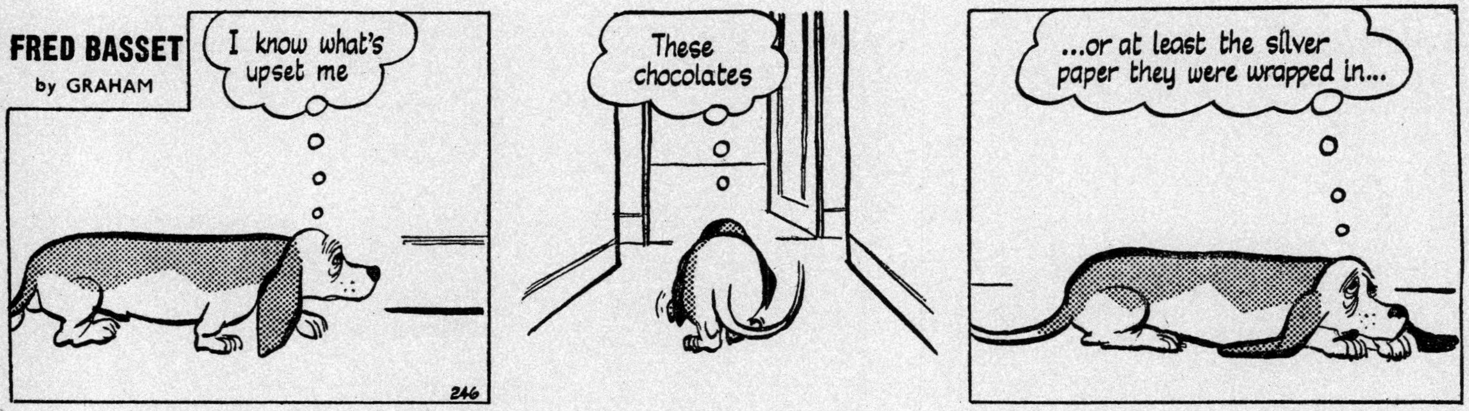
FRED BASSET
by GRAHAM
I know what's upset me
These chocolates
...or at least the silver paper they were wrapped in...
246

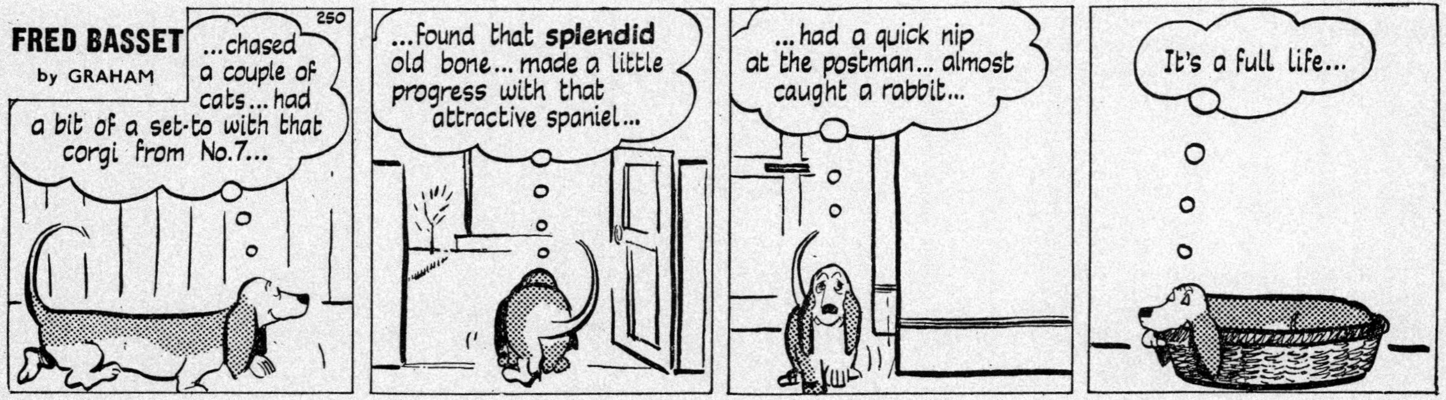
FRED BASSET
by GRAHAM
250
...chased a couple of cats... had a bit of a set-to with that corgi from No.7...
...found that **splendid** old bone... made a little progress with that attractive spaniel...
...had a quick nip at the postman... almost caught a rabbit...
It's a full life...

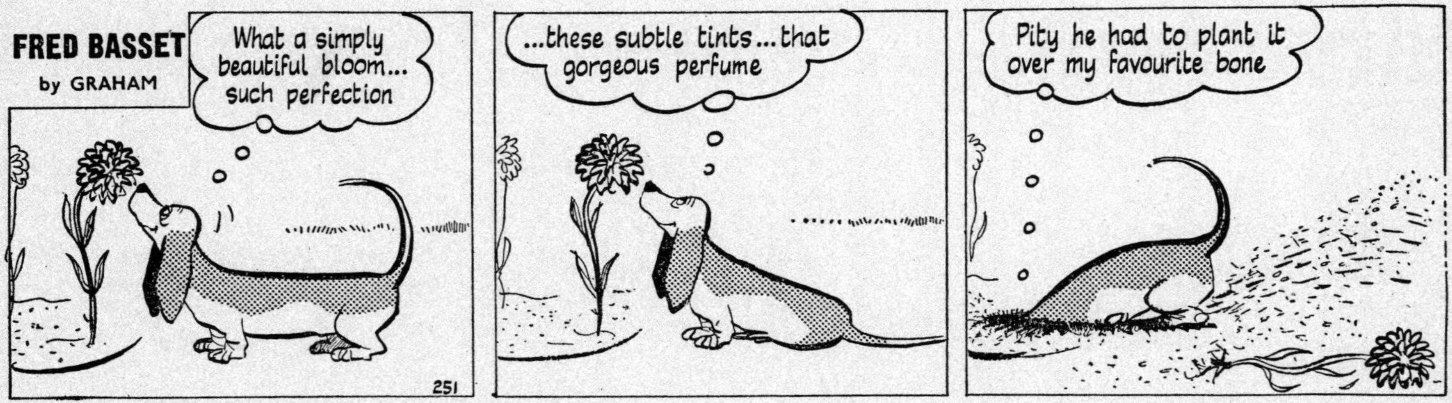
FRED BASSET
by GRAHAM
What a simply beautiful bloom... such perfection
251
...these subtle tints... that gorgeous perfume
Pity he had to plant it over my favourite bone

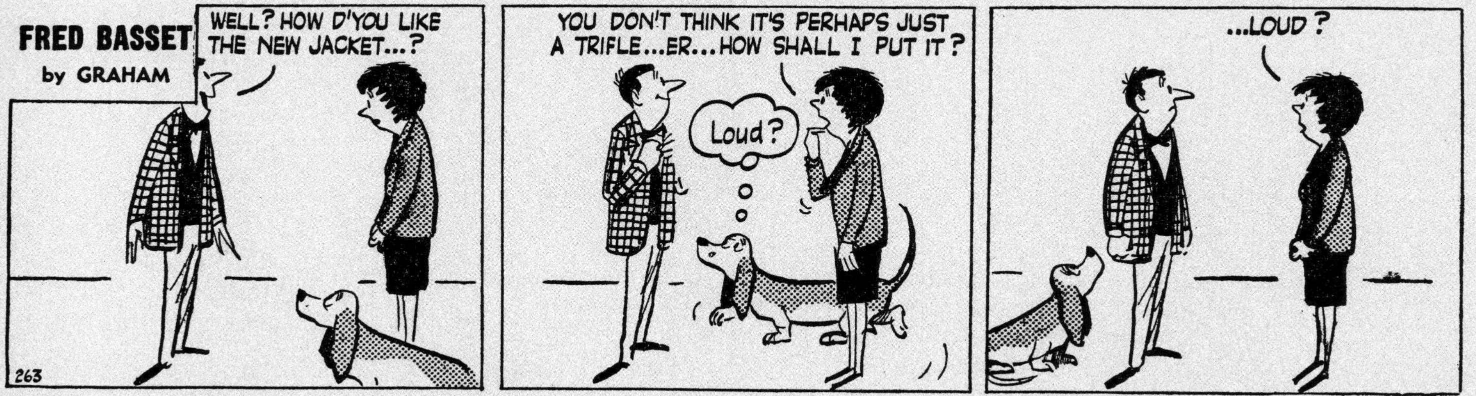
FRED BASSET
by GRAHAM
WELL? HOW D'YOU LIKE THE NEW JACKET...?
YOU DON'T THINK IT'S PERHAPS JUST A TRIFLE...ER...HOW SHALL I PUT IT?
Loud?
...LOUD?
263

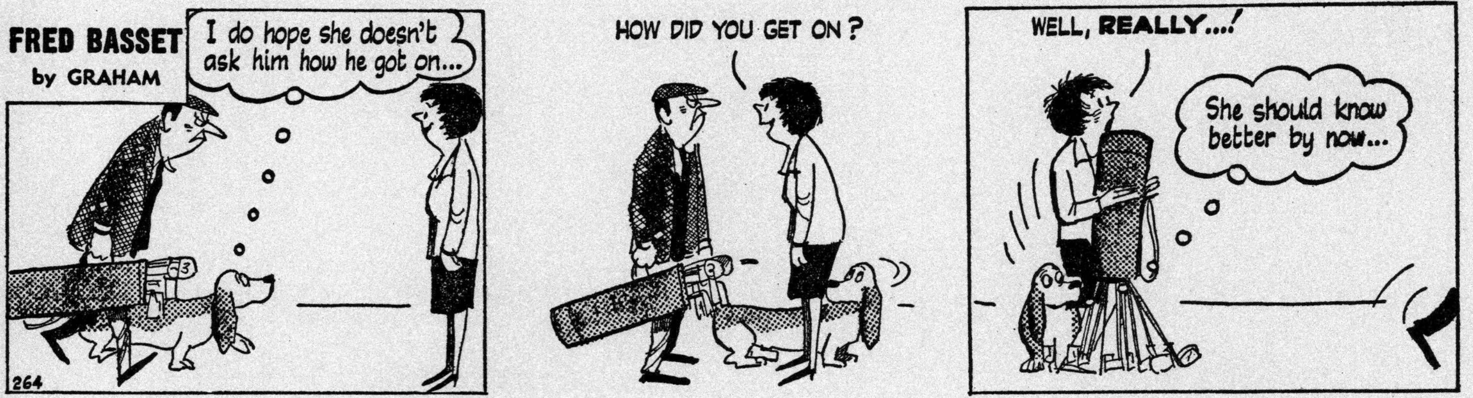
FRED BASSET
by GRAHAM
I do hope she doesn't ask him how he got on...
HOW DID YOU GET ON?
WELL, **REALLY**...!
She should know better by now...
264

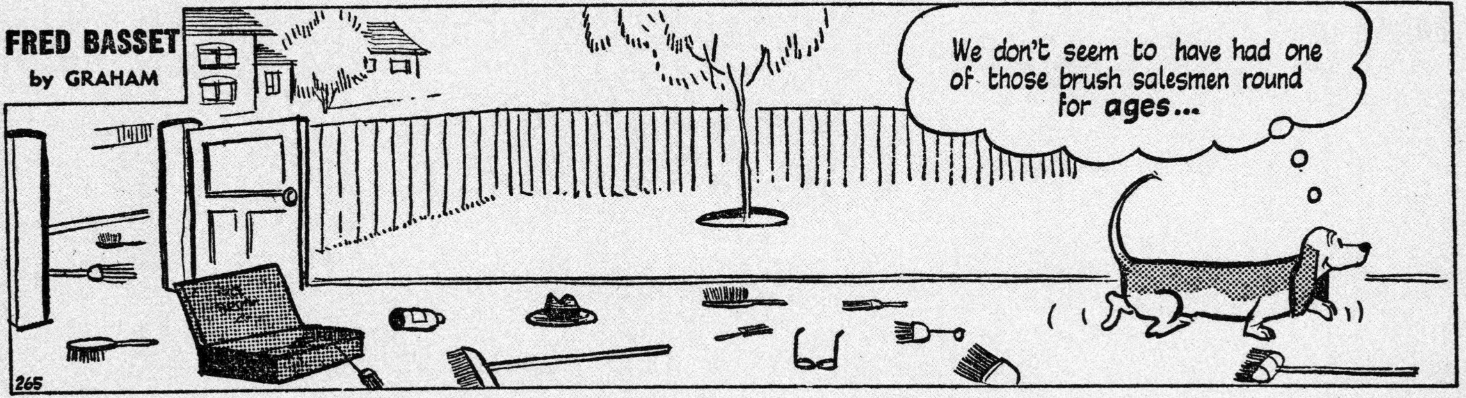
FRED BASSET
by GRAHAM
We don't seem to have had one of those brush salesmen round for ages...
265

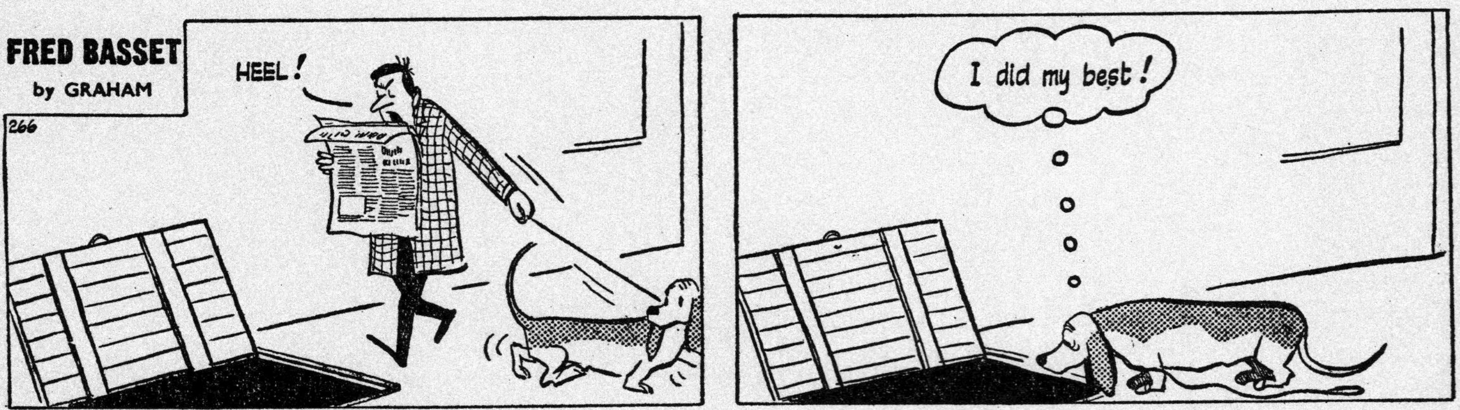
FRED BASSET
by GRAHAM
266
HEEL!
I did my best!

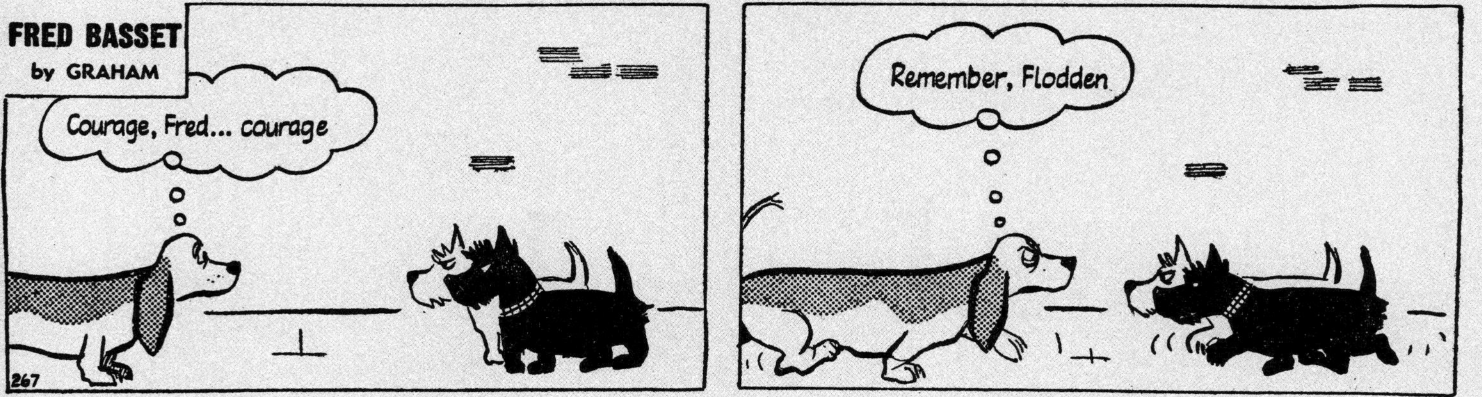

FRED BASSET
by GRAHAM
Courage, Fred... courage
267
Remember, Flodden

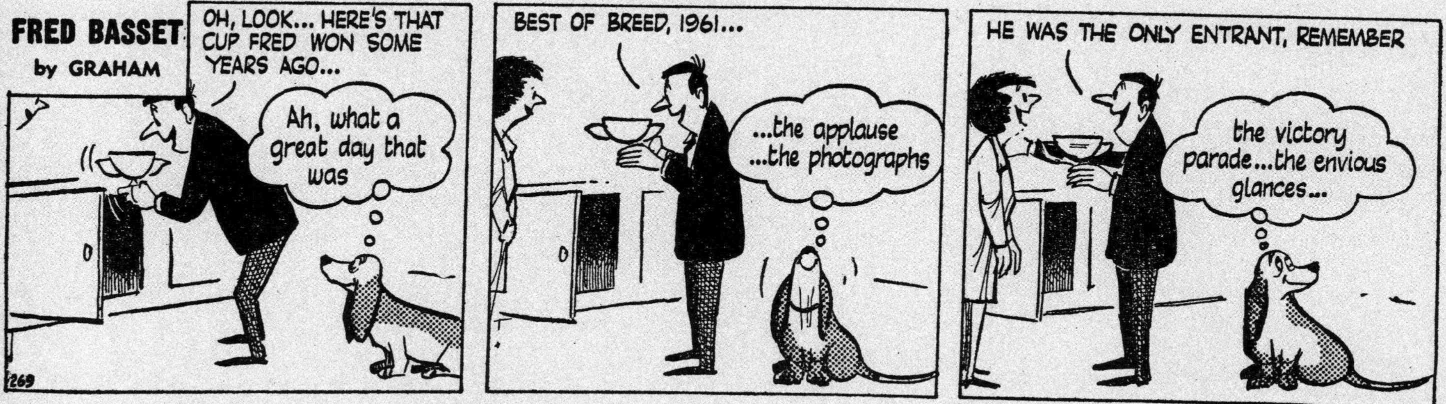

FRED BASSET
by GRAHAM
OH, LOOK... HERE'S THAT CUP FRED WON SOME YEARS AGO...
Ah, what a great day that was
269
BEST OF BREED, 1961...
...the applause ...the photographs
HE WAS THE ONLY ENTRANT, REMEMBER
the victory parade...the envious glances...

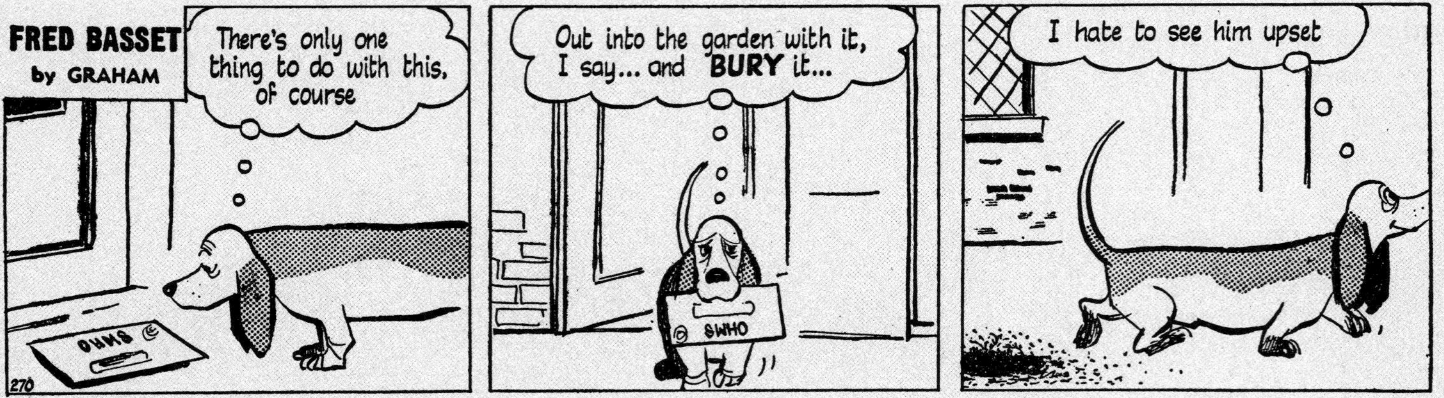
FRED BASSET
by GRAHAM
There's only one thing to do with this, of course
270
Out into the garden with it, I say... and **BURY** it...
SWHO
I hate to see him upset

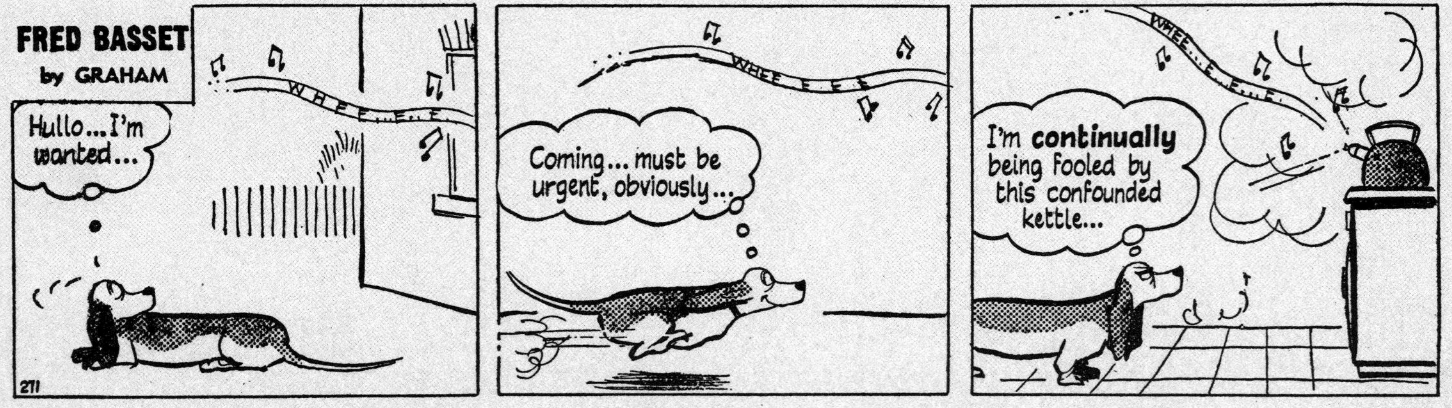
FRED BASSET
by GRAHAM
Hullo... I'm wanted...
271
Coming... must be urgent, obviously...
I'm **continually** being fooled by this confounded kettle...

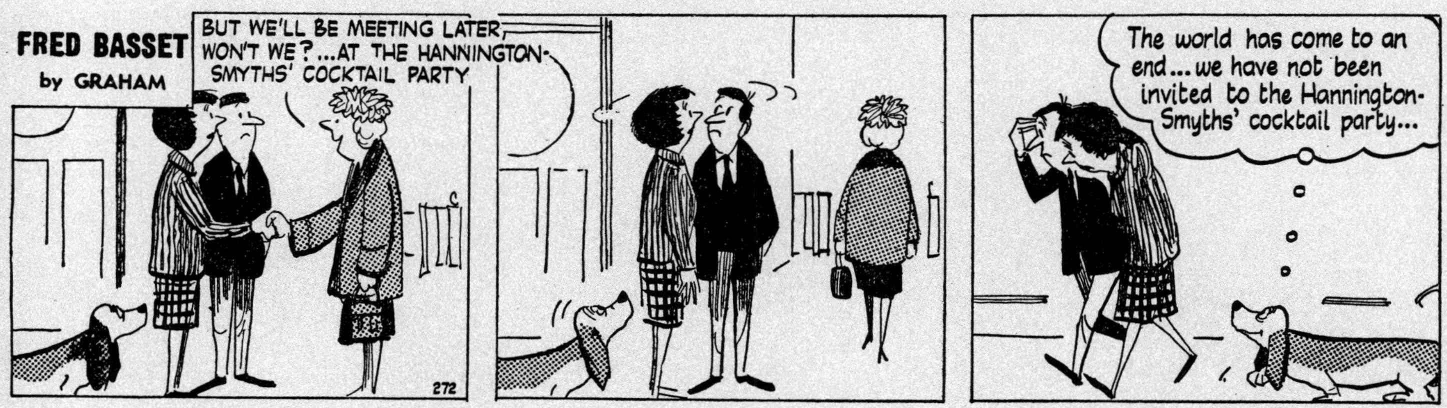
FRED BASSET
by GRAHAM
BUT WE'LL BE MEETING LATER, WON'T WE?...AT THE HANNINGTON-SMYTHS' COCKTAIL PARTY
272
The world has come to an end...we have not been invited to the Hannington-Smyths' cocktail party...

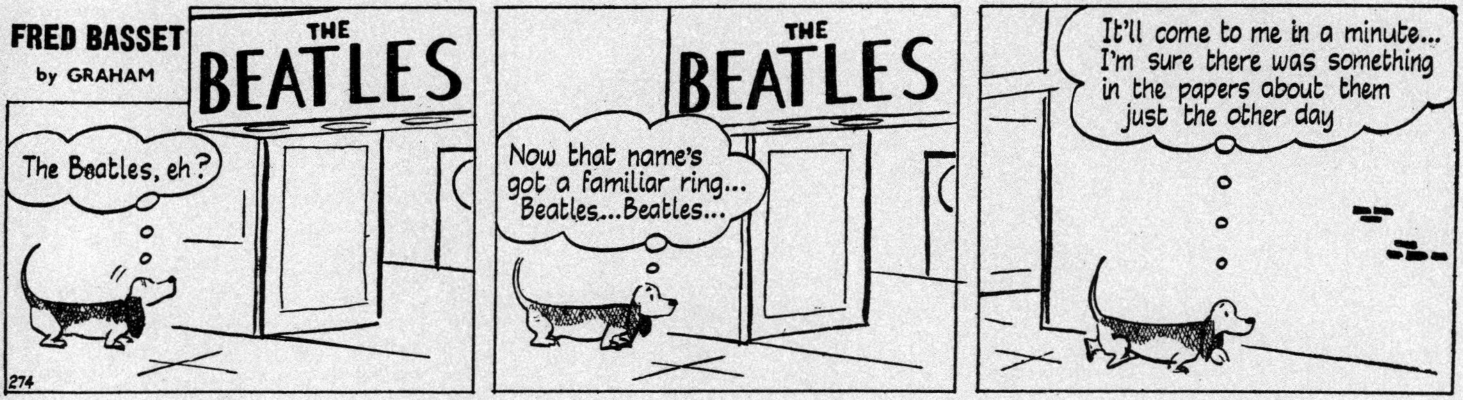
FRED BASSET
by GRAHAM
THE BEATLES
The Beatles, eh?
274
THE BEATLES
Now that name's got a familiar ring... Beatles...Beatles...
It'll come to me in a minute... I'm sure there was something in the papers about them just the other day

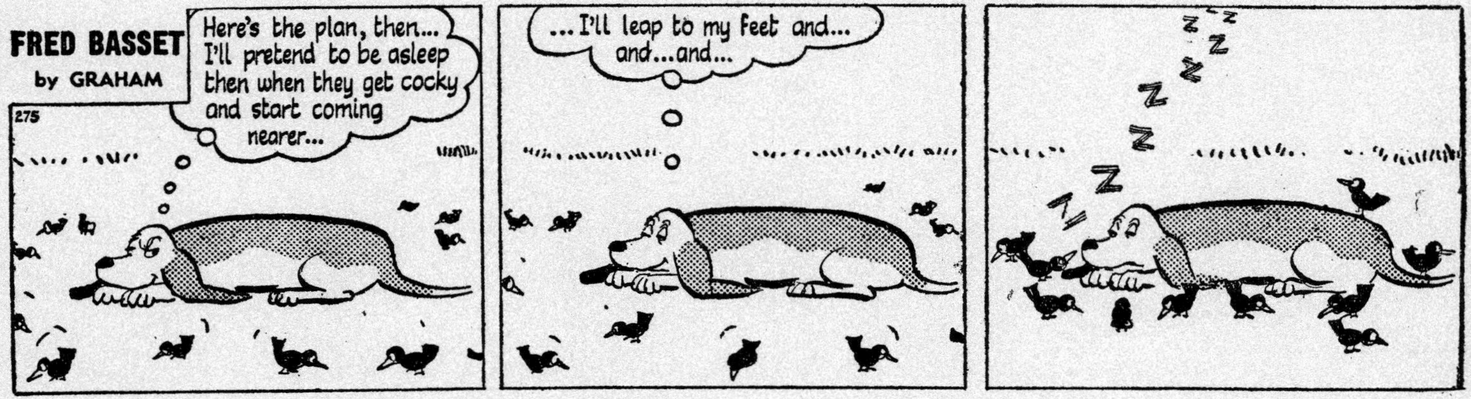

FRED BASSET
by GRAHAM
275
Here's the plan, then... I'll pretend to be asleep then when they get cocky and start coming nearer...
...I'll leap to my feet and... and...and...
Z Z Z Z Z Z Z Z

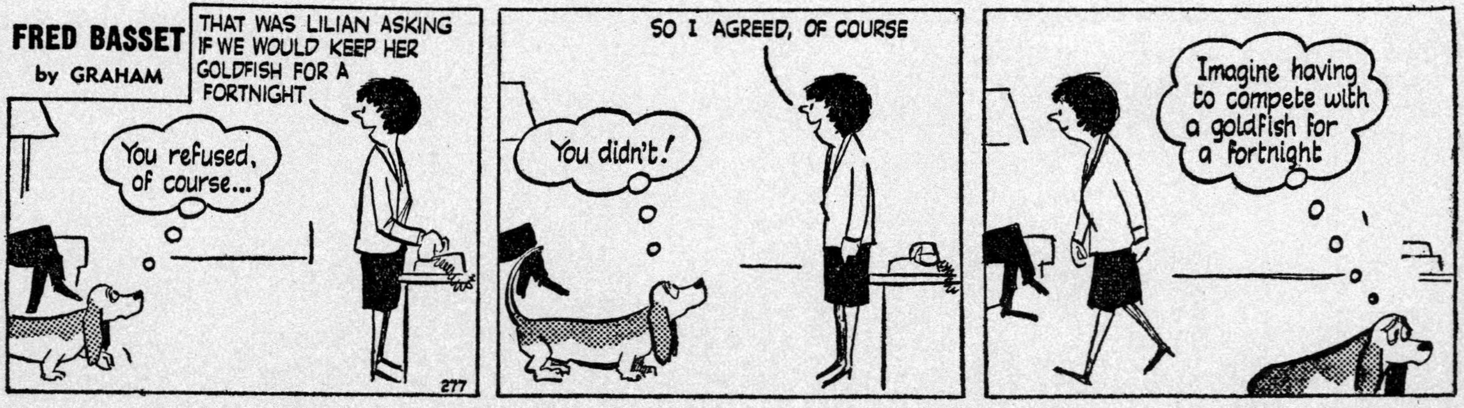

FRED BASSET
by GRAHAM
THAT WAS LILIAN ASKING IF WE WOULD KEEP HER GOLDFISH FOR A FORTNIGHT
You refused, of course...
277
SO I AGREED, OF COURSE
You didn't!
Imagine having to compete with a goldfish for a fortnight

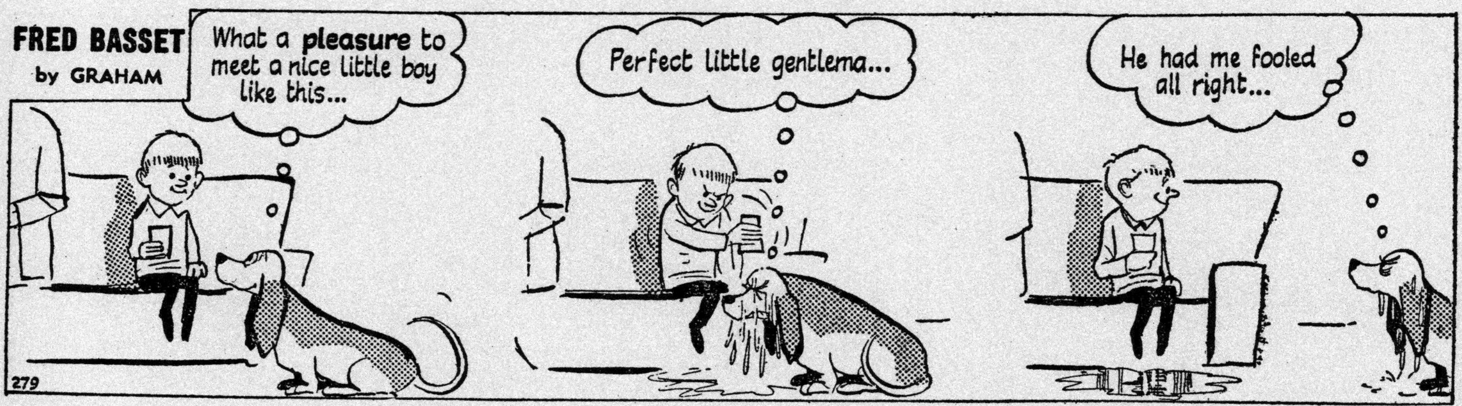
FRED BASSET
by GRAHAM
What a **pleasure** to meet a nice little boy like this...
Perfect little gentlema...
He had me fooled all right...
279

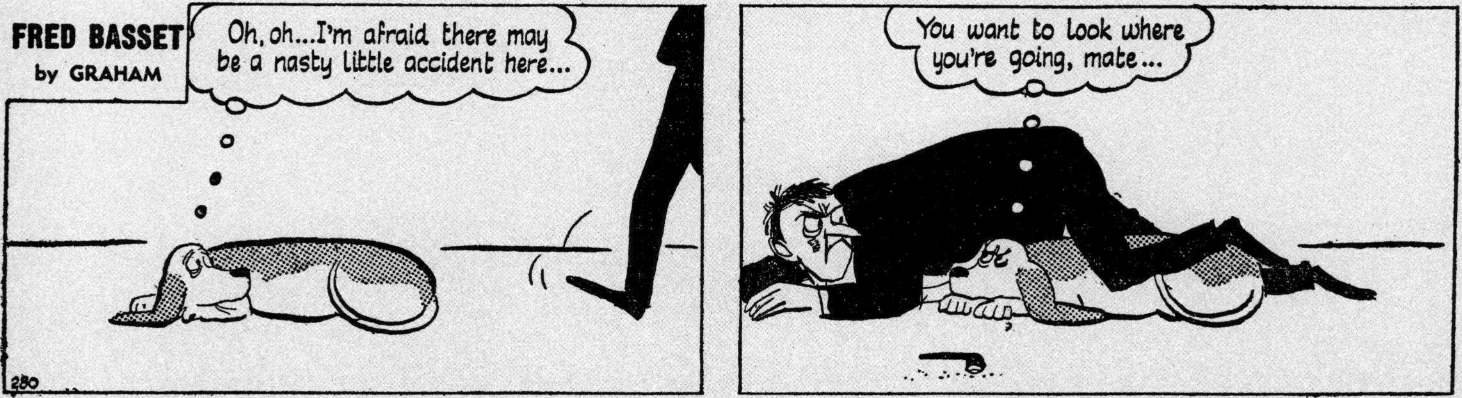
FRED BASSET
by GRAHAM
Oh, oh...I'm afraid there may be a nasty little accident here...
You want to look where you're going, mate...
280

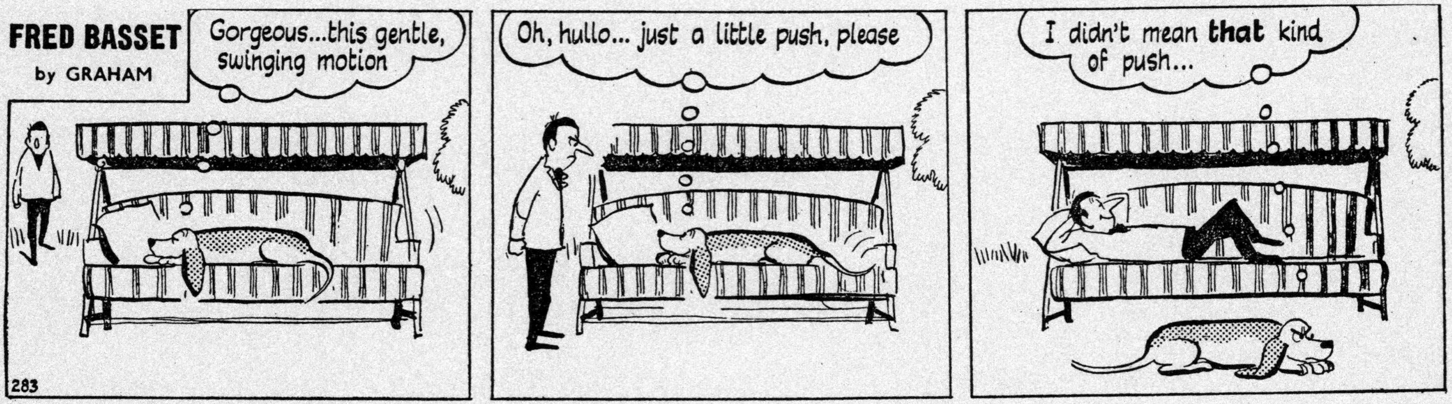
FRED BASSET
by GRAHAM
Gorgeous...this gentle, swinging motion
283
Oh, hullo... just a little push, please
I didn't mean **that** kind of push...

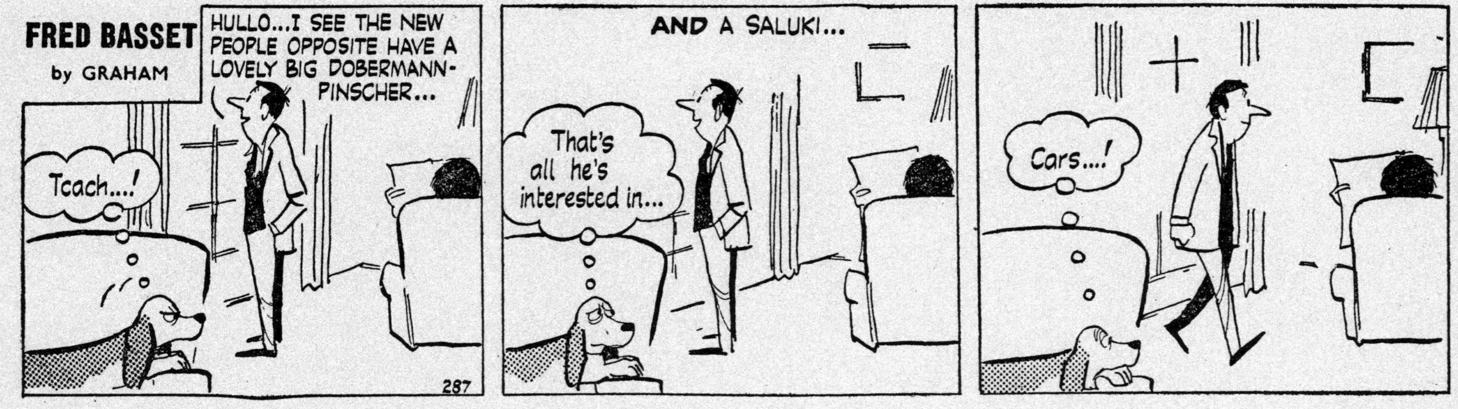
FRED BASSET
by GRAHAM
HULLO...I SEE THE NEW PEOPLE OPPOSITE HAVE A LOVELY BIG DOBERMANN-PINSCHER...
Tcach....!
287
AND A SALUKI...
That's all he's interested in...
Cars....!

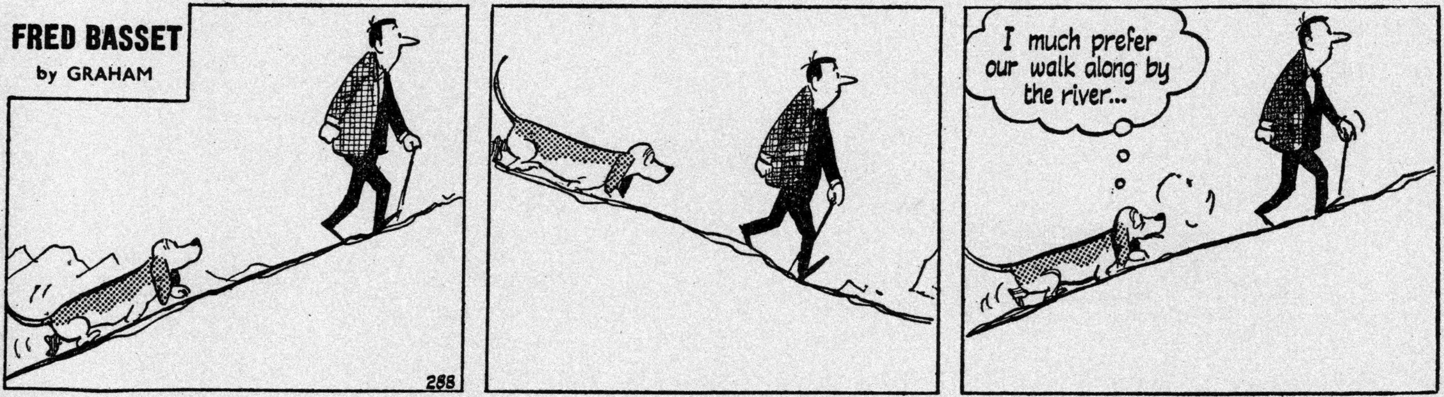
FRED BASSET
by GRAHAM
I much prefer our walk along by the river...
288

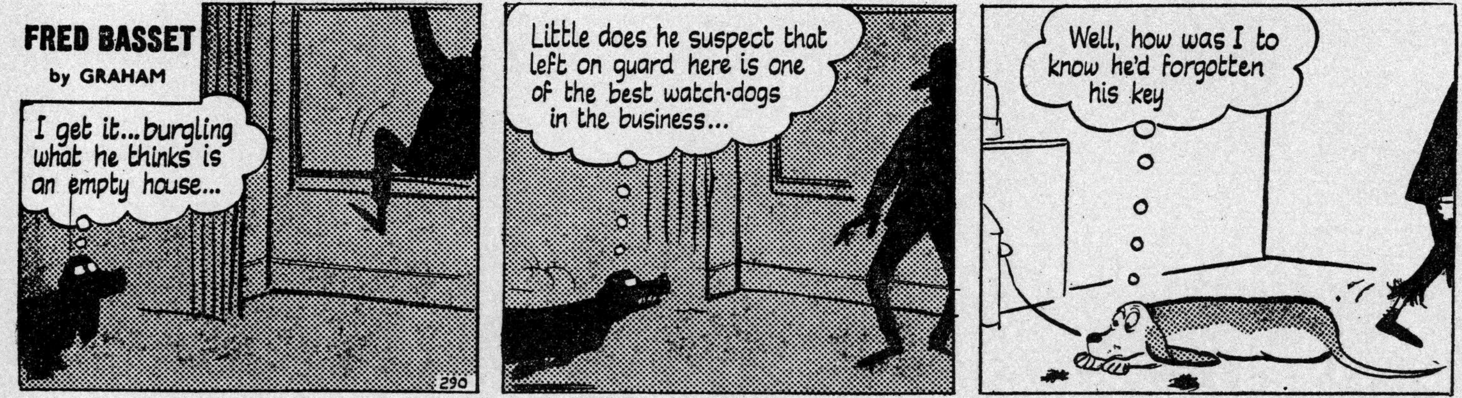
FRED BASSET
by GRAHAM
I get it... burgling what he thinks is an empty house...
Little does he suspect that left on guard here is one of the best watch-dogs in the business...
Well, how was I to know he'd forgotten his key
290

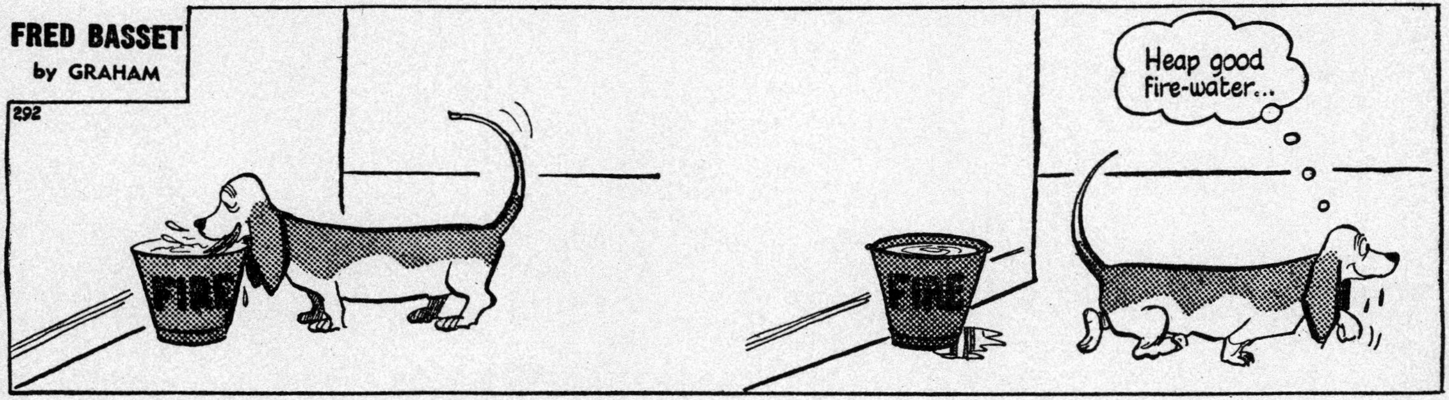
FRED BASSET
by GRAHAM
292
FIRE
FIRE
Heap good fire-water...

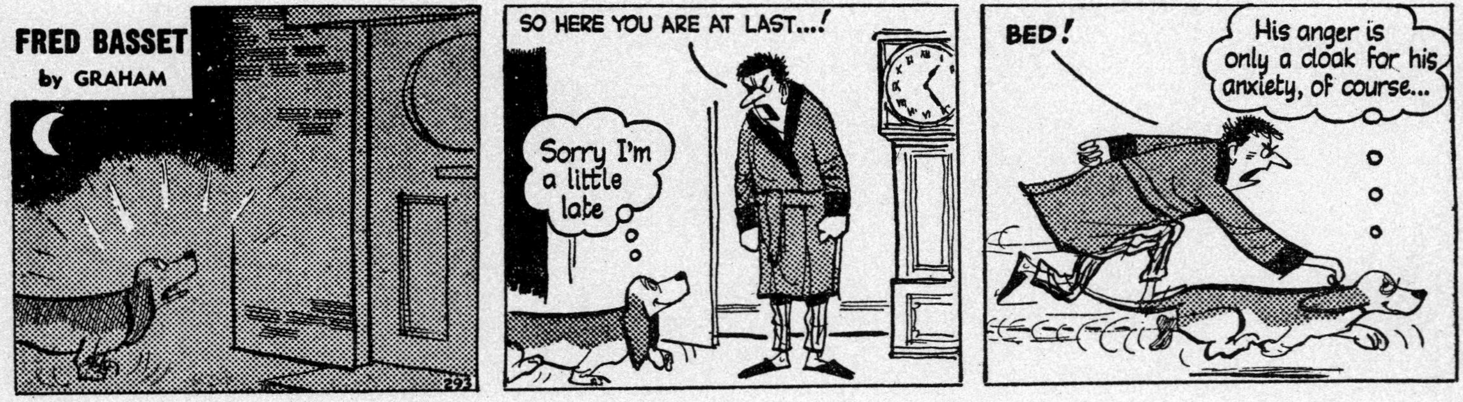
FRED BASSET
by GRAHAM
293
SO HERE YOU ARE AT LAST...!
Sorry I'm a little late
BED!
His anger is only a cloak for his anxiety, of course...

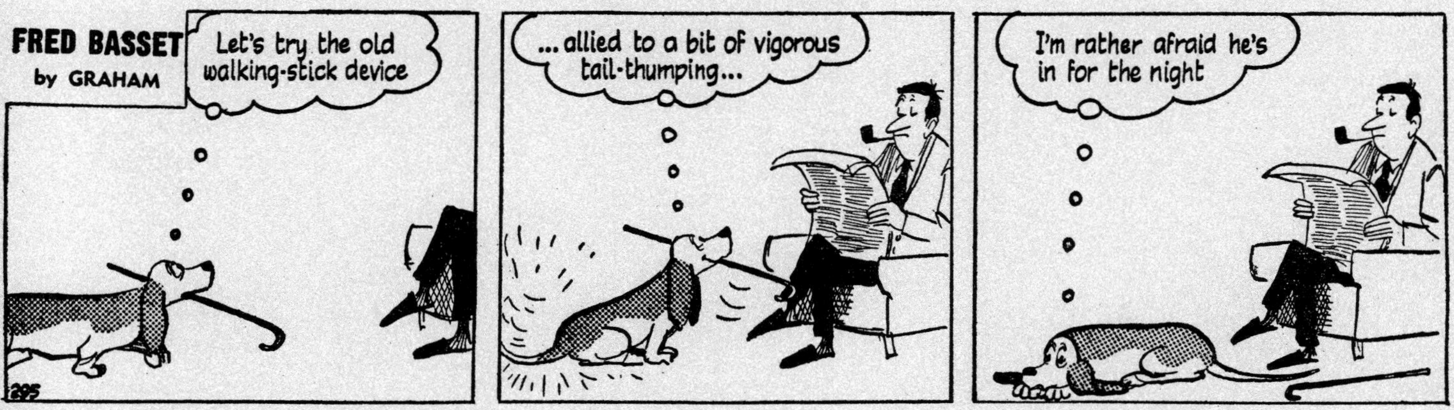
FRED BASSET
by GRAHAM
Let's try the old walking-stick device
...allied to a bit of vigorous tail-thumping...
I'm rather afraid he's in for the night
295

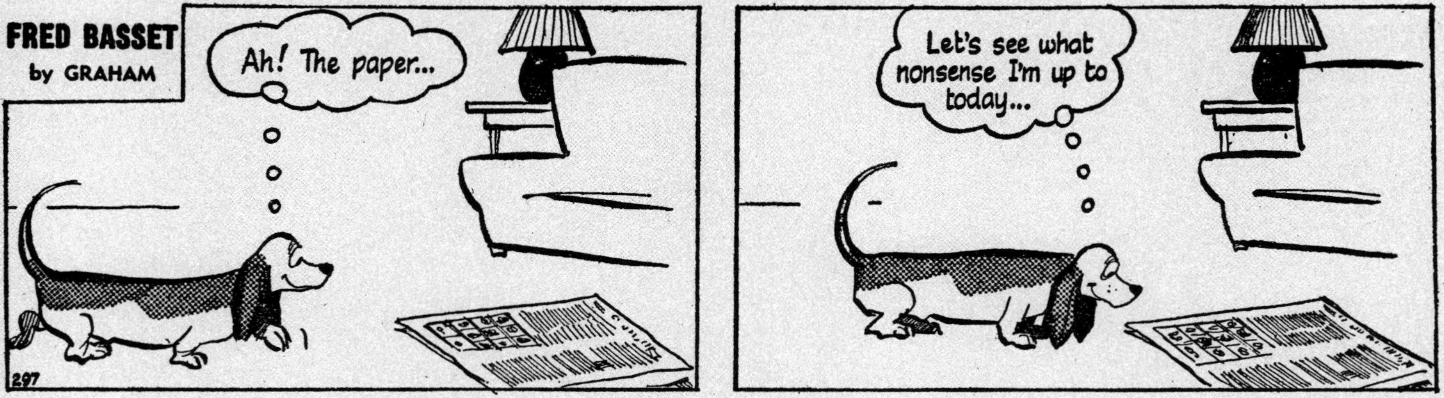
FRED BASSET
by GRAHAM
Ah! The paper...
Let's see what nonsense I'm up to today...
297

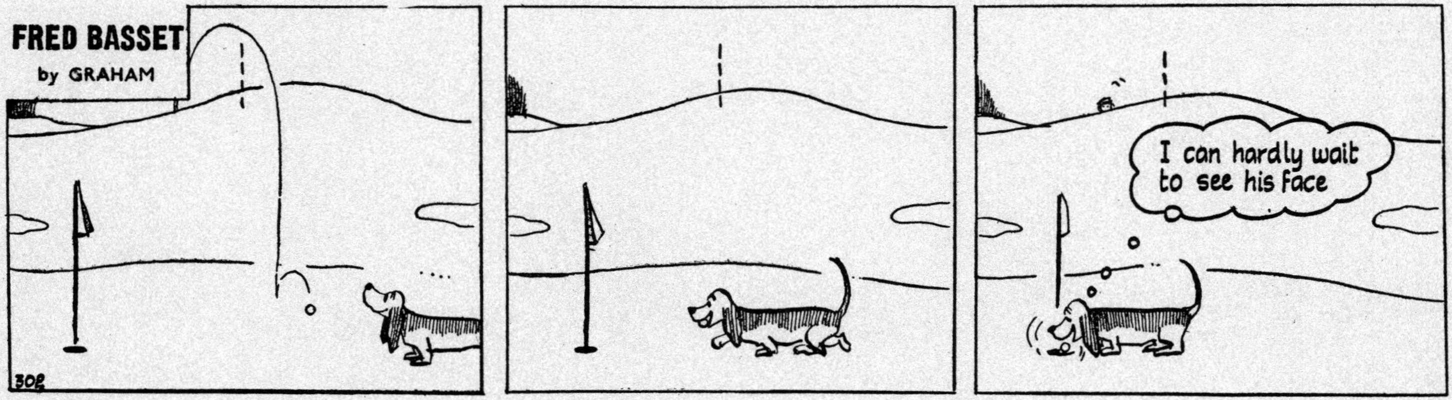

FRED BASSET
by GRAHAM
I can hardly wait to see his face

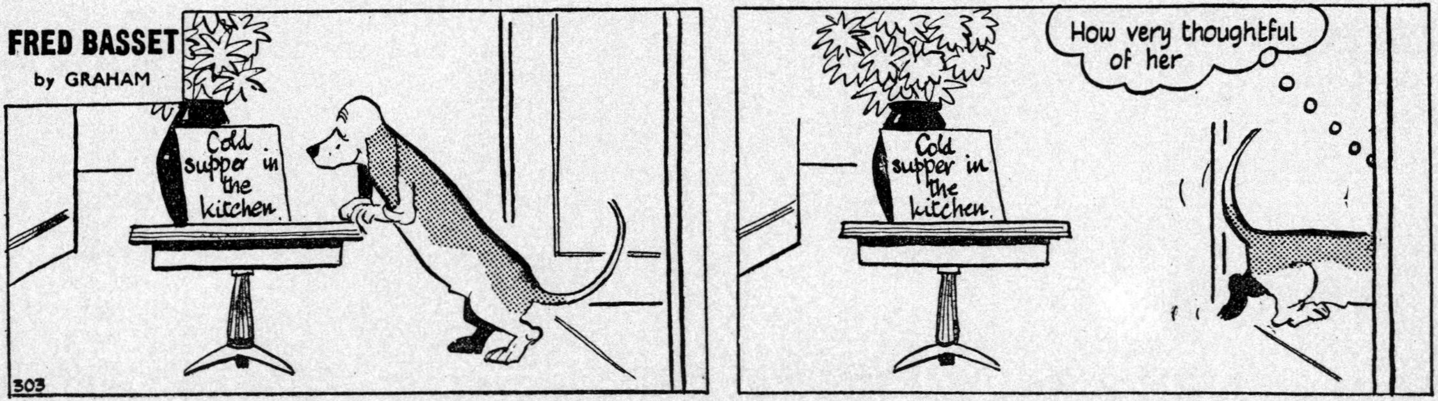

FRED BASSET
by GRAHAM
Cold supper in the kitchen
Cold supper in the kitchen
How very thoughtful of her

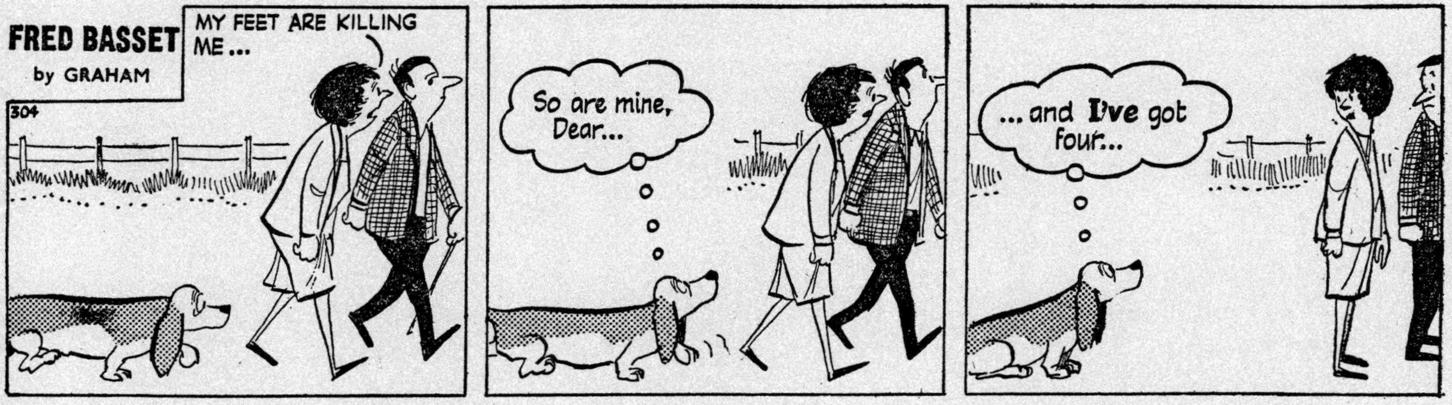
FRED BASSET
by GRAHAM
304
MY FEET ARE KILLING ME ...
So are mine, Dear...
... and I've got four...

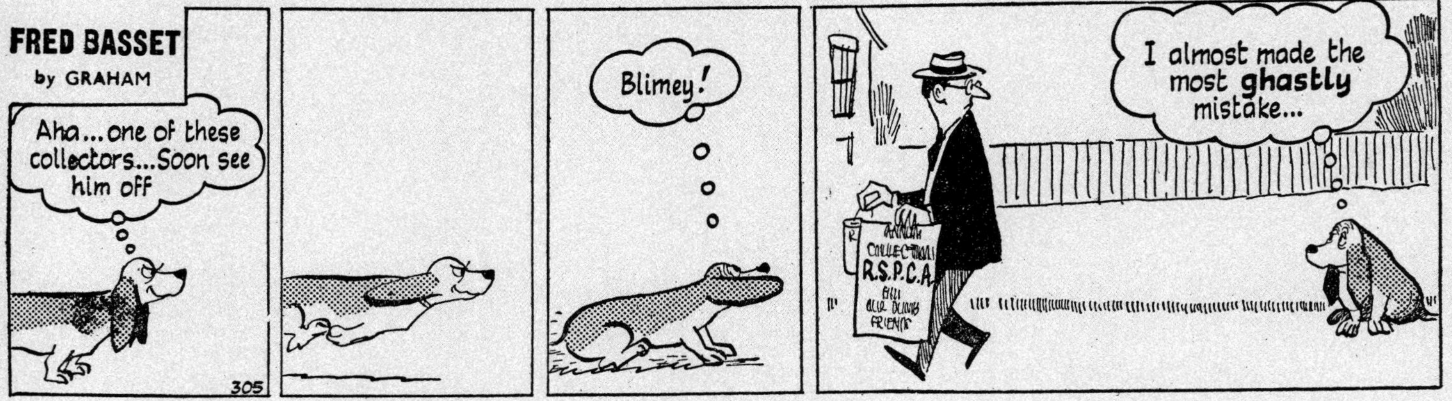
FRED BASSET
by GRAHAM
Aha...one of these collectors...Soon see him off
305
Blimey!
R.S.P.C.A.
I almost made the most ghastly mistake...

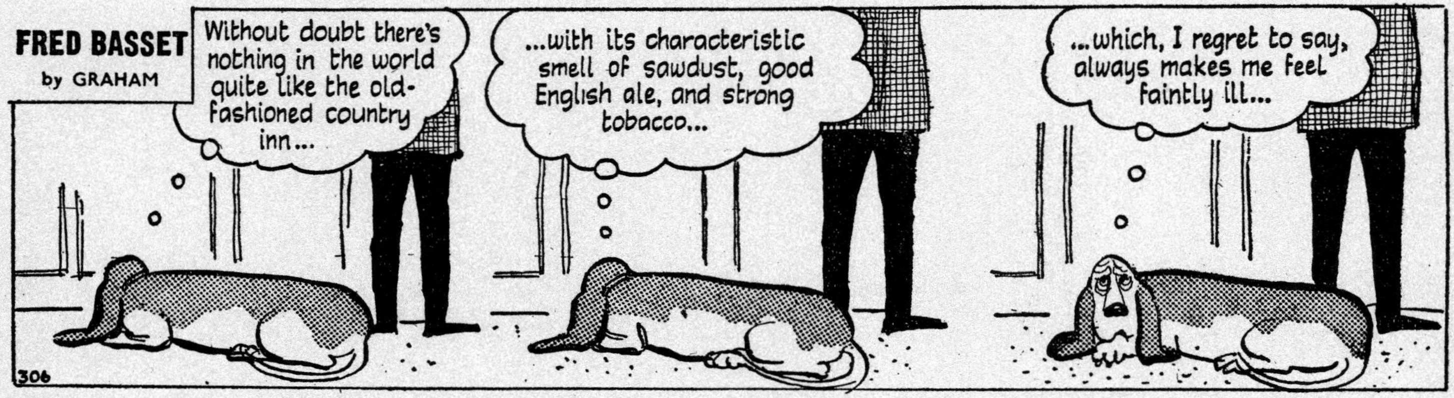
FRED BASSET
by GRAHAM
Without doubt there's nothing in the world quite like the old-fashioned country inn...
...with its characteristic smell of sawdust, good English ale, and strong tobacco...
...which, I regret to say, always makes me feel faintly ill...
306

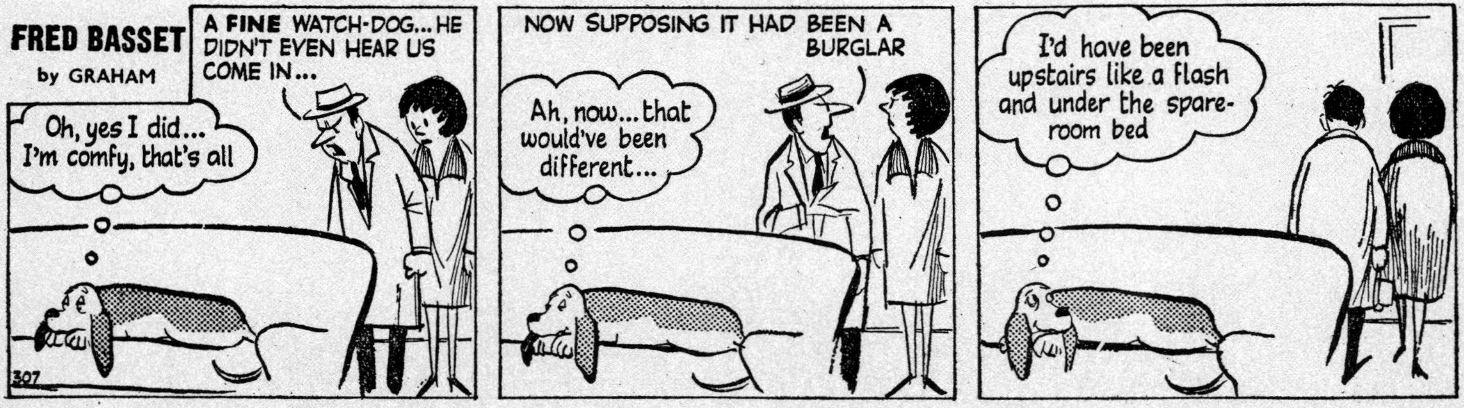
FRED BASSET
by GRAHAM
A FINE WATCH-DOG... HE DIDN'T EVEN HEAR US COME IN...
Oh, yes I did... I'm comfy, that's all
NOW SUPPOSING IT HAD BEEN A BURGLAR
Ah, now... that would've been different...
I'd have been upstairs like a flash and under the spare-room bed
307

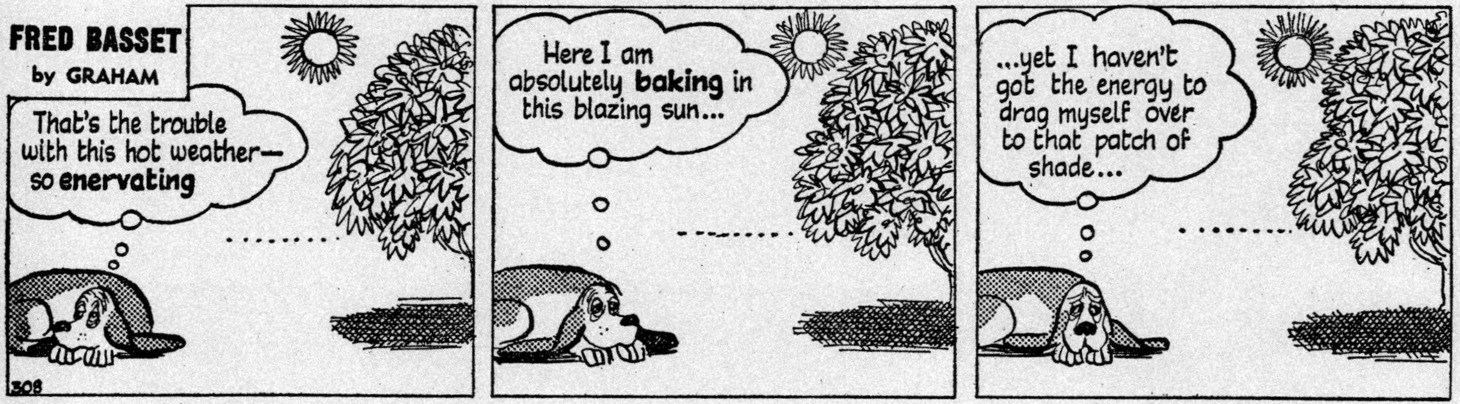
FRED BASSET
by GRAHAM
That's the trouble with this hot weather— so **enervating**
Here I am absolutely **baking** in this blazing sun...
...yet I haven't got the energy to drag myself over to that patch of shade...
308

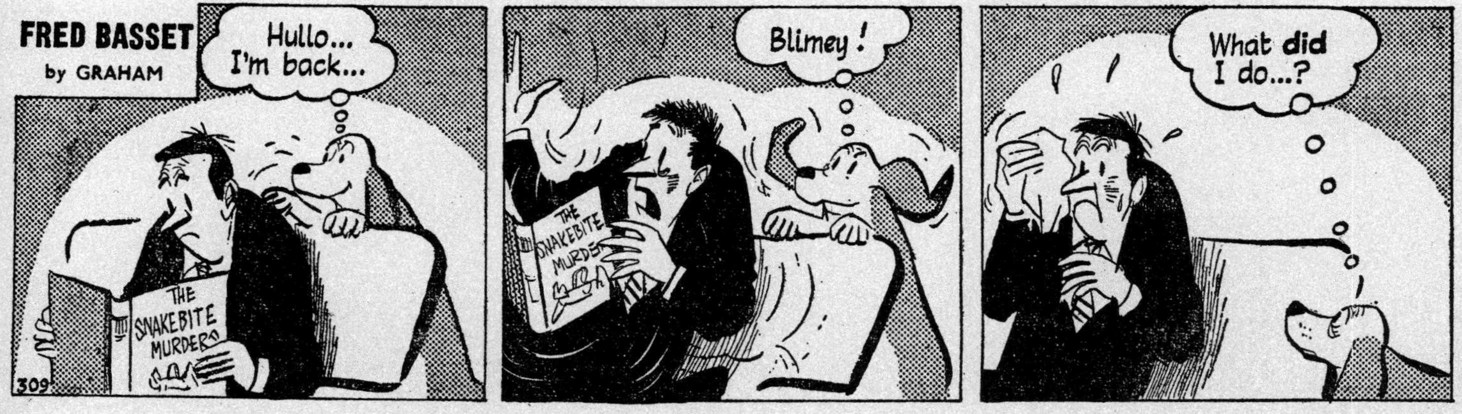
FRED BASSET
by GRAHAM
Hullo... I'm back...
THE SNAKEBITE MURDERS
Blimey!
THE SNAKEBITE MURDERS
What **did** I do...?
309

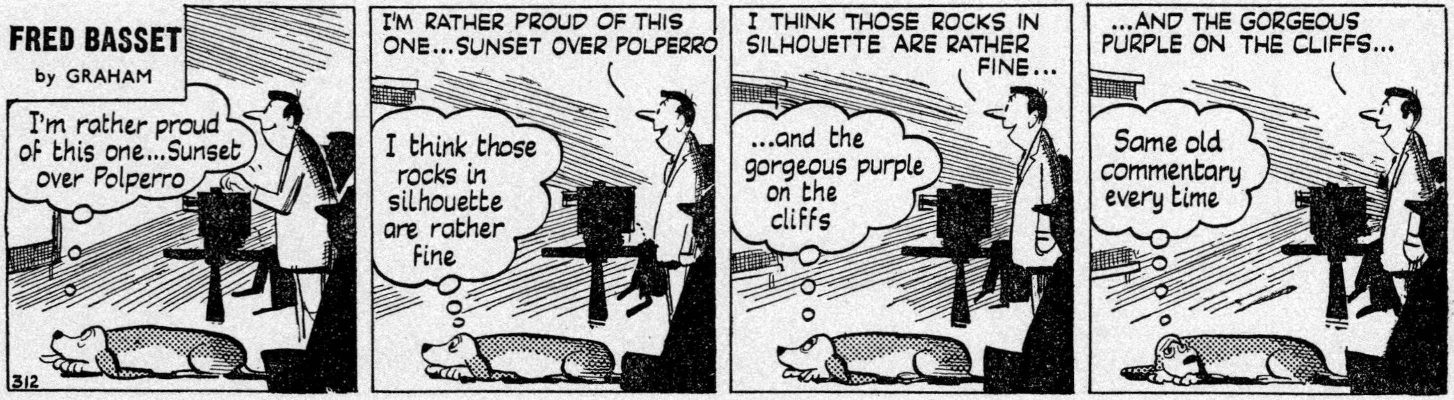
FRED BASSET
by GRAHAM
I'm rather proud of this one...Sunset over Polperro
312
I'M RATHER PROUD OF THIS ONE...SUNSET OVER POLPERRO
I think those rocks in silhouette are rather fine
I THINK THOSE ROCKS IN SILHOUETTE ARE RATHER FINE...
...and the gorgeous purple on the cliffs
...AND THE GORGEOUS PURPLE ON THE CLIFFS...
Same old commentary every time

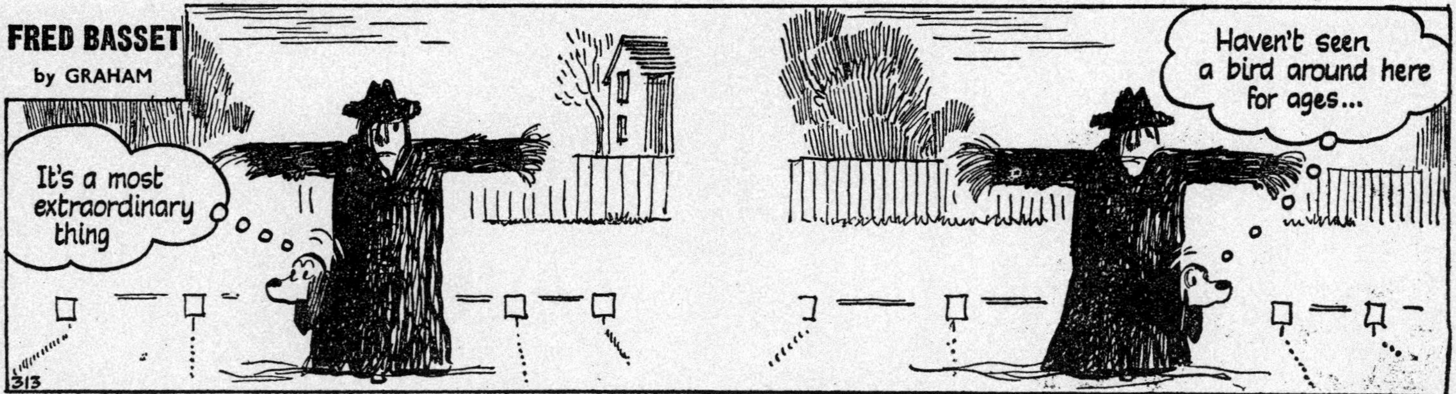
FRED BASSET
by GRAHAM
It's a most extraordinary thing
Haven't seen a bird around here for ages...
313

THE END

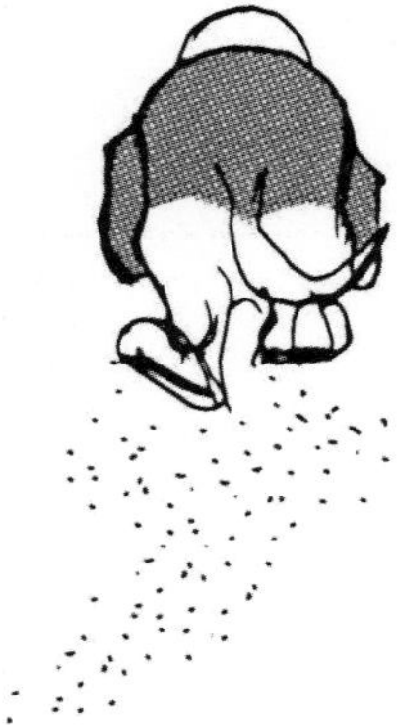

The publishers would like to thank the following individuals and institutions for permission to reproduce copyright material for this book. Every effort has been made to trace the copyright holders. The Orion Publishing Group apologise for any unintentional omissions and, if informed of such cases, shall make corrections in any future edition.

Associated Newspapers
Cartoonist Profiles
Alex Graham Ltd
Mac
Michael Martin
Jean Schulz
The Estate of P. G. Wodehouse